WOMEN
IN
THERAPY

WOMEN
IN
THERAPY

**DEVALUATION • ANGER • AGGRESSION • DEPRESSION
SELF-SACRIFICE • MOTHERING • MOTHER BLAMING • SELF-BETRAYAL
SEX-ROLE STEREOTYPES • DEPENDENCY • WORK AND SUCCESS INHIBITIONS**

Harriet Goldhor Lerner, Ph.D.

Jason Aronson Inc.
Northvale, New Jersey
London

10 9 8 7 6 5 4 3 2 1

Library of Congress Cataloging-in-Publication Data

Lerner, Harriet Goldhor.
  Women in therapy.

  1. Women—Mental health.   2. Women—Psychology.
3. Psychotherapy patients.   4. Women—Mental health.
I. Title.
RC451.4.W6L47 1988   155.6′33   87-19362
ISBN 0-87668-978-0

Manufactured in the United States of America.

The Chapters listed below in their original titles appeared in more than one publication. In addition to these credits, the author gratefully acknowledges all publishers who granted permission to use their material throughout the book, *Women in Therapy.*

Chapter 1   Origins of Envy and Devaluation of Women

(1974). Early origins of envy and devaluation of women: implications for sex-role stereotypes. *Bulletin of the Menninger Clinic* 38(6):538–553. Also in *Women and Mental Health,* ed. E. Howell and M. Bayes, pp. 26–40. New York: Basic Books, 1981. Also in *The Gender Gap in Psychotherapy: Social Realities and Psychological Processes,* ed. P. P. Rieker and E. (Hilberman) Carmen, pp. 111–124. New York: Plenum, 1984.

Chapter 2   Parental Mislabeling of Female Genitals

(1976). Parental mislabeling of female genitals as a determinant of penis envy and learning inhibitions in women. *Journal of the American Psychoanalytic Association* 24(5):269–283. Also in *Female Psychology,* ed. H. P. Blum, pp. 269–283. New York: International Universities Press, 1977. Also in *Psyche* 14:1092–1104, 1980, (German translation).

Chapter 5   Adaptive and Pathogenic Aspects of Sex-Role Stereotypes

(1978). Adaptive and pathogenic aspects of sex-role stereotypes: implications for parenting and psychotherapy. *American Journal of Psychiatry* 135(1):48–52. Also in *Women and Mental Health,* ed. E. Howell and M. Bayes, pp. 534–543. New York: Basic Books, 1981.

Chapter 6   Girls, Ladies, or Women? The Unconscious Dynamics of Language Choice

(1979). Girls, ladies, or women? the unconscious dynamics of language choice. *Comprehensive Psychiatry* 17(2):295–299. Also in *Nursing Dimensions* 7(1):1–3, 1979.

Chapter 7   The Hysterical Personality

(1974). The hysterical personality: a "woman's disease." *Comprehensive Psychiatry* 15(2):157–164. Also in *Women and Mental Health,* ed. E. Howell and M. Bayes, pp. 196–206. New York: Basic Books, 1981.

Chapter 8   Special Issues for Women in Psychotherapy

(1982). Special issues for women in psychotherapy. In *The Woman Patient: Medical and Psychological Interfaces,* ed. M. T. Notman and C. C. Nadelson, pp. 273–286. New York: Plenum. Also in *The Gender Gap in Psychotherapy: Social Realities and Psychological Processes,* ed. P. P. Rieker and E. (Hilberman) Carmen, pp. 271–284. New York: Plenum, 1984.

Chapter 11   Female Dependency

(1983). Female dependency in context: some theoretical and technical considerations. *American Journal of Orthopsychiatry* 53(4):697–705. Also in *The Gender Gap in Psychotherapy: Social Realities and Psychological Processes,* ed. P. P. Rieker and E. (Hilberman) Carmen, pp. 125–138. New York: Plenum, 1984.

This book is dedicated to feminist voices,
and to
The Menninger Foundation,
which is large enough in size and spirit
to encourage differences.

Contents

Acknowledgments

This book is a compilation of articles that I have written over a 15-year period, beginning when I was a postdoctoral fellow at The Menninger Foundation (1972–1974) and continuing to the present. During this time, I have had many fine teachers of psychoanalytic theory and practice. I would like to thank those people, too numerous to all be named individually, who have contributed to my professional development and encouraged my writing.

The Menninger Foundation is living proof of the old adage that "if you want something done, ask a busy person." My colleagues have always given generously of their time and expertise, providing extensive, thoughtful criticism. Special thanks go to Otto Kernberg, Paul Pruyser, Peter Novotny, Meredith Titus, Arthur Mandelbaum, Tobias Brocher, Leonard Horwitz, Sydney Smith, Donald Colson, and Marianne Ault-Riché, for their suggestions and comments on one or more of the chapters that appear in this volume. From outside the Foundation, Robert Seidenberg and Marie Badaracco offered valuable help on earlier pages. I am also grateful to Jean Baker Miller,

Rachel Hare-Mustin, Michelle Bograd, Patricia Klein Frithiof, Virginia Goldner, Ellen Safier, Jane Hirschman, Jeanne Marecek, and Nancy Chodorow, for their critical reading of Chapter 14. Thanks also to Roy Menninger, President of The Menninger Foundation, and to Irwin Rosen, director of the Adult Outpatient Department, for flexible work arrangements and for making it possible for me to pursue my own directions.

Others at The Menninger Foundation have helped with this volume over the years. I am grateful to Virginia Eicholtz for her reassuring editorial presence and generous assistance throughout my writing career. Thanks also to Alice Brand and the professional library staff for working beyond the call of duty, tracking down references, and helping with countless last-minute details during the final stage of this project.

Betty Hoppes has provided outstanding secretarial skills and has been a generous and important source of encouragement and assistance throughout my career. For as long as I can remember, Mary McLin and Sue Spicer have demonstrated exceptional competence in keeping things running smoothly. Jeannine Riddle and Aleta Pennington, in word processing, have typed manuscripts with the shortest notice and also deserve special thanks.

Teresa Bernardez left The Menninger Foundation before I arrived, but we connected nonetheless, and I remain grateful for her inspiring and energizing presence in my life. Anthony Kowalski, Dennis Farrell, Estela Beale, Shahla Chehrazi, Sherry Levy-Reiner, Diana Hartley, Deborah Levy, and Sally Davis were all important to me during our overlapping years at the Foundation, and I thank each of them for supporting my work at home base.

I am especially grateful to my publisher, Jason Aronson, who invited me to put this volume together, and who played the major role in getting this project under way. I was also fortunate to have Rachel Witty as my editor; she provided clear, valuable advice throughout the production of the book, and it was a pleasure to work with her. Nancy Morgan Andreola did an excellent job copy-editing the final manuscript.

My husband Stephen Lerner has offered thoughtful criticism of almost every chapter in this volume and, along with our two sons Matthew and Benjamin, has provided a loving atmosphere in which I could write. My love and gratitude also go to my first family—my parents and sister—whose influence is reflected in all my work.

I have learned most about systems thinking (in particular, Bowen Family Systems Theory) from Katherine Glenn Kent, and the last three chapters in this book reflect her influence. She has been the single most important mentor in my professional career; I thank her for all she has taught me and for more than a decade of generous friendship.

Last, but not least, I owe a special debt to the feminist movement, which has permitted me to think more freely, question more boldly, and draw more authentically from my own experience. From the beginning of my career, I have been blessed with a wonderful network of long-distance feminist colleagues and friends who have supported my work during the difficult times and have shown me a new meaning of intellectual community and camaraderie among women. Although I give special thanks to Teresa Bernardez and Jean Baker Miller, I could not begin to name the countless other women whose radical voices have made such a difference to me over the past fifteen years. It is to all feminist voices that this book is dedicated.

Author's Foreword

Toward a More Humble Psychology of Women

If today's woman were to bring her symptoms and dissatisfactions to ten different mental health experts, she would, more likely than not, receive ten different perspectives. All ten of these perspectives might be wrong. Or all ten might be correct, with each reflecting a different piece of the elephant. A great deal remains unknown about the psychology of women, although numerous theories continue to be generated, from which therapeutic interventions are derived. These theories, my own included, are rarely offered as tentative and partial beliefs, but rather are put forth as the scientific facts of the day. As generations of women have attempted to conform to prevailing notions of what is right and appropriate for their sex, the psychological costs have been incalculable.

It is unfortunate that theories of female psychology are reified as truth and viewed as possessing a life of their own apart from a specific context. No matter how sophisticated our research tools or how sincere our strivings for neutrality and objectivity, our formulations, at best, reflect how interactions unfold and how psychic structures develop in a particular family form at a particular point in patriarchal history. In addition, any useful theory of female development or behavior must account both for the profound impact of gendered family and work roles and for the psychology of dominant and subordinate groups. Finally, the ways in which we formulate research questions, generate theory, and conduct psychotherapy are never separable from our own gender and family experiences, which include unconscious fears, wishes, and assumptions about women. As family therapist Betty Carter[1] reminds us, we cannot *not* react out of our gender, class, sibling position, ethnic background, personal history, theoretical orientation, experience, and wisdom, or the lack of it. Our choice is whether we do so consciously or unconsciously—whether we glorify theory as higher truth or simply state what we believe.

Perhaps then, precisely *what* we think about the subject of women in therapy is less important than *how* we think. We can move toward developing a more useful understanding of female psychology when we recognize not only that we lack answers but also that we are still in the process of formulating the right questions and finding an appropriate language in which to discuss issues of gender. In this light, it has been a particularly humbling experience for me to lay out my own work on the theory and therapy of women, which spans a decade and a half. If one compares the final part of this volume to my earlier writings, it is evident that my current thinking differs from my earlier ideas in important respects and that these differences are reflected in changes in my clinical practice. Confronting these shifts in my own work over time helps me counteract my usual tendency to shout "Eureka!" at every point along the way.

The psychology of women, like this book itself, is a work in progress. Each of us adds a small piece to a picture that will continue to be changed and enlarged over time. This book is

---

[1]Carter, B. (1985). Ms. intervention's guide to "correct" feminist family therapy. *The Family Therapy Networker* 9(6):78–79.

neither comprehensive nor definitive; rather, it is a record of the evolution of certain ideas, which have shifted as feminist theory, and then family systems theory, enriched and challenged my psychoanalytic views. I hope that this volume reflects the spirit of openness and inquiry that feminist voices have inspired and made possible.

WOMEN IN CONTEXT

The earlier papers in this volume reflect my attempts to revise psychoanalytic assumptions about femininity and to reformulate phallocentric views of women which pathologize female functioning and perpetuate a narrow intrapsychic focus that obscures the larger context. Despite my commitment to viewing female behavior through a wide-angle lens, my focus in the 1970s was on the mother–child dyad, with the role of fathers and other family members rendered peripheral to the subject at hand. In contrast, the final chapter of this book critiques the psychoanalytic preoccupation with maternal power and with the mother–child dyad and describes the problems engendered when this encapsulated unit of mother and child, or the oedipal triad of mother, father, and child, remain the primary, if not exclusive, framework for observation and theory building. Here I argue that an understanding of female development and self-differentiation requires a systems perspective, in which the field of observation and inquiry is the reciprocal, circular patterns maintained by *all* family members. The implications for the psychotherapy of women from this perspective are profound.

What unifies the shifts and changes that are documented in this volume is my ongoing commitment to viewing female behavior within the broadest possible context. Feminist theory first challenged me to place the mother–daughter dyad within the cultural context and to show how difficulties in this arena could not be understood in isolation from the larger society in which mothering exists. Family systems theory then provided me with a new epistemological framework that allowed me to observe how the mother–daughter dyad is inextricably interwoven with the father–daughter dyad, the marital relationship, and other interlocking family relationships and triangles that often span several generations. Tracking family process and appreciating the complex circular interconnectedness between the individual, family, and culture is no small task. Indeed, I still struggle with a defensive wish to keep feminist theory, psychoanalytic theory, and family systems theory in separate, airtight pockets inside my head so that they will not rub up against each other and cause me trouble.

The chapters in this volume reflect my best attempt to move against this sort of compartmentalization—to reject the traditional notion that culture is not an appropriate focus of psychoanalytic inquiry or that the study of ongoing family processes is a less crucial or more superficial focus than internalized object representations evoked through transference. As a psychotherapist, I am able to be most useful to women when I can help them view their problems and behavior through the broadest possible lens, with an eye toward identifying the intrapsychic, familial, and cultural factors that thwart the differentiation of self and impede the ability to love and work.

Despite all good intentions, this book, like other scholarly volumes in the mental health field, reflects the narrow scope of one author's personal and professional experience. The clinical work from which my theoretical formulations are derived has been conducted largely (although by no means exclusively) with white, middle-class individuals and families. This is not to minimize the relevance of my ideas to other groups, nor to deny commonalities of experience among all women. Rather, I make this point because I am increasingly aware of how often my colleagues and I expound on the "psychology of women," as if we were speaking of *all* women—when indeed, we are not. With this reflexive use of language, we obscure differences and diversity among women, and we relegate women of different color, class, and sexual preference to a "special issues" category at best, or to a deviant or invisible subgroup at worse. Only when we have explored the interplay of race, class, sexual preference, and gender can we approach a more complex and inclusive analysis of female psychology. I wish, then, to re-emphasize the fact that my contribution is a very small piece of the larger mosaic that we are creating together in our efforts to depict the richness and diversity of female experience.

Ultimately, each individual woman we see in psychotherapy is the best expert on her own self. Ideally, it will be the voices of women that will continue to inform and shape our theories, and not the other way around. Ideally also, the future voices of women will evolve in a new context in which both sexes hold more equal power in families and in the public sphere. Our current understanding of the special strengths and vulnerabilities of women is inseparable from the psychology of subordinate-group functioning.

The task of examining the complexity and deep-rootedness of our patriarchal bias—a bias for which *sexism* is too glib a term—is one that we are still just beginning. It is precisely because the impact of patriarchy is so profound and pervasive that it is not possible to fully comprehend how it shapes our theoretical assumptions and our practice of psychotherapy. Only *after* patriarchal structures (including structures of language and thought) are challenged and changed can we begin to more fully realize the problems of the old way.

What would the psychotherapy of women look like in a society where women joined men equally as makers and shapers of culture, valued and represented in every aspect of public life? Would we, at such a time, still remain focused on gender issues or even require a special psychology of women?

Only the boldest and most radical thinkers among us can even begin to imagine.

Harriet Goldhor Lerner, Ph.D.
Staff Psychologist
The Menninger Foundation
Topeka, Kansas
January 1988

WOMEN
IN
THERAPY

PART I

EARLY YEARS AND THEIR INTERPRETATION

Chapter 1

Origins of Envy and Devaluation of Women

Psychoanalysts have long believed that penis envy is central to the understanding of women and have invoked this concept to explain everything from a woman's desire for a husband and child to her strivings to work and compete in traditionally male-dominated fields.[1] Those outside psychoanalytic circles have shown less enthusiasm for such explanations—particularly feminists who have pointed out that women have cause to be envious of men's position in society for reasons other than their possession of the desired penis. Certain psychoanalysts have, in turn, insisted that the women's liberation movement is itself a manifestation of penis envy and that discontent with the female role is a psychiatric problem.

Narrow and stereotyped notions concerning women's appropriate place in society are not confined to a mere handful of psychoanalysts. The most authoritative of psychoanalysts have concurred that the "true" nature of women is to find fulfillment in the traditional role of wife and mother (Chesler

---

[1]This chapter was first published in 1974 as "Early Origins of Envy and Devaluation of Women: Implications for Sex-Role Stereotypes" in the *Bulletin of the Menninger Clinic* 38(6):538–553, before the publication of Dorothy Dinnerstein's classic text *The Mermaid and the Minotaur: Sexual Arrangements and Human Malaise* (New York: Harper & Row, 1976).

1972). Without sharing Freud's views of the Oedipus complex and penis envy, Jung (1928) nevertheless stated "that in taking up a masculine calling, studying, and working in a man's way, woman is doing something not wholly in agreement with, if not directly injurious to, her feminine nature" (p. 169). Bettelheim (1965) commented that "as much as women want to be good scientists or engineers, they want first and foremost to be womanly companions of men and to be mothers" (p. 15). Women who are not happy with this state of affairs, according to Freud (1925), have refused adaptively to come to grips with their sexual inferiority and still have the "hope of some day obtaining a penis in spite of everything" (p. 191).

Although I am not in agreement with those who discredit the existence of penis envy, I do believe that psychoanalysts who rationalize certain maladaptive aspects of femininity as unavoidable biological necessities court contempt by carrying the concept of penis envy to untenable extremes. As Chesler (1972) has commented, "The 'Freudian' vision beholds women as essentially 'breeders and bearers,' as potentially warmhearted creatures, but more often as cranky children with uteruses, forever mourning the loss of male organs and male identity" (p. 79).

It is unfortunate, however, that feminist anger and misunderstanding have led to a global damnation of all psychoanalytic thinking, as well as to a somewhat more benign condemnation of other established modes of treatment. There have been numerous revisions of Freud's viewpoints on women, with frequent references to the unfortunate "phallocentric" bias of his theorizing and open acknowledgement that femininity and female sexuality are insufficiently understood (David 1970, Torok 1970). Even Freud expressed reticence and insecurity in the face of that "dark continent" of femininity, never failing to stress the incomplete and tentative nature of his theorizing. Recent psychoanalytic writers have, in fact, shown considerable appreciation of feminist protests and of the intense cultural pressures that combine with intrapsychic factors to encourage "women [to] accept [a] neurotically dependent, self-effacing solution in life" (Symonds 1971–1972, p. 224).

Long before the current feminist movement, however, there existed wide recognition that femininity in most cultures is much devalued and that frequent exaltation and idealization of women hardly mask the underlying contempt for them (Horney 1932). Writers from many disciplines, psychoanalysts among them, have described the quasiracial discrimination that exists against women. David (1970), for example, has noted one primitive tribe that refers to women as "the race which is not entitled to speak" (p. 50); and anthropologists have observed that the devaluation of women in many cultures is no less intense than the oppression of racial or ethnic minority groups.

The oppression of women is unique, however, in one important respect: Women may participate as vigorously in their own depreciation as do men. The "masochistic attitude" of many women can be easily recognized, and women's belittling of their own sex is observed daily in our consulting rooms, is demonstrated in experimental research (Goldberg 1968), and is inherent in cultural institutions around the world (Lederer 1968).

The devaluation of women is readily documented, but the reasons behind the complicity of both sexes are less clear. In addition to powerful cultural pressures on women to devalue themselves, there must be strong internal pressures as well, for institutionalized patterns are not so readily established and maintained unless there are advantages for all involved. For men as well, the reasons for complicity with a sexist solution are not obvious. Men have too frequently been described as having all the advantages and power of a "ruling class" when, in fact, the cost for their situation is no less dear. As one psychoanalyst has written:

> . . . on examining the question more closely, it is not obvious a priori that men should naturally want such a relationship of mastery. The falsity, the ambivalence, and the refusal of identifications it conceals should appear to him as so many snags on which his own full and authentic achievement comes to grief. . . . What interest has he in giving in to his need to dominate the

being through whom he could understand himself and who could understand him? To discover oneself through the other sex would be a genuine fulfillment of one's humanity, yet this is exactly what escapes most of us. [Torok 1970, pp. 168–169]

For many psychoanalytic theorists, the devaluation of women is an irreducible problem that stems from the genital deficiency (real or imagined) of the female sex. Intense hatred directed toward the mother because of her penis-less state and the resulting contempt not only for her but for all women is the inescapable lot of girls (due to their castration complex) and of boys (due to their castration anxiety). As long as men have penises and women vaginas, institutionalized sexism is an inevitable symptom of our anatomical destinies, for which phylogenesis alone must bear the responsibility.

By overextending the concept of genital inferiority in explaining the devaluation of women, however, we have failed to appreciate other important determinants. My opinion is that the devaluation of women as well as the very definitions of appropriate "masculine" and "feminine" behavior stem in large part from a defensive handling of the powerful and persistent affects of the early infant–mother relationship. The profound affects (i.e., envy, fear, rage, and shame) aroused by the child's helpless dependency on an all-powerful maternal figure have indeed received recognition, but their resulting impact on adult life has continually been underplayed and insufficiently elaborated. As Lederer (1968) commented, "of our fear and envy of women, we, the psychoanalytic-papers-writing men, have managed to maintain a dignified fraternal silence" (p. 153).

ENVY OF WOMEN

Although the concept of penis envy is familiar even to the layperson, psychoanalytic speculations regarding breast envy require a more arduous search through the literature. This fact is surprising, for society's intense idealization, devaluation, and literal obsession with breasts seems to point to the significance of such a phenomenon. Also of relevance is the critical importance of the mother's breast in early infancy: The breast is the earliest source of gratification and frustration and of love and hate, as well as the first vehicle of intimate social contact (Fairbairn 1952). Klein (1957), for example, has highlighted the infant's early relationship to the mother's breast: "in the analysis of our patients . . . the breast in its good aspect is the prototype of maternal goodness, inexhaustible patience and generosity, as well as of creativeness" (pp. 5–6).

Although the idea of breast envy has no formal conceptual status in psychoanalytic theory, it is of central importance in Klein's theoretical work. Defining envy as "the angry feeling that another person possesses and enjoys something desirable—the envious impulse being to take it away or to spoil it" (1957, p. 6), she writes: "My work has taught me that the first object to be envied is the feeding breast, for the infant feels that it possesses everything he desires and that it has an unlimited flow of milk and love which the breast keeps for its own gratification" (1957, p. 10). To Klein, the desire to internalize and thus possess the breast, so all the power and magic that the infant attributes to it will be his or her own, is of central importance. She reports that in the analysis of female patients, even penis envy can be traced back to envy of the mother's breast (or its symbolic representation, the bottle).

Freud (1909, 1918) also recognized that there is a counterpart to penis envy when he described pregnancy fantasies and the wish for a baby among men. In the analytic literature, one can find case studies describing pregnancy fantasies and enacted pregnancies both in grown men and young boys. Others, such as Brunswick (1940), have elaborated this theme, stating that in girls the wish for a child precedes the wish for a penis and that penis envy itself can be understood as the desire to possess the omnipotent mother and her attributes.

It is not my intention to popularize the notion of breast envy, but rather to suggest that male envy of female sex characteristics and reproductive capacity is a widespread and conspicuously ignored dynamic. Of greater importance is the fact that envy tends to be a larger phenomenon for both sexes, not typically confined to such part objects as penises and breasts. As Torok (1970) points out, it is not the absence of a thing (like the penis or breast) that produces such profound feelings of envy, despair, and self-hatred; rather, such envy is a symptom of unconscious desires, wishes, or fears that may have little to do with objective anatomical realities. Penis envy, for example, frequently has its origin in the dyadic relationship between mother and daughter and may be a symptom reflecting difficulties in identifying with and achieving differentiation from a mother who is perceived as jealous, destructive, and intrusive (Chasseguet-Smirgel 1970, Torok 1970). For men, it is unlikely that envy of women is derived simply from the feeding breast and reproductive capacities; rather, it is derived from the varied impressions of infancy and early childhood in which the mother is experienced as an omnipotent object who possesses inexhaustible supplies as well as the power both to inflict and to ward off all pain and evil.

Envy and Devaluation: Reversing an Early Matriarchy

Of central importance to the dynamic understanding of defensive sexism is the close relationship between envy and devaluation. Devaluation of an envied object is a typical defensive maneuver, for as long as an object is devalued it need not be envied. Klein has suggested that spoiling and devaluing are inherent aspects of envy and that the earliest and most important objects of envy and devaluation are the mother and her breast. Kernberg (1972) has also noted in his work with borderline and narcissistic patients that intense envy and hatred of women are conspicuous dynamics that impair the capacity to form love relationships. He finds that envy and hatred are defensively dealt with by depreciating and devaluating women.

The question arises whether envy and devaluation of women is confined to persons with serious psychopathology or whether it is a more pervasive, if not universal, dynamic. Although Kernberg implies that this constellation is a serious problem only for very disturbed patients, he also notes it is not a circumscribed clinical phenomenon: "One finds intense envy and hatred of women in many male patients. Indeed, from a clinical viewpoint, it seems the intensity of this dynamic constellation in men matches that of penis envy in women . . ." (1972, p. 14).

I agree with Kernberg's statement that devaluation of women is ". . . in the final analysis, devaluation of mother as a primary object of dependency" (1972, p. 14). However, I would further suggest that this dynamic is a pervasive one which is expressed in the institutionalized values and mores regarding gender in cultures around the world. In this culture, for example, I believe that the envy-devaluation constellation is reflected in the selection of what traits, qualities, behaviors, and roles are deemed appropriate for each sex. Our current notions of masculinity and femininity are such that enormous pressures are put on females to "let the man win," to avoid direct expressions of aggression, self-assertion, competitiveness, and intellectual prowess, and to suppress wishes to be leader and initiator rather than follower and helpmate (Lerner 1974, Lynn 1972). I suspect that these widely accepted gender definitions and sex-role stereotypes are themselves a reflection of a defensive devaluing of women, and thus of an early dependency relationship with mother.

Our gender definitions and sex role stereotypes also reflect an attempt to reinstate and retain in adult relations all the nurturant qualities of the "good mother." Thus, according to most cultural stereotypes, the desirable, "feminine" woman is one who embodies all aspects of the good mother (cleaning, feeding, providing emotional understanding, comfort, softness, warmth), but who possesses no elements of power, dominance, and control that are also factors within the imago of the omnipotent, envied mother. To put it somewhat differently, in conventional adult relationships, males stereotypically experience a *defensive reversal* of an early matriarchy, yet retain the nurturant functions of the good mother. A psychic and social situation is created in which the adult male retains the good aspects of mother but is now dominant and in control of a female object on whom, as in the case of his mother, he was initially dependent; that is, his wife (or female peer) becomes his own child. As long as this defensive reversal of an early dependency situation continues, envy and devaluation of women is subdued or seemingly eliminated; the devaluation of women achieves expression in the reversal itself.

But how are we to understand women's active participation in this system? For although women reverse the helpless dependency of their own infantile situation through the role of mother, they often "choose" in peer relationships with men to remain the dependent child. As Kernberg (1972) points out, envy and devaluation of the mother as a primal source of dependency is no less intense in women than in men. Thus, women's acceptance and perpetuation of feminine stereotypes (e.g., fragility, dependency, passivity, etc.) as well as idealization of men and the penis may also be an attempt to devalue the omnipotence and power of the maternal figure. This notion is compatible with Chasseguet-Smirgel's (1970) statement that images of women as castrated or deficient are a denial for both sexes of the imagos of the primitive mother (i.e., the good omnipotent mother is symbolized by the generous breast, fruitful womb, wholeness, abundance; the bad omnipotent mother is symbolized by frustration, invasion, intrusion, evil).[2]

Other theorists as well, while not focusing specifically on envy, have linked early maternal power to the depreciation of women. David (1970) speculates that profound narcissistic injuries inflicted on the infant by the omnipotent mother lead to a powerful need for revenge. He suggests that our distorted concept of femininity and female sexuality, the discrimination that women suffer by men and women, and the masochistic attitude that characterizes women are all the result of "revenge" for the radical narcissistic wounds inflicted on both male and female infants at the breast. Horney (1932) relates

---

[2]Penis envy and castration concerns in women reflect a defensive need to devalue the imagos of the primitive mother. Yet such symptoms may also reflect deep guilt and anxiety in identifying with this imago, especially when mother is experienced as a powerful, malevolent, and castrating figure in her relationship with father. Thus, women's self-experience of being "castrated" (and their idealization of men and the penis) is often a reaction formation against their own feared "castrating" and aggressive wishes. See Chasseguet-Smirgel (1970) for an excellent discussion of this issue.

both the idealization and the depreciation of women to the violently aggressive desires for revenge that stem from the mother's dominance and power and the small child's related feelings of weakness, impotence, and humiliation. Brunswick (1940) notes the powerful character of the primitive maternal image and emphasizes the early narcissistic injuries resulting from the child's dependency on the omnipotent mother ". . . who is capable of everything and who possesses every valuable attribute" (p. 304).

Chasseguet-Smirgel (1970) suggests another determinant of the need to reverse the infantile situation—namely, the fear and terror of women.

> I believe that a child, whether male or female, even with the best and kindest of mothers, will maintain a terri-fying maternal image in his unconscious, the result of projected hostility deriving from his own impo-tence . . . the child's primary powerlessness . . . and the inevitable frustrations of training are such that the imago of the good, omnipotent mother never covers over that of the terrifying, omnipotent, bad mother. [pp. 112–113]

Horney (1932) and Lederer (1968) each present an impres-sive amount of clinical, mythological, and anthropological evi-dence regarding man's terror of women. Although both au-thors comment on the remarkable lack of recognition and attention this topic has received, I suggest that perhaps it is not that the fear of women has gone unrecognized, but that the consequences of that fear for the patriarchal nature of societies have not been sufficiently appreciated. To what ex-tent has our concept of femininity been distorted by a need to discourage women from the recognition and expression of self-seeking, aggressive, competitive, ambitious strivings, in order to ensure that the primitive maternal imago can, in adult life, at last be controlled, dominated, and revenged? Similarly, if men were encouraged to experience and express so-called fem-inine qualities (e.g., dependency, passivity, and fragility), would they then feel in danger of returning to that dreaded (although wished for) condition of early maternal omnipotence? In keeping with this theme, Chasseguet-Smirgel (1970) has related religious mythology to the difficulties that maternal dominance and omnipotence present to both sexes.

> Man and woman are born of woman: before all else we are our mother's child. Yet all our desires seem designed to deny this fact, so full of conflicts and reminiscent of our primitive dependence. The myth of Genesis seems to express this desire to free ourselves from our mother: man is born of God, an idealized paternal figure. . . . Woman is born from man's body. If this myth expresses the victory of man over his mother and over woman, who thereby becomes his own child, it also provides a certain solution for woman inasmuch as she also is her mother's daughter: she chooses to belong to man, to be created *for* him, and not for herself, to be a part of him—Adam's rib—rather than to prolong her "attachment" to her mother. [pp. 133–134]

SEX-ROLE STEREOTYPES

At the cost of oversimplifying, I believe it may be worthwhile to examine how the values and mores of traditional male–female relationships in this country can be understood within the stated theoretical framework. The fact that the nurturant functions of the good mother (e.g., feeding, cleaning, providing emotional comfort and support) are retained by women in marriage hardly requires description or elaboration. The following points are offered to support the notion that the cultural stereotypes of adult gender interactions (apart from nurturant functions) involve a reversal for males of their early helplessness and dependency on a powerful female object.

1. Women are encouraged to be dependent and are frequently portrayed as lost and helpless without a male partner. "Little girl" qualities typically make women more attractive, and

it is of significance that women are affectionately referred to as "girls," "chicks," "baby," and "doll." Mothers tend to foster dependency to a greater degree in female children (Lynn 1972), and research indicates that adult men and women tend to equate assertive, independent strivings in girls and women with a loss of femininity (Baumrind 1972).

Expressions of dependency needs in men are considered unattractive, weak or effeminate, and are more frequently denied than cultivated. For males, the notion of men's greater independence is a reversal of the infant–mother paradigm, in which it is the child who is helplessly dependent on the powerful maternal figure.

2. In male–female relationships, intellectual ability and competence are frequently seen as the man's domain. A girl's sense of intellectual mastery and skill is progressively discouraged as she is trained to be "feminine"; she is encouraged to be smart enough to catch a man but never to outsmart him (Baumrind 1972, Lerner 1974). In the media, wives are often portrayed as silly, capricious, gossipy, illogical, and intellectually helpless; and mockery of a female's ability to think logically and critically is an extremely popular form of humor. Although women are acknowledged to have a type of wisdom that goes by the name of "feminine intuition," there is a persistent insinuation that for females, organized and sustained logical thinking is not critically involved. Research findings indicate that both sexes regard intellectual achievement as "unfeminine" and that college women tend to equate academic success with detrimental social consequences (Baumrind 1972).

Although many men do not value the "dumb blonde" stereotype, few seek love relationships with a female partner who is comfortably acknowledged to be an intellectual equal or superior. Similarly, a woman who assumes an intellectually aggressive, critical, or dominant stance is often labeled "masculine" or "castrating." Again, this social situation appears to be a reversal of the male's position as an infant, in which the intellectually helpless child is slowly taught to master his environment by a maternal figure who is experienced as infinitely capable and wise. The role of early teacher (and frustrator) moves systematically from mother to a continuing series of figures (governesses, babysitters, elementary-school teachers) who are predominantly female.

3. Physical strength and prowess, which are glorified and cultivated in men, are considered unattractive in women; the strong, athletic female or gymnast is generally not thought to be the most attractive of mates. Although men may be encouraged to go to painful extremes in body building, women are taught to exaggerate, and even feign, weakness in the interest of "femininity." Men enjoy treating women as weak and delicate creatures who cannot open their own doors or carry their own packages. Similarly, it is typically important for men to be physically taller than their mates. Short or small men are devalued. Again, for men, this paradigm reverses the infant's experiences of the small and weak child who is carried about with ease in the arms of the powerful mother. Horney (1932) emphasized the small boy's feeling of distress and humiliation at being small and weak in comparison with mother.

4. In love relationships, men are typically older than their female partner. While there is nothing unusual about a match between a 35-year-old man and a 23-year-old woman, the reversed situation is evaluated as eccentric, if not pathological. Similarly, when a man marries a woman "young enough to be his daughter," the match may be either criticized or condoned by society, but the desires of both parties are considered understandable. Were a woman to marry a man young enough to be her son, society tends to respond with scorn and shock. Again, for males, this situation reverses the infant–mother relationship, in which the "older woman" is the sole object of the young child's libidinal desires. One might further speculate that the intense pressures on women to look eternally like adolescent girls (rather than like "mothers") stems in part from the matronly woman's capacity to arouse infantile envy of the inexhaustible feeding breast as well as to stimulate anxiety-laden wishes for returning to a helpless state of dependency.

5. The perpetuation of personality characteristics and traits associated with infancy and childhood is encouraged in the female sex only. For example, crying, whining, and seductively manipulative and petulant behavior are all acceptable ways for women to make their demands felt and are portrayed in the media as typical feminine qualities. Such behaviors are unacceptable in men, who are encouraged to assert themselves in a more "manly" fashion. Similarly, females are most frequently portrayed as emotional and males as intellectual. The stereotype is of the "hysterical," overemotional wife who is kept in check by her husband, who allegedly makes decisions by the laws of logic and cool reason. Again, males experience a reversal of the infant's situation, in which it is the mother who supplies the intellectual controls to the child who has considerable affective lability and emotionality.

6. In courtship and sexual relations, women stereotypically assume a passive stance and men an overly active one. Men are taught to actively pursue what they want; women are taught to make themselves pretty enough to be sought after. Although females may learn "feminine wiles" to attract the men of their choice, they are discouraged from openly and directly pursuing a male figure. This state of affairs for males is again the reversal of the infant's situation, in which the baby is unable to actively determine whether it will get the breast or the mother's affection. The baby may actively attempt to "court" her in a number of ways (such as by crying or being cute), but it is the active mother who initiates or fails to initiate contact with the child.

7. Stereotyped notions of feminine sexuality tend to glorify naiveté and "innocence," whereas for males, "experience" tends to enhance their sexual attractiveness. (One might consider the difference between an "experienced man" and a "loose woman.") Similarly, in regard to the expression of aggressive impulses, Symonds (1971–1972) notes that what is called "strength of character" in boys is called "unfeminine" in girls. Stereotypes that have encouraged the stifling of sexual and aggressive expression in women and the frank

expression of impulse life in men are also for men a reversal of the infant–mother paradigm: It is the mother who inhibits the expression of "unacceptable" impulses early in the child's life. Many psychoanalytic writers, including Horney, Klein, and Freud, have stressed that mothers are experienced as punitive because they are the first to forbid a child instinctual activities.

It is, of course, naive to assume that the devaluation of women and the establishment and maintenance of traditional sex role stereotypes can be entirely understood according to the stated theoretical framework that emphasizes the early oral dyadic relationship between mother and child without regard for the complexities inherent in the oedipal triangle. Additional socioeconomic, biological, and psychodynamic factors are relevant to the present discussion, and the speculations offered here are to be considered partial rather than exhaustive explanations of complicated phenomena.

THE SIGNIFICANCE OF SEX-ROLE STEREOTYPES

I anticipate the objection that the generalizations presented here are oversimplified clichés that fail to account for the richness of individual differences in our culture. Clearly, both clinical knowledge and human experience reveal that there are varied bases for successful male–female relationships and that many stable and gratifying marriages involve variations if not thoroughgoing modifications of these general themes. Sydney Smith[3] points out that a common American cliché holds that the woman is the real decision maker in the family, despite the man's belief that he is the boss. This understanding of power relationships between the sexes is familiar and is well illustrated by the European saying "The man is the head of the family but the woman is the neck that carries the head and determines the direction." Underlying the notion that the woman gets her way despite the husband's stated authority as

---

[3]Personal communication.

boss is the idea that the woman wields her power in subtle and manipulative ways that allow the husband to retain his fantasies of being in charge. Many families are indeed matriarchal in their power balance, but the cultural ideal is that the man be the "head" of the household rather than a relatively submissive, passive (and thus "effeminate") figure. When we say that the wife "wears the pants" in the family, we imply that she has stepped into the role that rightfully belongs to the man.

That women surreptitiously wield power is further illustrated in movies, novels, and plays where one frequently runs across the theme of the egocentric, unrealistic male who meets his match in an eminently reasonable, practical woman. Smith also mentions A. J. Leibling's psychological and sociological studies of the American soap opera in which men are characteristically portrayed as weak, helpless, and impotent, or who become physically crippled and must be sustained by a good woman who alone maintains contact with the real world.

I do not purport to provide a factual description of all possible relationships between men and women, which are indeed infinitely variable and complex. Rather, what I present is an outline of widespread cultural values and ideal types—society's definition of the way relationships "should be" if both partners have fulfilled the criteria for appropriate masculine and feminine behavior. Thus, a frail, dependent, and intellectually inept man may indeed seek out a strong, assertive, and capable woman to protect and care for him; and the needs and dynamics of the two individuals might "fit" in a manner that results in a stable and satisfying marriage. Such a man is hardly the prototype of the successful male, however, and he is likely to be considered a poor, if not pathognomonic, role model for his son. Similarly, the woman married to such a man is perceived as having made a "bad catch," accompanied by the speculation that some neurotic problem kept her from "doing better." Men may indeed be passive, conforming, childlike, and unrealistically dependent but, as Chesler (1972) points out, they are hardly taught to romanticize these qualities as essential aspects of their masculinity.

Furthermore, the sex role stereotypes I have described are not peripheral to the culture but rather are powerful and ubiquitous forces affecting even the most "liberated" persons. Some authors (Baumrind 1972, Symonds 1971–1972) suggest that lifelong consequences exist for the growing girl whose concept of femininity is based on the model that to be more aggressive, assertive, or intellectually capable than one's male partner is to be unfeminine, unlovable, and even "castrating." Similarly, boys are deeply affected by current notions of masculine attractiveness that glorify such traits as power, dominance, and intellectual skill, and that do not allow for even realistic expressions of fear, dependency, childishness, and weakness. Although in intellectual circles there is a tendency to see such stereotypes as outdated and inapplicable to today's changing patterns of relationships, the psychic and social dynamics persist. Even if recent social changes were indeed substantial, there remains the important task of making sense of the intense subjugation and devaluation of women that has occurred throughout the world. The specifics of male–female sex role stereotypes may vary across time and place, but the ethos of male dominance and phallocentric prejudice is as old as humanity itself.

Rather than applying psychoanalytic principles toward understanding how our distorted notions of masculinity and femininity have been established and maintained, we have instead tended to incorporate these stereotypes into our theorizing and language, thus allowing myth and anxiety to prevail over scientific thought. A review of psychoanalytic writings reveals how practitioners and theorists pervasively and glibly label active displays of competitiveness, aggression, and intellectual ambitiousness in women as "phallic" or "masculine," and similarly label manifestations of passivity, submissiveness, malleability, childishness, emotionality, and dependency in men as "effeminate" or "feminine" (Young 1973).

For example, the character of the primitive maternal imago (and women's related fear of their castrating and destructive potential) may be such that the female sex has relatively greater difficulty acknowledging and directly expressing aggressive, competitive, and ambitious strivings. Labeling these qualities as masculine, however, only serves to increase women's guilt and inhibitions and to reinforce a masochistic position. Similarly, anxiety about reenacting an early matriarchy, with its related castration fears, may make men more fearful of acknowledging their own passive, dependent, and regressive longings, but it does not follow that these longings are "feminine" ones. There are indeed different developmental tasks that the two sexes must master based on anatomical differences; however, I believe that our present gender definitions are less a reflection of anatomical realities and more an expression of a defensive reaction to the imagos of the primitive mother. It is imperative that we gain greater conceptual clarity regarding the treatment implications and underlying theoretical rationale for labeling specific traits and behaviors as masculine or feminine.[4]

In order to defuse the character of the primitive maternal imago and to prevent excessive envy and fear of women, I suggest that shared parenting may be important. While the psychiatric literature is replete with the hazards of inadequate mothering, there has been only minimal concern with the infant–father relationship. The child's formula for mental health seems to involve spending the early years with a mother who ". . . is always present, alert and responsive to the child's needs . . ." (Mandelbaum 1973, p. 6), the later relationship with father being secondary to and dependent on the quality of this first interaction. Although many mental health professionals protest that we have held onto this model of mothering at a tremendous cost to women's growth and development, there has been less emphasis on its hazards for the growing infant and child. Is not defensive idealization and devaluation of women one pathological consequence of the child's world

---

[4]Research findings demonstrating sex differences along some dimension (e.g., relatively greater activity and aggressiveness in male infants) are often used to argue that a particular characteristic is a masculine or feminine one. Apart from the fact that there is always considerable overlap between the sexes, such conclusions are arbitrary ones. For example, female children are more verbal and articulate than male children; however, we do not label verbal skills as "feminine" and proceed actively to encourage these skills in girls or call them "feminine" to discourage them in boys. Group sex differences in no way imply that a trait or quality is healthy for one sex and less adaptive or important for the other.

being a matriarchal one, where the powerful figures that grat-
ify and frustrate the child's impulses and wishes are predominantly female? We have not as yet applied our sophisticated
psychoanalytic principles to understanding the consequences
of shared parenting or examining how such a system would
affect the developmental tasks that each sex must master.
Clearly, shared parenting would affect the maternal and paternal imagos that the child internalizes and may consequently
lead to a capacity for adult men and women to relate to each
other from a position of greater equality, openness, and
mutual respect.

REFERENCES

Baumrind, D. (1972). From each according to her ability.
     School Review 80(2):161–197.
Bettelheim, B. (1965). The commitment required of a woman
     entering a scientific profession in present-day American
     society. In *Women and the Scientific Professions: The
     M.I.T. Symposium on American Women in Science and
     Engineering*, ed. J. A. Mattfeld and C. G. Van Aken, pp. 3–
     19. Cambridge, Mass.: M.I.T. Press.
Brunswick, R. M. (1940). The preoedipal phase of the libido
     development. *Psychoanalytic Quarterly* 9:293–319.

Chasseguet-Smirgel, J. (1970). Feminine guilt and the Oedipus
     complex. In *Female Sexuality: New Psychoanalytic
     Views*, ed. J. Chasseguet-Smirgel et al., pp. 94–134. Ann
     Arbor: University of Michigan Press.
Chesler, P. (1972). *Women and Madness*. Garden City, N.Y.:
     Doubleday.

David, C. (1970). A masculine mythology of femininity. In
     Female Sexuality: New Psychoanalytic Views, ed. J.
     Chasseguet-Smirgel et al., pp. 47–67. Ann Arbor: Univer-
     sity of Michigan Press.

Fairbairn, W. R. D. (1952). *An Object-Relations Theory of the Personality*. New York: Basic Books.

Freud, S. (1909). Analysis of a phobia in a five-year-old boy. *Standard Edition* 10:3–149, 1955.

—— (1918). From the history of an infantile neurosis. *Standard Edition* 17:3–122, 1955.

—— (1925). Some psychological consequences of the anatomical distinction between the sexes. In *Collected Papers*, vol. 5, ed. J. Strachey. London: Hogarth Press, 1950.

Goldberg, P. (1968). Are women prejudiced against women? *Trans-action* 5(5):28–30.

Horney, K. (1932). The dread of women. *International Journal of Psychoanalysis* 13:348–360.

Jung, C. G. (1928). *Contributions to Analytical Psychology*, trans. H. G. and C. F. Baynes. London: Routledge and Kegan Paul.

Kernberg, O. (1971). Barriers to falling and remaining in love. In *Object Relations Theory and Clinical Psychoanalysis*, pp. 185–213. New York: Jason Aronson.

Klein, M. (1957). *Envy and Gratitude*. New York: Basic Books.

Lederer, W. (1968). *The Fear of Women*. New York: Grune & Stratton.

Lerner, H. G. (1974). The hysterical personality: a "woman's disease." *Comprehensive Psychiatry* 15(2):157–164.

Lynn, D. B. (1972). Determinants of intellectual growth in women. *School Review* 80(2):241–260.

Mandelbaum, A. (1973). Separation. *Menninger Perspective* 4(5):5–9, 27.

Symonds, A. (1971–1972). Discussion (of Ruth Moulton's paper, "Psychoanalytic reflections on women's liberation"). *Contemporary Psychoanalysis* 8:224–228.

Torok, M. (1970). The significance of penis envy in women. In *Female Sexuality: New Psychoanalytic Views*, ed. J. Chasseguet-Smirgel et al., pp. 135–170. Ann Arbor: University of Michigan Press.

Young, E. (1973). A review of feminine psychology. Unpublished manuscript, University of California at Berkeley.

Chapter 2

Parental Mislabeling of Female Genitals

As children grow up they are taught that boys have a penis and girls have a vagina.[1] That the little girl is taught she has a vagina, an internal organ difficult to examine in reality, but is not told she has a vulva that includes the clitoris and labia, may be a critical factor in her psychosexual development. Significantly, this incomplete labeling of female genitals is an almost ubiquitous phenomenon: If one interviews parents or reads literature on sex education, it is evident that the girl child is told that she has a vagina and nothing else. Even educational material written for an adolescent population typically communicates this same undifferentiated picture of female genitals. "A girl has two ovaries, a uterus, and a vagina which are her sex organs. A boy's sex organs are a penis and testicles. One of the first changes (at puberty) will be the growth of hair around the vaginal opening of the girl" (Taylor 1972, p. 47).

Such an incomplete, poorly differentiated and anatomically incorrect picture of female anatomy may have its most critical effect during the preoedipal and early oedipal phases of development, when the girl discovers her clitoris as the prime source of sexual stimulation and gratification. Surely it is of

---

[1]This chapter was first published in 1976 as "Parental Mislabeling of Female Genitals as a Determinant of Penis Envy and Learning Inhibitions in Women" in the *Journal of the American Psychoanalytic Association* 24(5):269–283.

serious psychological consequence to the child that she discovers an organ of pleasure that frequently is not acknowledged, labeled, or validated for her by the parents, and which is thus inevitably experienced as "unfeminine" (only boys have something on the "outside"). More specifically, this miseducation may be one contributing factor to penis envy in women, and I would speculate that penis envy is not simply the wish for a penis (i.e., the wish to have what boys have), but rather may reflect the wish to validate and have "permission" for female sexual organs, including the sensitive external genitals. I would suggest that at a deeper level penis envy is a symptom that may, in certain women, express an unfulfilled wish to have permission from mother to be a sexually operative and responsive female. This idea is in keeping with Torok's (1970) suggestion that penis envy is the girl's unconscious pledge to a jealous and possessive maternal imago that she will not achieve genital fulfillment and will deny herself pleasure with the penis for mother's sake.

Clinical Example

The following case presentation illustrates how the mislabeling of female genitals may contribute to penis envy as well as to symptomatic learning inhibitions.

> Ann was a married professional woman with children, whose initial decision to enter intensive psychotherapy was precipitated by a number of accumulating internal and external stresses. Three of her symptoms, which proved to be dynamically interwoven, will form the focus of the treatment fragment presented here.
>
> The first symptom that Ann reported was sexual inhibitions with her husband. While she experienced vaginal sensations during intercourse and felt that she "liked" her vagina, she had feelings of disgust, shame, and anxiety about her external genitals that greatly interfered with her capacity to experience sexual pleasure. She was unable to allow her husband to look at her vulvar area, and similarly was unable to examine herself, thus maintaining some uncertainty

about her own anatomical realities. She referred to her external genitals as "my outside stuff" and was unable, during the early part of treatment, to say the words clitoris, labia, and vulva without experiencing an acute sense of anxiety and humiliation.

Ann's second major symptom was a tendency to become confused and "stupid" in relation to what she called "time and place." For example, despite very superior intellectual ability, she would typically become disoriented in regard to time sequences—"Is fall before autumn, or are they the same thing? I can't remember." "Today could be Monday or Friday. Now I can't say which it is without stopping to figure it out." "If someone says to me, 'I went last spring,' I get confused. I may have to say the months and seasons to myself to place it in time." Ann was similarly disrupted in her thinking when it came to geography and spatial relations. She had difficulty picturing the location of a country, or relationships among countries or continents. She complained of having no "internal map" of the city in which she had lived for many years, and was characteristically confused about directions. In fact, she would often look at her wedding ring in order to distinguish with confidence the difference between left and right. The contrast, between the degree of helplessness and confusion she experienced in these areas of functioning and her otherwise rich and highly differentiated style of cognition, was indeed striking.

Ann's third symptom was penis envy: Her envy and idealization of male genitals was at times only thinly disguised. She was unable to comfortably assume the top and more active position in intercourse—a reluctance she later understood as reflecting the confusion she would experience in this position as to "who had the penis" and her conflicted wish that it be hers.

An important theme that became elaborated during the course of Ann's treatment was her confusion about what her own genitals looked like—a confusion she later linked with her inability to comprehend temporal and spatial structures or relationships. She spoke of the incomprehensible complexity of her external genitals: "What's between my legs is like a clock. A clock is simple on the outside. It has numbers and two hands. But if you look beyond the surface, the intricacy of a clock is too much to figure out. It's the same with me. If you look superficially, it's like having a crack like you see on statues. But if you really really look, then there's a lot of confusing parts. It seems like too much to figure out." Often, in a sequence of associations, she expressed her sense of helplessness about "figuring out" her genitals, followed by similar expressions of helplessness about her inability to comprehend her physical environment: "It's crazy, but I don't think I can ever comprehend where things are at [referring to her genitals]. I don't think men know either. They're always fumbling around. Sometimes my husband can't find my clitoris. It's like he needs a roadmap or something. When I direct him, I feel like a traffic cop. I'm not sure of my way around either." Ann used much the same language to describe her confusion about finding her way around the city: "It's like I don't have a map in my head no matter how often I've seen it or been there. It seems too confusing, almost hopeless, to try to figure out how everything is placed. It's always like seeing a place for the first time."

As Ann began to link her confusion about her anatomy to her temporal and spatial disorientation, she also began to associate her envy of the penis with the fact that the male organ is "neat and simple," "easy to figure out," and "without confusing or hidden parts." It was "validated" by others, whereas her external genitals were "unspeakable." "Everyone knows that men have a penis and everyone can say the word—even at parties. But the only word that people will say to describe what women have is 'vagina'."

With the progression of the treatment, the connection among these three themes (disgust and confusion about her external genitals, disorientation to time and place, and her envy of the penis) became clearer as I began to understand the salience of the word "permission." Ann sometimes experienced surges of anger or depression when referring to a vaguely defined feeling of "not having permission" for her external genitals, which she claimed had been "invalidated" and "denied" to her. Her sexual difficulties as well as her spatial and temporal confusions indeed proved to be symptomatic of her conflict around "having permission to have what I have."

Ann's feeling of "not having permission" achieved various expressions in her relationship with me. When I was absent for two weeks, she experienced increased feelings of disgust about her vulva and a decreased ability to enjoy sexual relations or even physical contact with her husband. On my return she complained at length about how the disruption of treatment had exacerbated her sexual difficulties. Later, she had a fantasy that I was secretly pleased by this course of events; her increased sexual inhibitions were a "gift" to me—an implicit statement that my presence and the treatment I offered were of "number one" importance. Having sexual pleasure in my absence was not permissible because it might make me feel irrelevant, pushed out, and even unhappy.

Similarly, Ann insisted that I wished to deny her pleasure with her clitoris. Armed with the information that I was a "Freudian," she became angrily preoccupied with the idea that I wanted her to be "totally vaginal" and that, as far as I was concerned, she only had permission for her internal genitals. When Ann understood the genesis of her feelings of "not having permission," her symptoms were significantly attenuated.

Two critical developmental events were linked to Ann's fantasy, "I do not have permission to have what I have." One was early punishments she received from her mother for masturbating, which, for Ann, meant that having pleasure with her genitals (and wishing to have sexual pleasure with father's penis) was destructive to her mother. The second was her early education that "boys have a penis and girls have a hole where the baby comes out." Ann's experience of discovering her external genitals and having pleasure with her clitoris and vulva was not prohibited solely by a masturbation taboo. More important, the incomplete information she received about her anatomy was for her "a message that I didn't have what I had." As she said, "What I had that felt good didn't have a name. It wasn't supposed to exist. Only boys had something on the outside. So I couldn't have my clitoris and still be a girl. No one can deny the penis to a boy. No one could not give it a name or make it into a secret. To have a penis is to have permission to have what you have."

Ann's inability to comprehend the "geography" of her genitals or of her external world was really a promise to mother that she "would not look." Looking meant that she would see something (her vulva, especially her clitoris) that wasn't supposed to be there for mother's sake. Penis envy, in Ann's words, was "a wish to have permission for what I really *did* have, which was more than a vagina where babies come from." Penis envy not only expressed Ann's wish to have her own sexuality "validated," it also served to block this forbidden wish by preventing sexual fulfillment, thus reassuring a prohibitive maternal imago that she (Ann) would not become a fully sexually responsive woman who took pride in femininity.

DISCUSSION

It is hardly necessary to stress that this treatment fragment is not intended to account for the complexities of feminine body image or to provide a comprehensive explanation of the symptoms of penis envy and disturbed cognition. Clearly, penis envy often has other meanings than that illustrated by Ann's case (Moulton 1973) just as a breakdown in sharply focused and differentiated perception and cognition may reflect a range of intrapsychic and cultural determinants (Shapiro 1965, Lerner 1974a).

Nor do I wish to imply that the inaccurate and incomplete labeling of female genitals will invariably convey to the girl child that she should deny herself sexual pleasure for mother's sake. The context of the parent–child relationship in which the sexual misinformation is conveyed is of considerable importance. In Ann's case, for example, there were additional aspects of her development that led to the internalization of a jealous maternal imago who did not want her to achieve genital fulfillment. Parental failure to label the components of female anatomy will have its most pathogenic effects when it occurs in the context of other sexual or oedipal prohibitions impeding normal development.

I would speculate, however, that even in the best of parent–child relationships, the failure to explicitly acknowledge and label the girl's external genitals, especially the clitoris, cannot help but have pathogenic consequences. This idea is in keeping with the suggestion that vague information regarding one's sexuality and sexual differences is an important etiological factor in disturbed reality testing and severe psychopathology (Bellak and Benedict 1958, p. 29). One consequence is to impair the girl's capacity to develop an accurate and differentiated psychic representation or "map" of her genitals and to impede her in the difficult developmental task of differentiating the internal from external genitals (see Kestenberg 1968). The fact that the girl's own exploration of her genitals is not corroborated or paralleled by information from her environment may lead to anxiety, confusion, and shame regarding her sexuality. Because neither sex is informed that the clitoris is part of "what girls have," this organ will be cathected as a small and inadequate penis rather than as a valid and feminine part of the girl's sexuality.

Of even greater dynamic significance is that this mislabeling will carry with it an implicit or unconscious communication to the girl child. In Ann's case, parental failure to label the external genitals was perceived as an unconscious message that she was to deny herself sexual pleasure and genital fulfillment for her mother's sake. While the unconscious message may vary in differing interpersonal contexts, something along the following lines will be communicated: The vulva (including the clitoris) is not important, must not be spoken of or thought about, or should not exist.[2]

Torok (1970) has emphasized the forbidding of masturbation as a central determinant of penis envy. She writes that the girl idealizes and envies the penis in order to reassure the possessive and intrusive mother that she will never achieve genital fulfillment, that she will abandon her desire to have pleasure with the penis, and that she will live out her days in unfulfilled longing for an unattainable object. According to Torok, the mother who forbids masturbation communicates that she would lapse into bitter emptiness and envy if the child could achieve satisfaction without her.

The forbidding of masturbation with a known and recognized body part is perhaps a more benign message to the child to relinquish female sexuality than is the neglect to "validate" and give a name to the girl's sensitive external genitals. I would further speculate that the ubiquity of the female "castration complex" does not stem primarily from the fact that the clitoris is a smaller (and thus inferior) organ compared to the penis. Rather, the girl's feeling of being "cheated" may reflect parental failure to explicitly acknowledge that the vulva (especially the clitoris) is an important aspect of "what girls have." It is interesting to note that in Freud's time, the words *clitoris, vulva,* and *labia* were not included in the dictionary and, in this country, the only word in Webster's dictionary to refer to female genitals was *vagina.* One might question how pride in femininity could flourish at a time when our language did not include a word for the part of the female anatomy most richly endowed with sensory nerve endings and with no function but that of sensual pleasure.

---

[2]Unlike boys, who characteristically masturbate by focused and specific genital manipulation, girls are reported to more commonly engage in nonspecific, indirect forms of masturbation (Clower 1976). I suspect the avoidance of focused manual clitoral stimulation may in part reflect the failure to acknowledge and label this organ for the girl child.

While the appropriate additions to Webster's dictionary have since been made, little has changed, linguistically speaking, since Freud's day. Not only do parents fail to tell their daughters that they have a vulva which includes a clitoris, but my interviews reveal that the very idea of such communication produces a curious reaction of embarrassment and discomfort in the parent. In addition, it is surprising how many educated parents report never having heard the word vulva (including a large number who think the term refers to a Swedish automobile). Many of these parents think the word *vagina* means both the internal and external genitals. In our professional circles, as well, the avoidance of the world *vulva* is striking, even when the context specifically calls for it. For example, in Martin Mayman's Rorschach scoring manual, which is used by clinical psychologists at The Menninger Foundation, the word *vagina* is repeatedly misapplied to Rorschach percepts of the external female genitals. Similarly, patients who take this test frequently report seeing "vaginas," although subsequent inquiry, as well as the stimulus attributes of the inkblot, demonstrate that it is the female external genitals that are being perceived. The appropriate term *vulva* is very infrequently used even when residents, medical students, and professional staff are tested.

Although failing to appreciate the significance of parental mislabeling of female genitals, psychoanalytic theorists have been particularly sensitive to the complexities and difficulties that female anatomy presents to the growing girl. It has been noted, for example (Moulton 1973), that while boys have ". . . the obvious advantage of possessing a neat, visible organ" (p. 213) which can be handled without reprimand during urination, the girl's genitals are less accessible to either visual or manual inspection. Attention has also been given to the unconscious vagina–mouth equation, which may cause the girl or woman to fear this organ because of its fantasied castrating, oral-devouring, and destructive potential. In addition, the external genitals may be frightening because they may be perceived as resembling a wound, an idea that is reinforced by menstrual bleeding (Abraham 1920). De Beauvoir (1953) has written:

> The sex organ of a man is simple and neat as a finger;
> it is readily visible and often exhibited to comrades
> with proud rivalry; but the feminine sex organ is mys-
> terious even to the woman herself, concealed, mucous,
> and humid, as it is; it bleeds each month, it is often
> sullied with body fluids, it has a secret and perilous life
> of its own. . . . [p. 386]

It must be stressed, however, that the "mysterious" and
concealed nature of female anatomy does not necessarily prevent the girl child from discovering the components of her genitals. She will inevitably discover her external genitals, including
the clitoris, in the course of masturbation and maternal care.
Further, vaginal activity and possible orgastic potential may
exist during infancy and childhood. Vaginal stimulation may
occur in early infancy during sucking (Brierley 1936), during
infant toilet training (Greenacre 1950, Moulton 1973), and in a
vareity of indirect ways during child care (Kestenberg 1968). In
addition, the child's clitoral masturbation may lead to intense
sensations in the inner genitals via nervous and vascular con-
nections. In contrast to Freud's belief that the vagina is nonexistent until puberty (1905), pediatric reports suggest that little
girls may begin vaginal masturbation at a very early age. More
important, those children who are "ignorant" of their vaginas as
a tangible organ that can be examined and explored may still
discover their vaginas in terms of internal sensations.

All things considered, however, it seems to be a relatively
more difficult task for the female child to achieve a comfortable, accurate, and differentiated appreciation of her genitals.
Whether the girl's greater difficulty reflects anatomical realities, or whether it stems primarily from parental failure to
corroborate the girl's own sexual explorations and genital sensations, is a question deserving careful investigation. Clearly,
many intrapsychic and cultural factors may combine to prevent the growing girl from achieving a full understanding and
appreciation of her own sexuality.

Before Masters and Johnson (1966) published their research
findings, the clitoris was literally considered to be a vestigial

organ in adult sexuality; clitoral stimulation was considered "masculine" or "phallic" and was written off as a manifestation of penis envy or sexual immaturity. Psychoanalytically speaking, the adult woman was given the same message as the little girl: The most physiologically sensitive part of her anatomy, which has no function other than that of sensual pleasure, is "unfeminine," of "masculine character," and should be denied; that is, it does not or should not exist. While it is recognized that the intensity of clitoral sensations never ceases, we have only recently acknowledged that the clitoris is a valid and important organ of adult sexuality.

Partially under the impact of the current feminist movement, psychoanalytic circles have given increased attention to the phallocentric bias of our theorizing, with attempts being made to correct certain misconceptions about femininity (Lerner 1974b) and female sexuality (Chasseguet-Smirgel 1970). In our eagerness to reevaluate Freud's theories about women, we may bypass an equally significant theoretical task, which is to make dynamic sense of those distortions and misconceptions that have, in fact, been established and maintained. Giving the clitoris its rightful role in female sexuality is no more important than gaining dynamic understanding of why the clitoris and the external genitals have been "denied" to begin with—a denial well illustrated by current parental teachings, our own past theorizing, and, in its most extreme form, by the custom of excising the clitoris and ablating the labia, which has been practiced on millions of women in certain cultures (Ploss, Bartels, and Bartels 1965). Clearly, this denial must stem from powerful feelings of anxiety that both sexes share regarding female sexuality and the external female genitals. Perhaps it is a sympton of this anxiety that so much psychoanalytic attention has been directed, instead, to the fear of the internal genital, the vagina.

It is not accurate, however, to say that psychoanalysis has ignored the anxiety associated with the external female genitals. Technically speaking, castration anxiety in males does not occur from seeing the vagina (which is hardly accessible to visual inspection), but rather from seeing "the hairy maternal vulva" (Lederer 1968, p. 3) and the vulva of the young girl. It is the vulva and not the less visible vagina that may give the appearance of a "wound," and it is the clitoris that may arouse or reinforce men's fears that the penis can indeed be lost, reduced in size, or drawn into the body. Freud himself (1940) recognized the anxiety that the vulva may inspire and recalls a passage from Rabelais in which the exhibition of a woman's vulva puts the devil himself to flight.

Perhaps it is not so much that the fear of the vulva has been ignored by psychoanalytic theorists, but rather that the consequences of this fear have not been fully appreciated. Parental failure to label the girls' external genitals may be one important symptom or manifestation of this fear, although it is unlikely that this neglect derives solely from anxieties that have their origin in the anatomical structure of female genitals. My interviews with parents suggest that additional factors are at work as well, such as the parents' anxieties about acknowledging the female child as a sexual individual who has pleasure with her genitals. (As one mother explained: "It's easy to talk about the vagina because it's a reproductive organ, but telling my daughter about her clitoris seems like telling her to go masturbate.") More careful and systematic investigation is necessary to further elucidate both the dynamics underlying such parental discomfort and the failure to acknowledge and name the girl's sensitive external genitals.

It is relevant to note that the clitoris is only one aspect of female experience that has been denied or invalidated by nonrecognition or by application of the label "masculine." Women have been inhibited in numerous aspects of personal development and achievement by their conscious and unconscious fears that ambitious, competitive, self-seeking strivings are "masculine." Having valued aspects of one's self-experience labeled as gender inappropriate may lead not only to conflicts and inhibitions, but to cognitive and intellectual impairments as well. It is a challenging task for psychoanalysis to seek greater understanding of the unconscious meanings of femininity and of the labeling of specific traits, strivings, and behaviors as "masculine" or "feminine," and to further assess both the adaptive and pathogenic implications these labels may have for the growing child.

In sum, a survey of sex education literature confirms parents' self-reports regarding sex information imparted to their children. With relatively few exceptions, young children (and even teenagers) are taught that "boys have a penis and girls have a vagina," without further linguistic distinctions regarding the sensitive external genitals of the female child. This incomplete, undifferentiated, and often inaccurate picture of female genitals may prevent the growing girl from achieving pride in femininity, and may lead to anxiety and confusion regarding her sexuality. In the case example presented in this chapter, the failure to label the girl's external genitals was a contributing factor to penis envy, as well as to conflicts about "looking," which led to symptomatic learning inhibitions.

It is suggested that the ubiquity of the female "castration complex" may not stem primarily from the fact that the clitoris is a smaller (and thus inferior) organ compared to the penis. Rather, the girl's feeling of being "cheated" may reflect parental failure to explicitly acknowledge that the vulva (especially the clitoris) is an important aspect of "what girls have." Because visible and sensitive aspects of the girl's genitals are not labeled for her, the girl may feel that she does not have "permission" to develop into a sexually responsive and complete woman. As in the case presented, penis envy may be a symptom which expresses the wish to have one's female sexuality "validated," but which also serves to block this forbidden wish by inhibiting sexual responsiveness and pride in femininity.

REFERENCES

Abraham, K. (1920). Manifestation of the female castration complex. In *Selected Papers of Karl Abraham, M.D.*, trans. D. Bryan and A. Strachey, pp. 338–369. London: Hogarth Press, 1927.

Beauvoir, S. de (1953). *The Second Sex*. New York: Knopf.
Bellak, S., and Benedict, P. K., eds. (1958). *Schizophrenia: A Review of the Syndrome*. New York: Grune & Stratton, 1966.

Brierley, M. (1936). Specific determinants in feminine development. *International Journal of Psycho-Analysis* 17:163–
180.

Chasseguet-Smirgel, J. (1970). *Female Sexuality: New Psy-
choanalytic Views*, ed. J. Chasseguet-Smirgel et al. Ann
Arbor: University of Michigan Press.
Clower, V. L. (1976). Theoretical implications in current views
of masturbation in latency girls. *Journal of the American
Psychoanalytic Association* 24(5):109–125.

Freud, S. (1905). Three essays on the theory of sexuality.
Standard Edition 7:125–244, 1953.
—— (1940). Medusa's head. *Standard Edition* 18:273–275,
1955.

Greenacre, P. (1950). Special problems of early female development. In *Trauma, Growth, and Personality*, pp. 234–258.
New York: International Universities Press, 1969.

Kestenberg, J. S. (1968). Outside and inside, male and female.
Journal of the American Psychoanalytic Association
16:457–520.

Lederer, W. (1968). *The Fear of Women*. New York: Grune &
Stratton.
Lerner, H. G. (1974a). The hysterical personality: a "women's
disease." *Comprehensive Psychiatry* 15:157–164.
—— (1974b). Early origins of envy and devaluation of
women: implications for sex role stereotypes. *Bulletin of
the Menninger Clinic* 38:538–553.

Masters, W. H. and Johnson, V. E. (1966). *Human Sexual
Response*. Boston: Little, Brown.
Moulton, R. (1973). A survey and reevaluation of the concept of
penis envy. In *Psychoanalysis and Women*, ed. J. D. Miller,
pp. 207–230. New York: Brunner/Mazel.

Ploss, P., Bartels, M., and Bartels, P. (1965). *Femina Libido Sexualis.* New York: The Medical Press.

Shapiro, D. (1965). *Neurotic Styles.* New York: Basic Books.

Taylor, K. (1972). *Almost Twelve.* Wheaton, Ill.: Tyndale House.
Torok, M. (1970). The significance of penis envy in women. In *Female Sexuality*, ed. J. Chasseguet-Smirgel, et al., pp. 135–170. Ann Arbor: University of Michigan.

Chapter 3
Penis Envy

The concept of penis envy has been revised considerably, and the wish for a penis is no longer viewed as a ubiquitous force in female development.[1] A woman's desire for self-actualization and growth, be it through motherhood or professional development, is now regarded as a primary feminine striving rather than as a defensive reaction to real or imagined genital inferiority. While either sex may adopt an ambitious, competitive, production-oriented stance as a means of compensating for a sense of narcissistic injury and damage, today's analyst is less quick to label women's aggressive, ambitious, and competitive strivings as "masculine" or to interpret them a priori as a manifestation of penis envy. In sum, penis envy has been relegated to a less universal and necessary place in the onset of femininity than earlier writings would suggest (Blum 1977).

In contrast to Freud's viewpoint that femaleness does not come into being until puberty (Kleeman 1977), the female child's femininity is now viewed as primary. At the same time, there remains wide agreement that penis envy and the castration complex may exert a crucial influence upon feminine development, and penis envy continues to be a conspicuous symptom among some women. Indeed, coveting the male sex

---

[1]This chapter was first published in 1980 as "Penis Envy: Alternatives in Conceptualization" in the *Bulletin of the Menninger Clinic* 44(1):39–48.

organ may be such a powerful and pervasive dynamic that the sociocultural legitimacy of penis envy may hardly seem sufficient to explain the profound feelings of defectiveness and inferiority that certain women feel toward their own sex. While the existence of symptomatic penis envy is a clinical fact, there remains a lack of psychoanalytic agreement regarding the etiology and meaning of the symptom. My task in this chapter is to make explicit certain important theoretical differences regarding the symptom and to note implications for clinical practice.

THE ROLE OF ANATOMICAL DIFFERENCES

The psychoanalytic literature reveals that there remains considerable disagreement regarding the importance of actual anatomical differences in the etiology of penis envy. According to Freud (1905), penis envy stems from the genital inferiority (either real or imagined) of the female sex and occurs as a consequence of the female child's traumatic observation of sexual differences. In contrast to this widely held point of view, a growing number of psychoanalytic writings are in keeping with Torok's (1970) seemingly paradoxical notion that "the penis itself is not involved in penis envy" (p. 138). These writings suggest that the awareness of objective anatomical differences does not account for the idealization of male genitals and, further, that the absence of a body part, such as the penis, does not in itself produce pathological envy or self-depreciation. It is worthwhile to examine these two theoretical positions in greater detail.

Penis Envy as a Reflection
of Actual Anatomical Realities

Many female patients relate their sense of deficiency specifically to their lack of male genitals. As Torok (1970) has noted, "Many women have the fanciful idea that the male sex organ possesses supreme qualities: infinite power for good or evil, a guarantee of its possessor's security, absolute freedom, immunity against anxiety or guilt, and a promise of pleasure, love, and the fulfillment of all his wishes" (p. 139). It would seem to follow logically, then, that penis envy stems from the girl's reaction to actual or perceived anatomical differences. This viewpoint, put forth by Freud, has been summarized by Stoller (1973) as follows:

> Because it is visible, can change so in size, is shaped like a weapon, can penetrate, frightens women, and is such an intense source of sensation from infancy on, it [the penis] also demonstrates its superiority. Then, when it is contrasted with the female genitals, the case is again made. The female phallus, the clitoris, is much smaller, not visible, cannot penetrate, has not seized mankind's imagination, is never symbolized or exalted, and—Freud thought—is not a competent source of pleasure. Its significance is further weakened since it must share its fate with another organ, the vagina, which Freud felt was universally considered as an inferior organ—it is hidden, dark, mysterious, uncertain, unclean, and an undependable source of pleasure. [pp. 244–245]

Similarly, in his classic paper on the female castration complex, Abraham (1920) suggests that anatomical realities are such that "the female genital is looked upon as a *wound*, and as such it represents an effect of castration" (p. 340). This viewpoint suggests that penis envy is a bedrock phenomenon whose etiology rests on the girl's observation, or at least her conviction, that she lacks or has lost a superior genital.

There is an additional way to conceptualize the role that anatomical realities play in symptomatic penis envy. This alternate viewpoint suggests that it is not the actual or perceived superiority of the penis which leads the girl to envy it, but rather the anxiety-provoking nature of her own genitals that predisposes her toward penis envy. There is, in fact, little question that the anatomical structure of female genitals presents special problems to the little girl, who may have far greater difficulty than the boy in arriving at an accurate, comfortable, and differentiated appreciation of her sexual anatomy (Kestenberg 1968, Lerner 1977). The primitive anxieties that both sexes share about the vagina and vulva have received considerable attention in the literature (Lederer 1968) and need not be elaborated here. What is significant is that the vagueness, confusion, and anxiety that the little girl experiences about her genitals may well predispose her to the fantasy that her intrapsychic life would, indeed, be more manageable if she possessed male genitals in place of her own.

The conceptual difference just outlined is subtle but important. The first viewpoint assumes that the critical determinant in penis envy is the actual or perceived superiority of the penis in the little girl's mind (it is bigger, visible, a more intense source of pleasure, etc.). The second viewpoint assumes that the girl's envy of the penis is a secondary reaction to anxiety about her own genitals (fear of penetration or intrusion; fear of intense, diffuse, inner-genital sensations; fear of the vagina as a castrating, oral-destructive organ; etc.). Although these two viewpoints need not be mutually exclusive, the conceptual difference is significant, as differing clinical interventions follow from each. In the first case, interpretive work may focus concretely on the patient's wish to be a boy/man and to have male genitals in place of her own. In the second case, interpretive work may focus on the patient's wish to be a girl/woman and to have a full appreciation of her own genitals, while acknowledging that she is unable to do this because of anxieties and conflicts about what she actually has. Envy of male genitals is understood as a secondary or defensive elaboration rather than as a bedrock experience. Clinical interventions of the first kind run the risk of exacerbating the patient's devaluation of femininity and, in my opinion, block further analysis of the problem.

Penis Envy as an Expression of Unconscious Conflict

In contrast to the two viewpoints outlined above, a growing number of psychoanalysts believe that actual anatomical differences play little or no primary etiological role in penis envy. For example, Torok (1970) states that the penis, when considered as an objective biological organ, is not of importance in understanding penis envy: "Only an inquiry which disregards the object nature of the penis reveals the general significance of penis envy, the conflict which the symptom is trying to solve and the way it attempts to do this" (p. 183). The analyst's task is to probe beyond penis envy to uncover the unconscious desire, fear, or wish that produced penis envy as a solution.

Within this conceptual framework, Grossman and Stewart (1977) suggest that penis envy is a "metaphor" which reflects or expresses narcissistic injuries and issues of envy at all psychosexual levels of development. While the focus on a missing and unobtainable organ may provide a concrete and understandable explanation for dissatisfaction and envy, anatomical differences in themselves may not be of etiological significance. These authors note that severe feelings of damage, deprivation, and envy, existing before the discovery of sexual differences, are among a number of psychological factors that can create a traumatic vulnerability to the discovery of genital differences, which is one among many experiences of deprivation.

Other authors (Chasseguet-Smirgel 1970, Torok 1970) suggest not only that penis envy may be unrelated to the object nature of the penis, but, further, that the symptom may have little to do with envy. It is my belief that the most clinically sound and useful understandings of penis envy view the symptom as reflecting some disturbance in object relations, often with the mother.

If the female child or woman devalues femininity and desires the penis, one can ask: "Why does she? What unconscious internalized drama with the parental figure is expressed by this wish?" A number of possible solutions have been suggested: The female child may desire a penis in order to better express her hatred toward her mother, or as a means of possessing the envied omnipotent mother and her magical attributes, or as a means of extricating herself from a dependent and frustrating relationship with mother—that is, as a desperate attempt at separation and differentiation. Penis envy may be an expression of a revolt against the narcissistic wounds inflicted by the omnipotent mother or may be the girl's attempt to protect a jealous, intrusive, maternal imago by making an unconscious "oath of fidelity" to the mother that she (the daughter) will not achieve genital fulfillment (Chasseguet-Smirgel 1970, Torok 1970, Lerner 1977).

Chasseguet-Smirgel (1976) later observed that symptomatic penis envy is most severe in families in which the mother is experienced as dominant and controlling and the father as weak and passive. This finding is in keeping with my own clinical observation that envy and idealization of men and the penis are often associated with the girl/woman's attempt to separate herself from maternal overcontrol and to avoid a fearful identification with a destructive, castrating, "bad mother." That is, the defensive shift in self-experience from "castrating" to "castrated" is common among women. As Chasseguet-Smirgel (1970) notes, images of women as castrated or deficient are a denial for both sexes of the imagos of the primitive mother.

The foregoing summary is not meant to do justice to the multiplicity of meanings that the symptom of penis envy may have for a particular woman. The point is, rather, that certain psychoanalysts continue to view penis envy as a symptom reflecting girls' difficulties in coming to terms with anatomical differences. Other analysts view the symptom as a conscious mental content whose unique unconscious meanings (which may have little to do with either envy or anatomy) must be analyzed and understood.

IMPLICATIONS FOR TREATMENT

Grossman and Stewart (1977) note that when penis envy is conceptualized in concrete terms as reflecting the patient's envy of male genitals, it may be dealt with clinically as a final, immutable truth about anatomical differences or about the patient's wish to be a male. They point out that such interventions reduce the multiple source of dissatisfaction to a single cause and prevent analysis of underlying meanings of the symptom. Further, the clinical effect of such interventions may be to confirm the patient's worst fears of her inferiority and to exacerbate her sense of "real" deprivation. It is my observation, as well, that such interpretations strengthen the patient's defensive focus on anatomical or genital deficiency and prevent both patient and analyst from examining the underlying, more anxiety-arousing and painful wishes and conflicts that are bound up in and expressed by the symptom.

I believe that interpretations of penis envy are invariably antitherapeutic if the female patient believes the analyst/therapist is saying, "Really, you would like to be a man." This pronouncement is experienced as an irretrievable and final judgment of depreciation of the patient's femaleness and femininity. It is a communication that must make the woman feel misunderstood, for what she wants is to be more of a woman, although her conflicts and symptoms prevent her from achieving this goal. Symptomatic penis envy is encountered commonly enough in psychoanalytic practice, but the numbers of female patients who truly wish to be men (as a primary, rather than a defensive, experience) are few indeed, and I suspect are limited to transsexuals.

A related point of importance is that female patients are often quick to agree with the notion that they "have penis envy" (in concrete anatomical terms) for a multiplicity of defensive reasons; this agreement should not be mistaken for "validation" of the concept. Grossman and Stewart (1977) have observed that interpretations of penis envy may readily be embraced by the patient as true because they have an organizing effect; that is, they function like a delusion to bring order to what was otherwise a free-floating envy or a vague dissatisfaction with femininity. As noted earlier, certain patients may unconsciously focus on issues of anatomical or genital deficiency in order to block more anxiety-arousing exploration of the underlying affects and anxieties bound up in the symptom. I have informally interviewed a surprising number of women who report having "gone along" with interpretations of penis envy, which "felt true" at the time but were later (after treatment or in a subsequent treatment) experienced as insulting, inhibiting, or false. I believe that the unconscious motivations leading a patient to comply with analytic interpretations of penis envy (especially when the analyst is male) are complex and deserve further attention.

Penis Envy and "Masculine Strivings"

The idea that penis envy is a symptom that derives from society's neglect and distortion of women's true sexual, social, and intellectual needs is a point of view that has stirred considerable controversy among contemporary clinicians. While most psychoanalysts are unsympathetic to this viewpoint, a minority (Seidenberg 1970) agree with Thompson's (1943) surprisingly early view that penis envy reflects the attitude of an underprivileged or subordinate group toward those in power.

Irrespective of one's viewpoint on this matter, the controversy has helped bring to light a lack of conceptual precision on the part of many theorists and practitioners who attach the label of "penis envy" to any woman who rebels against societal definitions of femininity or expresses envy of male prerogatives and privileges. For certain analysts, "penis envy" is synonymous with a lack of acceptance of the "feminine role" (as it is culturally defined) despite growing psychological research demonstrating that such "rebels" may be healthier than their stereotypically "feminine" sisters (Bem 1976, Kaplan and Bean 1976). The equation between penis envy and so-called masculine strivings is conceptually unsound and characteristically leads to countertherapeutic consequences.

I have found that women who rebel against culturally defined notions of femininity, as well as express envy and resentment of men, do so for a multiplicity of neurotic as well as healthy and adaptive reasons. A great number of these women who manifest "masculine strivings" do not have penis envy, but rather take deep pride and pleasure in their femaleness. However, these women do struggle with unconscious anxiety and guilt regarding their own ambitious and competitive strivings for mastery and success in the world outside the home—strivings that they view men as expressing with apparent ease. The inhibitions these women share frequently have their roots in an undifferentiated relationship with their mothers which leaves the woman unable to tolerate the experience of autonomous functioning associated with intellectual mastery or professional success. In addition, such strivings may be experienced unconsciously as "too masculine" or "phallic"—a perception greatly reinforced by cultural pressures.

When the patient's "phallic" strivings are interpreted in treatment as masculine or viewed as an expression of penis envy, guilt regarding ambitious and competitive strivings increases. In addition to exacerbating the woman's inhibitions, such interpretations inevitably deepen her resentment of men, who she feels have permission to be successfully competitive without having their gender identity brought into question. I agree with Kronsky's (1971) observation that, too frequently, symptomatic penis envy is paradoxically reinforced by the very interpretation that is aimed at leading to its dissolution. In many cases envy and resentment of men disappears by itself when the woman becomes able to fulfill herself in broad and varied aspects of functioning.

When penis envy is conceptualized in concrete anatomical terms (that is, as indicative of the patient's wish to be male or to possess male genitals), analytic interpretation may further lend itself to a kind of absurd reductionism. Take, for example, Ritvo's (1977) often-heard statement that the mind–penis equation makes the mind's good functioning a source of pride and satisfaction to women. He writes, "One successful and satisfying sublimation of penis envy, seen particularly in college students, is in intellectual functioning and achievement" (p. 132). Is the author implying here that the truly feminine woman (free from penis envy) lacks pride and pleasure in intellectual functioning and achievement? Or that bright and ambitious women are motivated by an unconscious sense of anatomical defectiveness? Or that the creative use of one's mind is a "masculine" pursuit? Probably not, for we know that the pleasure an individual takes in achieving and in being intellectually masterful has a wealth of psychological meanings for both sexes. These strivings reflect adaptive sublimatory capacities, healthy identifications with either or both parents, the ego's natural pleasure in mastery and learning, the narcissistic gratification derived from receiving praise from others, and the feeling of self-respect and well-being inherent in the knowledge that one is competent and successfully competitive. Although analytic work has demonstrated that competing, achieving, and "measuring up" may have pathological underpinnings and may serve to compensate for an underlying sense of defectiveness or inadequacy, this finding is no more the case for women than for men.

It is my impression, however, that comments such as Ritvo's (despite their intentions) may be heard in the consulting room as suggesting that the woman's competitive, intellectual, and ambitious strivings are not "fully feminine" and womanly, thus making it unlikely that these can be incorporated in the patient's self-experience in a pleasurable and ego-syntonic way. Psychoanalysis has at times failed to appreciate sufficiently the deep guilt and anxiety a woman experiences when some valued aspect of her self-experience is labeled "masculine." For example, one psychotherapy patient of mine owned a treasured leather briefcase which had belonged to her deceased father, whom she had loved dearly. She put it away in the closet "forever" when a previous therapist interpreted her attachment to it as her wish for a penis. In her later work with me, she was able to reclaim and again enjoy this valued possession.

Psychoanalytic interpretations of penis envy may be countertherapeutic or useful, depending on the analyst's capacity to explore the unique, varied, and complex meanings that the symptom may serve for a particular woman. There remains a great diversity of psychoanalytic opinion regarding the meaning of penis envy, although disagreements have not always been explicitly stated. Because psychoanalytic interpretation derives specifically from the way in which penis envy is conceptualized, the attainment of further conceptual clarity is of special clinical and theoretical importance.

References

Abraham, K. (1920). Manifestation of the female castration complex. In *Selected Papers of Karl Abraham, M.D.,* trans.

D. Bryan and A. Strachey, pp. 338–369. London: Hogarth Press, 1927.

Bem, S. L. (1976). Probing the promise of androgyny. In *Beyond Sex-role Stereotypes: Readings Toward a Psychology of Androgyny*, ed. A. G. Kaplan and J. P. Bean, pp. 47–62. Boston: Little, Brown.

Blum, H. P., ed. (1977). *Female Psychology: Contemporary Psychoanalytic Views*. New York: International Universities Press.

Chasseguet-Smirgel, J. (1970). Feminine guilt and the Oedipus complex. In *Female Sexuality: New Psychoanalytic Views*, ed. J. Chasseguet-Smirgel et al., pp. 94–134. Ann Arbor: University of Michigan Press.

—— (1976). Freud and female sexuality: the consideration of some blind spots in the exploration of the "dark continent." *International Journal of Psychoanalysis* 57(3): 275–287.

Freud, S. (1905). Three essays on the theory of sexuality. *Standard Edition* 7:130–243, 1953.

Grossman, W. I. and Stewart, W. A. (1977). Penis envy: from childhood wish to developmental metaphor. In *Female Psychology: Contemporary Psychoanalytic Views*, ed. H. P. Blum, pp. 193–212. New York: International Universities Press.

Kaplan, A. G. and Bean, J. P., eds. (1976). *Beyond Sex-role Stereotypes: Readings Toward a Psychology of Androgyny*. Boston: Little, Brown.

Kestenberg, J. S. (1968). Outside and inside, male and female. *Journal of the American Psychoanalytic Association* 16(3): 457–520.

Kleeman, J. A. (1977). Freud's views on early female sexuality in the light of direct child observation. In *Female Psychology: Contemporary Psychoanalytic Views*, ed. H. P. Blum, pp. 3–27. New York: International Universities Press.

Kronsky, B. J. (1971). Feminism and psychotherapy. *Journal of Contemporary Psychotherapy* 3(2):89–98.

Lederer, W. W. (1968). *The Fear of Women*. New York: Grune & Stratton.

Lerner, H. G. (1977). Parental mislabeling of female genitals as a determinant of penis envy and learning inhibitions in women. In *Female Psychology: Contemporary Psychoanalytic Views*, ed. H. P. Blum, pp. 269–283. New York: International Universities Press.

Ritvo, S. (1977). Adolescent to woman. In *Female Psychology: Contemporary Psychoanalytic Views*. ed. H. P. Blum, pp. 127–137. New York: International Universities Press.

Seidenberg, R. (1970). *Marriage in Life and Literature*. New York: Philosophical Library.

Stoller, R. J. (1973). Overview: the impact of new advances in sex research on psychoanalytic theory. *American Journal of Psychiatry* 130(3):241–251.

Thompson, C. (1943). "Penis envy" in women. *Psychiatry* 6(2):123–125.

Torok, M. (1970). The significance of penis envy in women. In *Female Sexuality: New Psychoanalytic Views*, ed. J. Chasseguet-Smirgel et al., pp. 135–170. Ann Arbor: University of Michigan Press.

Chapter 4

Internal Prohibitions against Female Anger

D ifficulty in the management of anger and aggression is not exclusively a woman's problem.[1] In clinical work, we see individuals of both sexes who are inhibited in the direct expression of realistic anger or are prone to impulsive, poorly modulated aggressive outbursts. Indeed, the management of anger and aggression presents intrapsychic difficulties for all of us, interfering in varying degrees with our capacity to work and to love.

However, there are also conspicuous sex differences, as well as similarities. Simply put, women tend to be overly inhibited, and men not inhibited enough, in the direct expression of anger and aggression. Although there are many exceptions to the rule, the greater aggressivity of the male sex is an observable fact of life, documented by clinical and experimental research (Lewis 1976). That men wage war, and women do not, is noted by Lewis to be the clearest and most indisputable difference between the sexes, apart from the biological reality that only women give birth and nurse babies.

It is perhaps surprising that mental health professionals have failed to examine the vicissitudes of anger and aggression for each sex separately. The work of Bernardez-Bonesatti

[1]This chapter, which was presented in May 1978 at the 131st annual meeting of The American Psychiatric Association in Atlanta, Georgia, was first published in 1980 in *The American Journal of Psychoanalysis* 40(2):137–148.

(1978) was the first serious attempt to carefully elucidate the intrapsychic and cultural factors that are specific to women's difficulties with anger and aggression. Clearly, women's problems in this area merit special study, for men and women have different anatomical structures to come to terms with, different developmental tasks to master, and different socialization inputs from parents and the culture at large throughout a lifetime.

Differences in socialization inputs for each sex are dramatic with regard to anger and aggression. From birth, the parent's awareness of the child's sex ("My baby is a girl!") organizes and directs that parent's response to the child's expression of anger, rebelliousness, and protest. Despite changes brought about by the feminist movement, expressions of anger and aggression are still considered masculine in men, and unfeminine in women. So strong are societal prohibitions against female anger that the angry woman may be condemned, even if she is waging a bloodless and humane revolution for her own legitimate rights. I cannot count the number of times I have heard it said, "I agree with much of the women's liberation movement, but those angry women just turn me off!"

Unlike male heroes who fight and even die for what they believe in, the angry or aggressive woman may, indeed, repel us all. For what images come to mind? The envious, castrating "man-hater" venting her rage and resentment against men? The passive-aggressive housewife who bitterly dominates and controls her husband from behind the scenes? The infantile, irrational, "hot-tempered" female who hurls pots and pans from across the kitchen and carries on like a hysterical bitch? These familiar images are more than just cruel, sexist stereotypes. They are neurotic positions that real women adopt when intrapsychic and cultural pressures combine to inhibit the direct and appropriate expression of legitimate anger and protest. In addition, Bernardez-Bonesatti (1978) has noted that such images serve to reinforce cultural definitions of the healthy, "feminine" woman as one who is devoid of anger and aggressiveness, especially toward men. Although women may express anger in defense of others more helpless than themselves, anger toward men is held in check "by continuous warnings about the danger of becoming one of the frightening and despicable stereotypes which depict women as ferocious, envious, vengeful, or 'castrating'" (Bernardez-Bonesatti 1978, p. 216).

Women's difficulties with anger have been conceptualized by feminist writers as a consequence of the feminine socialization process (Kaplow 1971). Clinical and research evidence does, in fact, indicate that girls are raised in a manner that restricts their freedom to express anger and aggression and inhibits their capacity for competitive and self-assertive behavior (Gornick and Moran 1971, Kaplan and Bean 1976). But why have such cultural pressures been established and maintained? The myth of the feminine woman as devoid of anger and aggressiveness could not have so vigorously survived over the ages unless both sexes shared deep intrapsychic fears of female anger.

In this chapter I will discuss two intrapsychic determinants that I believe are central in understanding women's fear of their own anger. The first involves women's irrational fears of their own omnipotent destructiveness, a topic that has received attention from a number of writers (Lederer 1968, Lerner 1974, Bernardez-Bonesatti 1976). The second involves separation-individuation difficulties in the mother–daughter relationship, which may leave the girl/woman unable to tolerate the sense of separateness and difference inherent in the experience of anger. My theoretical position derives from diagnostic testing and intensive clinical work with adult female patients who share a common cluster of characteristics. They assume a protective, placating, "good-girl" stance in relationships with others. In some cases, passivity, weakness, and vulnerability to victimization may emerge as salient features of their character style. These women characteristically avoid the direct experience and expression of anger, tending instead to report feeling "hurt" in situations that might more realistically evoke anger or protest. These women all share deep unconscious anxieties about "fighting" which interfere not only with their ability to express anger, but also with their capacity to be adaptively self-assertive and competitive.

FEARS OF OMNIPOTENT DESTRUCTIVENESS

Although both sexes have frightening fantasies about the devastating effects of their unmodulated rage, such primitive anxieties are, as a rule, more powerful and inhibiting in women (Lederer 1968, Bernardez-Bonesatti 1978). It may at first appear paradoxical that women, who present themselves in our consulting rooms as the weaker and "castrated" sex, should have relatively greater anxiety regarding their own power and destructiveness. This seeming contradiction is resolved when we appreciate that women's self-experience of being weak and castrated is often a defensive retreat from a more frightening self-experience—that of an omnipotently destructive, castrating individual whose archetypal expression is beautifully captured in the character of Nurse Ratched in *One Flew Over the Cuckoo's Nest.*

To understand the fear of female anger that both sexes share, we must appreciate that the infant's and child's world is a matriarchal one in which power and authority are predominantly, if not exclusively, in the hands of women (Lerner 1974). It is the mother who not only gratifies the child's impulses, but also is the first to forbid their expression. It is the mother, along with a host of other women (governesses, baby-sitters, elementary-school teachers), who not only provides rewards and pleasures but also inflicts the unavoidable punishments and narcissistic injuries that are part of the day-to-day task of socializing a child. Most important, it is the mother who is the primary object of the child's dependency; it is with this woman that the child must move from the experience of a fused, undifferentiated symbiosis, in the direction of increasing individuation, separateness, and autonomy. The strength of this struggle with mother—the struggle between regressive dependent wishes and more autonomous strivings toward separation and autonomy—inevitably generates aggression and rage at the object of the dependency. Because of the child's heavy reliance on primitive projection, one aspect of the early maternal imago that persists in the unconscious of even the most "rational" adults is that of a vengeful, angry, possessive, all-powerful bad mother who restricts her child's autonomy, freedom, and growth.

One dilemma that the girl faces in identifying with her mother is that she is confronted with an internalized maternal imago that includes elements of the bad, omnipotent, destructive mother. To avoid such a fearful identification, the girl/woman may defensively shift to a self-experience of being castrated and reassuringly helpless. This self-experience, and the related idealization of men, frequently masks its opposite—a self-experience of being destructive and castrating, especially in relationship to men (Chasseguet-Smirgel 1970, Lerner 1974, Bernardez-Bonesatti 1978). The defensive shift from castrating to castrated frequently achieves a concrete anatomical expression. In the case of symptomatic penis envy, for example, the woman's devaluation of her genitals as mutilated and inferior may defend against a more fearful unconscious experience of her vagina as a dangerous oral-incorporative organ that will literally destroy the penis during intercourse.

Frightening fantasies about women's omnipotent destructiveness need not be based on actual "bad" qualities of the mother, although in my clinical experience, such fears are most powerful when the mother is, in fact, possessive and controlling in relationship to a passive and unavailable father. Nevertheless, in cultures where parenting is not shared, irrational anxieties about female anger and power may be the inevitable consequence of the child's world being predominantly, if not exclusively, a matriarchal one (Lerner 1974, Dinnerstein 1976). In addition, women's primitive fears about their own destructiveness are profoundly reinforced by cultural stereotypes that teach women to "play dumb," "let the man win," "pretend he's boss," or any variety of maneuvers that encourage women to feign weakness when it does not come naturally. These cultural teachings are paradoxical warnings of how hurtful and destructive the "weaker sex" might be to men if women were simply to be themselves.

FROM ANGER TO HURT: SEPARATION ANXIETY

In order to understand the dynamics of women who character-istically become "hurt" in situations that might more realisti-cally evoke anger, a distinction must be made between the phenomenology of anger and of hurt. It is important to appre-ciate that the experience of anger is one that involves the feeling of being separate, different, and alone. Any angry con-frontation is a statement of differences between people, which elicits a heightened sense of standing on one's own two feet, separate and apart from a relational context. In the midst of an angry confrontation, a woman no longer feels like the wife of her husband, the daughter of her mother, or the mother of her child. She is herself, separate and alone.[2] Bernardez-Bonesatti has noted that "In anger, the person establishes automatic aloneness and makes herself temporarily separate from the object of the anger." (1978, p. 216). She writes that women are so afraid of this loss of connection that their expressions of anger are frequently accompanied by tears, guilt, and sorrow, which contaminate the anger or serve to nullify it entirely.

The experience of hurt (which may be behaviorally ex-pressed by tears, self-criticism, displays of depression, and/or guilt-inducing statements) contrasts markedly with the expe-rience of anger. When, in the midst of an angry confrontation, a woman shifts from anger to hurt or tears, she is retracting her statement of being separate and alone. Expressing hurt draws the object closer and emphasizes his or her importance to the self. Hurt, in contrast to anger, emphasizes the relational "we" rather than the autonomous "I."

In keeping with Bernardez-Bonesatti's observation, I have noted that female patients, in particular, have difficulty toler-ating the feeling of separateness and aloneness inherent in the experience of anger. The feeling of separateness stirs separa-tion anxiety and an unconscious fear of object loss, which

---

[2]In my book *The Dance of Anger* (New York: Harper & Row, 1985), I illustrate how expressions of anger do not always evoke a greater sense of separateness from the other; rather they may reflect anxiety about differences and serve to maintain the experience of fusion and "stuckness" in relationships.

mobilizes the woman to attempt to "get back" the person at whom she is angry by, for example, crying, apologizing, criticizing herself, or expressing hurt or depression. I believe that this separation anxiety is independent of fears the woman may have about the destructive effects of her aggression or the possible retaliation of the other. Rather, it stems from the phenomenological experience of lacking an attachment to an object and of being "all on one's own"—an experience not unique to the expression of anger, but felt during periods of creative and intellectual achievement as well. Certain women find this "aloneness" tolerable, or even exhilarating. For others, however (whose characteristics I have just described), this "aloneness" feels dangerous, as if it threatens a bond with a mother who would herself be left emptied out and depleted if her daughter should feel whole and complete unto herself, apart from a relational context. At the heart of the problem is the girl's special difficulty achieving an adequate degree of separation and autonomy from her own mother.

An old folksaying goes, "A son's a son till he gets a wife; a daughter's your daughter for the rest of her life." While this quotation reflects the special closeness that exists between mothers and daughters, it also hints at the girl's greater difficulty in making her declaration of independence from mother. My own clinical work has convinced me that the task of declaring one's separateness and difference from mother is a relatively more difficult and complex task for the girl. It is the daughter, in particular, who may unconsciously experience moves toward autonomy as dangerous, as if to be separate and complete without mother constitutes a disloyal betrayal of the relationship between them. When mother and daughter cannot negotiate an adequate degree of separation between them, the daughter may sacrifice her own growth and avoid autonomous functioning in order to preserve an unconscious tie with the mother, who is experienced as too possessive or fragile to tolerate the girl's developing autonomy. When it is not safe to express one's separateness and difference from mother, the experience of separateness and difference inherent in the expression of anger may also be taboo. Healthy expressions of anger and protest may be replaced by masochistic solutions;

by the daughter's becoming the hurt or dependent child, an unconscious bond with the mother is maintained.

Next, I will comment generally on the developmental task of separation-individuation, and then speculate about why the daughter, more than the son, may be especially vulnerable to experiencing anxiety and guilt in association with declaring her separateness and difference from mother. Although many cultural and intrapsychic factors are relevant, I will focus on one difference that I believe to be critical to the issue at hand. I refer to the fact that the female child must differentiate herself from a maternal figure with whom she is to identify, whereas the male child must differentiate himself from a maternal figure whose qualities and behaviors he is taught to repudiate within himself in his efforts to become "masculine."

SEPARATION-INDIVIDUATION FROM MOTHER: SEX DIFFERENCES

Issues of fusion and individuation have been addressed by such psychoanalytic thinkers as Searles (1965, 1973), Fairbairn (1952), Guntrip (1961), and Mahler (1963), as well as by family therapists, including Bowen (1978) and Minuchin (1974). Drawing upon both individual and relational theories, Karpel defines individuation as "the process by which a person becomes increasingly differentiated from a past or present relational context. . . . Individuation involves the subtle, but crucial, phenomenological shift by which a person comes to see him/herself as separate and distinct in the relational context in which s/he has been embedded. It is the increasing definition of an 'I' within a 'we.'" (1976, p. 67). The process of separation-individuation begins with the mother, but does not end with her. Rather, struggles for individuation are never entirely resolved, but are worked on in a variety of intrapsychic and interpersonal relationships throughout one's lifetime. The process of moving from fused to individuated relationships is a "universal developmental and existential struggle and . . . a fundamental organizing principle of human growth" (Karpel 1976, p. 67).

Central to the struggle to individuate are the child's attempts to express her or his differences from the mother and the mother's reaction (i.e., approval and love, or withdrawal of approval and love) to the child's assertion of differences. Attempts to separate and individuate from mother (and, later, father) through the assertion of differences are manifested by a variety of behavioral expressions throughout a lifetime. The small toddler may assert her differences from mother by active locomotion, thus demonstrating that she is an individual entity, physically separate and different from mother. The little boy may delight in his penis as a symbol of his separateness and difference from mother. The adolescent girl may express her separateness from mother by violating an unwritten family rule that mother will select the children's clothing. The adolescent boy may wear his hair in a fashion that irritates his family or may refuse to go into the family business. Although such assertions of differences may in part derive from a counterdependent and hostile stance toward parental figures, they are frequently the best means available to the child, at a particular time, to assert his or her autonomy and independence from mother and father. When the parent characteristically reacts to the child's assertion of differences as a threatened "loss" of the child, or as a disloyalty or violation of the bond between them, the child, in response, may lapse into chronic passivity, conformity, and helplessness as an attempt to restore and preserve the threatened object relation (Masterson 1976).

Why should the female child have relatively greater difficulty making her statement of being separate and different from her mother? Why should the male child have a relatively easier and more comfortable time making such a declaration? Although there is little question that much of the feminine socialization process predisposes girls toward dependent, rather than autonomous, solutions (Kaplan 1976), these cultural realities are not my primary concern, here. Rather, as previously noted, I wish to focus on one particular and rather dramatic sex difference in the complex task of separation-individuation from mother. That is, the girl goes through this developmental struggle with a same-sex parent; the boy, with an opposite-sex parent.[3] The girl assimilates *sameness* to the mother; the boy assimilates *difference* from the mother. Margaret Mead long ago noted that the boy's "earliest experience of self is one in which he is forced, in the relationship to his mother, to realize himself as different, as a creature unlike his mother" (Mead 1949, p. 167).

I believe that the boy's struggle for individuation with the opposite-sex parent may grant him a certain "permission" to be separate and different from mother from the time he is old enough to understand the concept "I am a boy." In addition to the fact that a boy is anatomically dissimilar from his mother, bipolar concepts of masculinity and femininity encourage the mother to help her son assert his differences. This is not to imply that the developmental task of separation-individuation is easily accomplished between mother and son; in many families male children are unable to develop a firm sense of autonomy and may remain enmeshed with parents who themselves unconsciously place powerful obstacles in the way of their sons' growth. It is rather to suggest, generally speaking, that bipolar definitions of masculinity and femininity offer mothers special help in encouraging their sons to be separate and different from themselves. No matter how undifferentiated and possessive the mother herself is, no matter how intense is her wish that her son reflect herself and remain forever tied to her, she also wants her son to be masculine, and thus different from herself.

The girl child may have less "permission" from her mother to assert her differences and declare her independence. Not only is she anatomically similar to mother, but the developmental task of differentiating herself from mother is coupled with the task of identifying with her and acquiring a sense of

---

[3]These ideas were written for presentation in 1978, in the same year, but before Nancy Chodorow published her classic book *The Reproduction of Mothering* (Berkeley and Los Angeles: University of California Press, 1978). Chodorow's work also rests on the psychoanalytic concept that the differentiation process (within traditional family structure) occurs within the mother–child dyad and that difficulties for girls arise accordingly. See Chapter 14 for a critical reevalutation of this assumption.

"sameness." Also, the masculine-feminine polarity that exists in all cultures may serve to discourage the daughter in her attempts to be different from mother; when girls behave in ways that are out of keeping with the traditional scripts that their mothers have followed, they are likely to be labeled "unfeminine" or "masculine." A number of factors combine to predispose the mother to respond to the girl's display of "differences" as a rejection or a disloyalty. In such a case, the girl's assumption of so-called feminine qualities (i.e., passivity, conformity, and the inhibition of direct expressions of anger) may be a small price to pay in order to pledge her allegiance to a mother who is unconsciously experienced as too fragile to withstand her daughter's developing autonomy.

Although the focus here is on the boy's greater ease declaring his separateness and difference from mother, it should be noted that his experience with opposite-sex caretakers presents him with unique problems as well. More specifically, the relative absence of primary male caretakers leaves him vulnerable to persistent primitive fantasies about female omnipotence (Lerner 1974, 1978), as well as to greater uncertainty regarding his own gender identity (Lewis 1976). The latter problem is especially conspicuous in father-absent, patri-local cultures in which severe male initiation rites (e.g., cutting the penis) become necessary to establish a firm "masculine" identity over a primary feminine one (Burton and Whiting 1961). Men's greater vulnerability to symptoms involving gender identity has been documented in this society by both clinical and empirical research (Lewis 1976). From an anthropological perspective, Chodorow (1972) has discussed other disadvantages males face in being socialized predominantly by women.

While space does not permit a detailed discussion of other intrapsychic and cultural factors that make it especially difficult for mothers and daughters to negotiate an adequate degree of separation from each other, a few deserve brief mention. First, the girl child faces the uniquely difficult developmental task of negotiating a "change of object" (see Chasseguet-Smirgel 1970)—that is, shifting from mother to father as the primary love object. Difficulties at this stage may leave the girl especially vulnerable to experiencing real or imagined maternal envy or fragility, which interferes with the daughter's moves toward autonomous functioning and heterosexual genital fulfillment. Furthermore, the strong identification that exists between mother and daughter pulls for a greater reliance on reality-distorting projection for both. The daughter, more easily than the son, may become the vehicle through which the mother hopes to achieve the pleasures and gratifications which, in fantasy or reality, have been denied her. While parents may live vicariously through either their sons or their daughters, the identification between mother and daughter predisposes the mother to envy her daughter (at least unconsciously) more than her son. She may thus encourage her daughter to be autonomous and self-seeking, yet subtly undermine the girl's attempts to get for herself what she (the mother) does not have. Her envy may be especially intense at the time of her daughter's adolescence, when the girl's activity, exuberance, and heightened sexuality may coincide with the mother's experience of declining sexual attractiveness and her growing awareness that her children need her less, and soon not at all. The issue of oedipal rivalry per se may be secondary to the crisis that a woman faces at this time in a culture in which her decorative and nurturant qualities may comprise much of her identity and sense of worth.

It is important to recognize that problems in the mother–daughter relationship cannot be conceptualized as reflecting "bad mothering" as such. Indeed, mothering cannot be understood apart from the role of the father (often conspicuous by his absence), and both must be considered within the cultural context in which parenting exists (Seidenberg 1970, Rich 1976). Much of the feminine socialization process, as well as the very structure of the traditional nuclear family, may predispose both mother and daughter to seek enmeshed, dependent relationships. The overpossessive or jealous mother who restricts her daughter's moves toward autonomy may herself be the product of a distorting and constricting feminine socialization process which has left her with little else but her own children to possess (Seidenberg 1970). The intense ambivalence that often characterizes a mother's reactions to her daughter (especially during adolescence) is particularly under-standable in today's society, which encourages women to self-lessly relinquish their own self-seeking strivings in order to be the best of mothers, while at the same time questioning whether such sacrifices are necessary or even laudable. In the final analysis, difficulties mothers and daughters face in nego-tiating separation-individuation issues must take into ac-count both intrapsychic and cultural factors, which are inex-tricably interwoven, mutually reinforcing, and difficult to separate from each other.

IMPLICATIONS FOR TREATMENT

The expression of legitimate anger and protest is more than a statement of dignity and self-respect; it is also a statement that one will risk standing alone, even in the face of disapproval or the potential loss of love from others. For our female patients, this requires a particular degree of courage. Not only have women been taught that their value, if not their very identity, rests largely on their loving and being loved, but also, even more to the point, many women have not achieved the degree of autonomous functioning that would permit them to stand separate and alone in the experience of their anger (Lerner 1977, Bernardez-Bonesatti 1978).

A central task of psychotherapy is to help women under-stand the unconscious irrational fears as well as the external realities that prevent them from the direct, open, forthright expression of legitimate anger and protest. In this task, direct work on problems of anger and aggression is a necessary, but not sufficient, focus for exploration. In addition, unresolved issues of autonomy and separation from mother must be ex-plored and resolved. Women who have unconscious loyalties to remain their mother's child and avoid autonomous function-ing are inhibited not only in the expression of anger and protest, but in any activity that demands the subjective expe-rience of feeling alone and standing on one's own two feet. Such women will have difficulty tolerating the experience of separateness and difference inherent in having an original idea, in entertaining a critical or innovative thought that is theirs alone, or in tolerating the competition necessary to achieve professional success. Such acts may unconsciously be experienced as a violation of an unconscious oath to remain their mother's child and avoid autonomous functioning.

By the time we see adult women in treatment, they frequently have transferred this internalized drama from mother to husband. They may have found for themselves possessive, undifferentiated lovers or husbands with whom to continue the earlier drama with mother. The man's outward dominant and controlling stance may barely mask his underlying fragility and insecurity. Replicating the woman's experience of her mother, the husband may thwart his wife's attempts to change and grow, experiencing her moves toward increased autonomy as a disloyalty that will threaten the predictable security of the relationship between them. To view the woman's dilemma only in the "here-and-now"—that is, as a struggle with an oppressive husband—is to miss the opportunity to analyze an undifferentiated relationship with mother that may predispose her to accepting patriarchal solutions rather than moving ahead to true autonomy.

In helping female patients toward increased autonomy, we are helping them to stand firm and strong in the expression of legitimate anger and protest, which is essential to one's sense of dignity and self-regard. But the experience of autonomy carries with it its own burdens. To experience autonomy is to experience our essential aloneness—to recognize that we determine our own choices, decide on our own risks, and assume the primary responsibility for our own growth and development. It is perhaps simpler for all of us to direct our energy toward seeking love and approval from others, to enter into relationships comprised of endless cycles of guilt and blame toward the person who is failing to provide for our happiness and to preserve forever the fantasy that some other person can complete and fulfill us, as the nursing mother does for her child. My own patients who have made significant moves toward autonomous functioning inevitably go through a painful feeling of mourning and loss for the comforting undifferentiated relationship with a parent (or internalized parental imago) that they have courageously left behind. Still, the goal of achieving increasing autonomy is one that we strive for with each of our patients, male and female, and also with ourselves. For it is through the capacity to be separate, different, and alone that we become free not only to express anger in response to the violation of our rights, but also to love from a position of true equality and mutual respect.

REFERENCES

Bernardez-Bonesatti, T. (1976). Unconscious beliefs about women affecting psychotherapy. *North Carolina Journal of Mental Health*, 7(5):63–66.

—— (1978). Women and anger: conflicts with aggression in contemporary women. *Journal of the American Medical Women's Association*, 33(5):215–219.

Bowen, M. (1978). *Family Practice in Clinical Practice*. New York: Jason Aronson.

Burton, R., and Whiting, J. (1961). The absent father and cross-sex identity. *Merrill-Palmer Quarterly*, 7:85–95.

Chasseguet-Smirgel, J. (1970). Feminine guilt and the Oedipus complex. In *Female Sexuality: New Psychoanalytic Views*, ed. J. Chasseguet-Smirgel et al., pp. 99–134. Ann Arbor: University of Michigan Press.

Chodorow, N. (1972). Being and doing: cross-cultural examination of the socialization of males and females. In *Women in Sexist Society: Studies in Power and Powerlessness*, ed. V. Gornick and B. Moran, pp. 259–291. New York: New American Library.

Dinnerstein, D. (1976). *The Mermaid and the Minotaur: Sexual Arrangements and Human Malaise*. New York: Harper & Row.

Fairbairn, W. R. D. (1952). *Psychoanalytic Studies of the Personality*. London: Tavistock.

Gornick V., and Moran B., eds. (1971). *Woman in Sexist Society*. New York: Basic Books.

Guntrip, H. J. (1961). *Personality Structure and Human Interaction*. New York: International Universities Press.

Kaplan, A., and Bean, J., eds. (1976) *Beyond Sex-Role Stereotypes*. Boston: Little, Brown.

Kaplow, S. (1971). Getting angry. Notes from the Third Year. In *Women's Liberation*, ed. A. Koedt and S. Firestone, 15–17.

Karpel, M. (1976). Individuation: from fusion to dialogue. *Family Process* 15(1):65–82.

Lederer, W. (1968). *The Fear of Women*. New York: Grune & Stratton.

Lerner H. G. (1974). Early origins of envy and devaluation of women: implications for sex-role stereotypes. *Bulletin of the Menninger Clinic* 38:538–553.

—— (1977). Taboos against female anger. *Menninger Perspective* 8(4):4–11.

—— (1978). On the comfort of patriarchal solutions: some reflections on Brown's paper. *Journal of Personality and Social Systems* 1(3):47–50.

Lewis, H. B. (1976). *Psychic War in Men and Women*. New York: International Universities Press.

Mahler, M. S. (1963). Thoughts about development and individuation. In *The Psychoanalytic Study of the Child*, vol. 18. New York: International Universities Press.

Masterson, J. F. (1976). *Psychotherapy of the Borderline Adult: A Developmental Approach*. New York: Brunner/Mazel.

Mead, M. (1949). *Male and Female*. New York: Morrow.

Minuchin, S. (1974). *Families and Family Therapy*. Cambridge, Mass.: Harvard University Press.

Rich, A. (1976). *Of Woman Born*. New York: W. W. Norton.

Searles, H. F. (1965). *Collected Papers on Schizophrenia and Related Subjects*. New York: International Universities Press.

—— (1973). Concerning therapeutic symbiosis. *The Annual of Psychoanalysis* 1:247–262.

Seidenberg, R. (1970). *Marriage in Life and Literature.* New York: Philosophical Library.

PART II

FEMALE PSYCHOLOGY AND PSYCHOTHERAPY

Chapter 5

Adaptive and Pathogenic Aspects of Sex-Role Stereotypes

and psychotherapy will be discussed. I will not attempt to present an exhaustive and definitive account of the issues at hand; rather, my goal is to add balance and conceptual clarity to an important area that has remained clouded by prejudice, cultural mythology, and a counter-productive battle of the sexes.

PATHOGENIC AND ADAPTIVE CONSEQUENCES

The pathogenic consequences of sex-role stereotypes have been discussed at length in the feminist and psychiatric literature. There is little question that stereotyped notions of masculinity and femininity have a constricting and inhibiting effect on development. Children are encouraged to conform to idealized generalizations of what males and females "should be," rather than being allowed to develop their own unique potentials, interests, and skills (Seidenberg 1976, Lerner 1973). The inevitable pathogenic consequence of any masculine-feminine dichotomy is that the child will be made to feel that some valued and desired aspect of herself or himself is gender-inappropriate and must be denied or relinquished (Badaracco 1974). The question of biological or constitutional sex differences is not relevant in this regard. Rather, the question is whether one respects the temperament and biological predisposition of each unique child, which may or may not conform to statistical group differences between the sexes.

There has recently been a growing appreciation of the deep guilt, anxiety, and inhibition that result when a child is told that his or her interests, skills, or behaviors are gender-inappropriate (Badaracco 1974). No little boy can tolerate being called feminine, and no little girl can tolerate being called masculine. It is hardly surprising, then, that early in a girl's life she experiences anxiety and guilt about strivings in directions that are not domestic (Seidenberg 1970). Numerous publications in the psychoanalytic literature suggest that many women who seemingly choose to relinquish self-seeking ambitious strivings do so because they cannot freely and without guilt fulfill themselves through personal achievement. This guilt is linked to the fact that professional capability and competence are unconsciously experienced as masculine (Chasseguet-Smirgel 1970, Moulton 1973). Clinical and life experience demonstrate that few women are resilient enough to tolerate internal and external threats to their femininity. As one psychoanalyst put it, "No woman will treasure any fame or glory she can achieve at the price of being called unfeminine. This below-the-belt blow sends most women into despair" (Seidenberg 1970, p. 134). Pressures on men to relinquish so-called feminine aspects of themselves are equally, if not more, intense.

In addition to having pathogenic consequences, it may be argued that sex-role stereotypes, irrespective of their content, are conceptually unsound. Dichotomous notions of masculinity and femininity implicitly embrace a dichotomous concept of mental health for the two sexes that is difficult to justify on theoretical grounds. Research findings demonstrating statistically significant differences between the sexes cannot be interpreted to mean that a trait or quality is healthy for one sex and less adaptive or important for the other. Rather, it is more likely that a trait, quality, or behavior is either healthy or unhealthy for a particular individual, irrespective of sex. Both sexes, for example, should be able to express a healthy degree of aggression, competition, and self-assertion that allows one to persist and work for what one believes in, even in the face of anger or disapproval from others. For both sexes, however, aggression, competition, and self-assertion may have pathological underpinnings; competing, winning, or "measuring up" can become ends in themselves, perhaps to compensate for an individual's underlying feelings of narcissistic inadequacy.

Let us turn now to the positive or adaptive aspects of sex-role stereotypes. First, we should pay due respect to the fact that in all places and times there has existed some masculine-feminine dichotomy that has included a clear division of labor based on sex, as well as a sharp division in the attributes, traits, and qualities valued for each sex. The universality of sex-role stereotypes does not necessarily prove them to be virtuous (scapegoating, prejudice, and war have also achieved such universal status), but it does suggest that a masculine-feminine polarization serves significant adaptive functions.

It is important to note that the defenses of splitting and projective identification that are involved in a masculine-feminine polarization are not just pathogenic defenses; they also facilitate personality organization for the growing organism (Cooper 1976). As Klein noted, the placement of experiences into bipolarities orders the universe and "allows the ego to emerge out of chaos and to order its experience" (Segal 1967, p. 22). She suggested that splitting might be a precondition for the later, more complicated, although internally more whole, experience of integrating bipolarities within one's self (e.g., good-bad, active-passive, dependent-independent).

One adaptive function of bipolar concepts of masculinity and femininity is to make the consolidation of gender identity a simpler task for the child. The child's cognitive labeling of herself or himself as girl or boy is the basic organizer for subsequent gender experience (Kleeman 1976), and dissimilarities or bipolarities in socialization may facilitate this labeling process. In addition, establishing and reinforcing clear-cut differences between the two sexes may help the child to manage certain anxieties regarding sexual differences—the boy's fear that he will lose his penis and become a girl, for example, or the girl's fear that she has lost a penis and is thus a castrated male.

It is likely that dichotomous notions of masculinity and femininity are of greater psychological value to the male child, in part because of the intensity of castration anxiety. In addition, an exaggeration or polarization of the differences between the sexes (whether real or imagined) may help the boy in the task of achieving autonomy and separation from the mother. This has characteristically been a more difficult developmental task for the girl, who is anatomically similar to the mother and cannot rely on a sense of masculinity to bolster differences from or defiance of her mother. At the same time, however, the boy is in the uniquely difficult situation of identifying with and learning from a primary caretaker whose qualities he is taught to repudiate within himself.

Although the exaggeration or polarization of sex differences, whether real or contrived, may simplify the establishment of gender identity, it does not follow that a similar sex-role socialization for both sexes would lead to a disturbance in gender identity. Psychiatric writings often suggest or imply that adherence to dichotomous concepts of masculinity and femininity, however culturally defined, is essential for the development of normal gender identity (Kleeman 1976, Stoller 1976). This theoretical viewpoint is put forth without acknowledging or studying those healthy children who are being raised in normal families in which sex-role stereotypes are neither adhered to by the parents nor especially encouraged in the children. I am speaking of families in which parents have a deep sense of gender identity that transcends and is independent of societally prescribed role behaviors and culturally defined notions of masculinity and femininity.

IMPLICATIONS FOR PARENTING

The viewpoint that sex-role stereotypes have a consolidating and facilitating effect as well as restrictive and pathogenic consequences raises the question of the optimum degree to which sex-role stereotypes should be adhered to for the growing child. Should parents try to free themselves entirely from thinking in terms of a masculine-feminine dichotomy? Should stereotypes be adhered to rigidly, at least while the child is young? Or is there some middle ground in which we can retain our cultural definitions of masculinity and femininity while broadening them and making them more flexible, thus providing a wide range of choice for both sexes?

This question, so long as it is posed as a search for general rules and guidelines, cannot be answered. Sex-role stereotypes and bipolar concepts of masculinity and femininity provide a structure for the child. The extent to which this structure is necessary and valuable—or restrictive and inhibiting—depends on the child's unique qualities and the family constellation. My clinical work suggests that the degree to which sex-role stereotypes are adaptive and facilitating (as opposed to restrictive and inhibiting) is inversely related to the extent to which an individual has established a stable and integrated sense of self and has consolidated a solid gender identity.

It may be helpful to define the concept of gender identity as it appears in this paper. Stoller (1976) defines *core gender identity* as "the sense we have of our sex—of maleness in males and of femaleness in females" (p. 61). *Gender identity* is a broader concept involving a conviction about one's self and one's role, or a sense of masculinity and femininity. The concepts of masculine and feminine are elusive, since they refer to subjective experiences that can achieve a multiplicity of behavioral expressions. I define gender identity (i.e., masculinity and femininity) as a stable, subjective sense of comfort and liking for one's sex and for those functions which are sex-specific. In women, this means comfort and liking for female genitals and reproductive capacities without undue envy or fear of men and the penis. In men, this means a comfort and liking for male genitals without undue envy or fear of women and female genitals and reproductive capacities.

Consider first the child who is being reared by two mature parents, each of whom has established a sense of autonomy and self-worth and a stable, nonconflictual gender identity. That is, the mother has a secure and comfortable sense of being female and feminine, and the father of being male and masculine. If such parents are not split along traditional masculine-feminine lines, their child may receive considerable psychological benefits with few costs. If the mother and father are both nurturant and intellectual, if they cook together, clean together, and share authority in a spontaneous collaborative way that defies traditional stereotypes, the child does not become confused or anxious. Rather, such parenting allows the girl (or boy) to incorporate a definition of femininity (or masculinity) that permits or sanctions acknowledgment, appreciation, and enjoyment of a wide range of behaviors, feelings, and experiences.

In contrast, consider the child reared in a family in which self–other boundaries between parents are poorly maintained and in which the father and/or mother has an unstable or conflict-laden gender identity. For such children, who may be developing unassimilated, confused maternal and paternal imagoes, the parents' adherence to traditionally defined masculine-feminine roles can have a clarifying-consolidating effect.

In such families, culturally defined bipolar concepts of masculinity and femininity may be reassuring not only to the child but also to the parents. As Kleeman (1976) noted, the parents' cognitive awareness of the child's sex—"my baby is a girl"—organizes and directs a whole set of cues, rewards, and sanctions. Sex-role stereotypes simplify the task of parenting by providing explicit rules and guidelines for child rearing. This is essential for parents who themselves lack stable and clear inner directives.

IMPLICATIONS FOR PSYCHOTHERAPY

The viewpoint that sex-role stereotypes have a consolidating, supportive function for certain individuals and restrictive, inhibiting consequences for others has important implications for treatment. For example, it is not therapeutic to attempt to "liberate" a patient from cultural sex-role stereotypes if that patient relies on them to shore up and maintain a shaky sense of gender identity. The following brief vignette is illustrative.

Clinical Example

When Ms. A. came to her first therapy hour, she had an ultrafeminine appearance and manner that had an imitative or "tacked-on" quality. There was a striking absence of so-called masculine strivings in her history. She had never gone through a tomboy stage and had always avoided rough or aggressive play. In many ways she had always been a model if not a caricature of domesticity and femininity.

Ms. A. had managed to maintain a somewhat stable existence until she began to feel pressure from the feminist subculture in California and from a man with whom she was involved to become more "liberated." As she yielded to such pressure, the potentially disorganizing effects were quickly apparent. For example, on a camping trip she dressed in her first pair of blue jeans and a work shirt and suddenly felt "unfeminine" and unattractive, and the thought crossed her mind that perhaps she was not "totally female." Subsequently, she noted that when she was dressed in "men's clothing" (in this category she included women's jeans with a fly front) she "talked differently," took "bigger strides," and began to have mild episodic feelings of depersonalization and unreality. In the face of this anxiety and confusion, Ms. A., at the age of 25, sought psychotherapy.

Early in the course of treatment, which by practical necessity was once-a-week therapy, it became evident that Ms. A. was a severely disturbed individual who maintained her tenuous sexual identity primarily through strict conformity to behaviors ascribed to her sex that were clearly differentiated from those ascribed to men. Given the practical limitations on the extensiveness of treatment and the very precarious nature of the patient's ego functioning, I chose a supportive approach and helped her to reestablish the sense of femininity that in the past she had been able to consolidate through her strict adherence and even caricature of traditional feminine behaviors. Part of this therapeutic approach was actively helping Ms. A. to resist surrounding cultural pressures toward androgyny. A strict feminist therapist might have failed to appreciate the consolidating, supportive effect of sex-role stereotypes for this woman.

While the severity of Ms. A.'s disturbance is atypical, the phenomenon illustrated by this vignette is widespread. One neurotic female patient, for example, was unable to assume the top, more active position in intercourse because it made her feel like she "had the penis," a conflicted wish for her. A neurotic male patient was unable to comfortably let his wife drive while he was in the car because this made him feel "feminine." Some conflicts and anxieties about gender identity may be ubiquitous. To the degree that a particular individual experiences such conflicts or anxieties, sex-role stereotypes or the "rules of the game" may be helpful. The therapist's decision to

analyze or to support defensive conformity to sex-role stereotypes should be made not on the basis of personal ideology but
rather on a careful assessment of the function that sex-role
stereotypes may serve for a particular individual.

In treating relatively healthy patients who have established a stable gender identity, the most common therapeutic
error is failure to question conformity to sex-role stereotypes.
This happens frequently when the patient is seemingly comfortable in complying with her or his culturally defined role.
The following case is illustrative.

Clinical Example

Ms. B., a 28-year-old woman in intensive psychotherapy, announced to her therapist that she would be
moving to a new city at the end of the year because of
her husband's professional advancement. Although
she was sad about leaving psychotherapy as well as her
friends and her teaching job in a Montessori school,
she expressed excitement about the challenges that
the move would bring and pride in her husband's
success. Initial inquiry by the therapist as to any less
enthusiastic feelings she might have met with a re-
statement of her positive reaction to the anticipated
change. Certainly, it entailed losses for her, but these
were well overshadowed by the gains. Further, Ms. B.
was thinking about starting a family soon and
thought she might stop work entirely for several years.
She clearly communicated that she would like the
issue dropped, and it was dropped for some time.

Months later, when Ms. B. was discussing some
pains and pleasures of her work, the therapist once
again commented that he was struck by how easily she
made her own job unimportant in regard to the
planned move, and how adept she was at convincing
him that this was the case. He also speculated as to why
she might need to avoid taking her own professional
life seriously, and commented that it was difficult for
her to be in competition with her husband or to ask

him to make professional sacrifices for her, although she had done so earlier for him. His questioning, which occurred in the face of her initial insistence that there were no further issues to discuss, led to her increased understanding of the neurotic anxieties that caused her to devalue her work, to treat it as less important than her husband's, and even to be ready to drop it entirely. The therapist's persistence in this line of questioning also had significant transference implications, since it communicated to the patient that he took her work seriously. The fact that he had dropped the issue, even though she had more than invited him to do so, had for her the unconscious meaning that he, like her mother, did not really want her to be a fulfilled individual. Ms. B. and her husband did not move, and she has continued to advance professionally and now has a challenging position with considerable authority.

This therapist's skillful handling of Ms. B.'s treatment may be more the exception than the rule. Many therapists fail to analyze defensive and maladaptive aspects of the life choices of patients who conform to predominant cultural stereotypes, especially when the patient is seemingly content (e.g., the "feminine" woman who opts for full-time motherhood because of neurotic anxieties regarding intellectual achievement, competition, and success). This is an especially important issue for women patients, who so often begin treatment with intense unconscious guilt and anxiety about acknowledging wishes or longings that are not in keeping with the feminine role. Even therapists who are deeply committed to facilitating women's struggles for self-realization may unwittingly contribute to their inhibitions by an implicit acceptance or approval of a patient's neurotic compliance with culturally defined notions of femininity.

It is to be hoped that mental health professionals will continue to reexamine and clarify their thinking regarding sex-role stereotypes and bipolar concepts of masculinity and femininity. While radical feminist writings are sometimes naive in their global damnation of sex-role stereotypes, the traditional psychiatric literature has more frequently erred in the direction of blanket condemnation of the current trend toward depolarization of the sexes. Some of this literature warns of impending pathology for children who are not raised in conformity to traditional masculine-feminine stereotypes and suggests that nonsexist child rearing will lead to identity problems, sexual confusion, and to gray, affectless, "neuter" children (Landman 1974). Terms such as *role blurring, role confusion,* and *role reversal* are applied to parents in a pejorative manner, often without discriminating between healthy parents who, for adaptive reasons, do not choose to organize their lives along traditional masculine-feminine lines and those chaotic, unstable parents who may make a similar "choice" for pathogenic reasons.

In addition to being theoretically unsound, such writing has the consequence of discouraging certain people from seeking our services and has led individuals to turn to more progressive, nonestablishment therapists who may be less qualified to offer help. There is unquestionably a powerful trend in this country away from dichotomous concepts of masculinity and femininity; many young couples today choose not to live like Jack Spratt and his wife. In fact, a report from the Group for the Advancement of Psychiatry (GAP) quoted a study finding that 50 percent of college students expressed a belief in equal and shared parenting (GAP 1975). Clearly, such trends are in the direction of greater equality and more functional modes of relatedness for both sexes, despite the fact that pressures towards androgyny may evoke heightened anxiety and confusion in certain individuals. Perhaps it is because issues related to the topic of masculinity and femininity are anxiety-producing and emotionally laden that so much of our writing on this topic fails to do justice to either the precision of scientific thinking or the complexity of human experience.

REFERENCES

Badaracco, M. R. (1974). Recent trends towards unisex: a panel. *American Journal of Psychoanalysis* 34:17–23.

Chasseguet-Smirgel, J. (1970). *Female Sexuality: New Psychoanalytic Views*, ed. J. Chasseguet-Smirgel et al. Ann Arbor: University of Michigan Press.

Cooper, L. (1976). Cotherapy relationship in groups. *Small Group Behavior* 7:473–498.

GAP, Committee on the College Student (1975). *The Educated Woman: Prospects and Problems* 9(92). New York: GAP.

Kleeman, J. A. (1976). Freud's views on early female sexuality in the light of direct child observation. *Journal of the American Psychoanalytic Association* 24:3–27.

Landman, L. (1974). Recent trends toward unisex: a panel. *American Journal of Psychoanalysis* 34:27–31.

Lerner, H. G. (1973). Women's liberation. *Menninger Perspective* 4:11–13, 20–21. (10)

——(1974). Early origins of envy and devaluation of women: implications for sex-role stereotypes. *Bulletin of the Menninger Clinic* 38:538–553. (6)

Moulton, R. (1973). The myth of femininity: a panel. *American Journal of Psychoanalysis* 33:45–49.

Segal, H. (1967). *Introduction to the Work of Melanie Klein.* New York: Basic Books.

Seidenberg, R. (1970). *Marriage in Life and Literature.* New York: Philosophical Library.

Stoller, R. (1976). Primary femininity. *Journal of the American Psychoanalytic Association* 24:59–78.

Chapter 6

Girls, Ladies, or Women? The Unconscious Dynamics of Language Choice

Recently, at a case conference, one of my colleagues made a slip of the tongue and referred to a 33-year-old male patient as a boy.[1] This slip was recognized as significant, and it led to productive group discussion about this patient's immaturity, dependency, and general lack of adult masculine qualities. In a culture in which we clearly separate the men from the boys, it is hardly surprising that this linguistic distinction is an important one. Boys early learn to look forward to becoming men, and encouragement to "Act like a man!" implies that one should strive for strength, independence, maturity, courage, and integrity. For men, it is evident that differences in language reflect differences in self-experience and in the experience of others.(Consider, for example, the difference between a "colored boy" and a "black man.") The *Random House Dictionary of the English Language* notes that the word *boy*, when applied to a young adult, suggests that the person in question lacks maturity and judgment, or is considered by the speaker to be inferior.

In clinical settings, female patients are frequently referred to as girls, regardless of whether they are 13 or 30. Further, I have noticed that when I question my colleagues about blanketly

---

[1]This chapter was first published in 1976 in *Comprehensive Psychiatry* 17(2):295-299.

labeling all females "girls," many will use the term *gal* or *lady* (respectively, according to age) but assiduously avoid the word *woman*. Because the preferred use of either the term *girl* or the term *lady* is a ubiquitous phenomenon in this culture, the linguistic distinction is often seen as a mere cultural habit that is of no particular psychological relevance. However, one's choice of language reflects one's unconscious assumptions, and for mental health professionals it is imperative that such assumptions be recognized, made explicit, and understood. The task of this chapter is to examine the assumptions underlying the preferred use of the terms *girl* and *lady*, to explore why this choice in language has been established and maintained, and to note the significance it may have in regard to treating patients.

WOMAN AS A DIRTY WORD

Although it might first appear that *woman, lady,* and *girl* are interchangeable terms—one's choice of words reflecting habit rather than attitude—people are indeed cognizant (at least unconsciously) that only the term *woman* has sexual and aggressive implications and connotes reproductive functioning. One can see, for example, by completing the following sentences, that these terms are hardly interchangeable.

- She feared that after her hysterectomy she might no longer feel like a real _____ .
- Jane is sweet, soft-spoken, and modest. She is truly a _____ .
- When Sue began to menstruate, she knew she was on the road to becoming a _____ .
- Why are you always fighting and screaming? Can't you behave like a _____ ?
- She felt very passionate with him; he made her feel very much like a _____ .

As linguists have noted, the term *lady* functions as a euphemism, in that it removes the sexual and reproductive implications inherent in the word *woman* (Lakoff 1974). The fear that both sexes commonly experience regarding female genitals and reproductive capacities is a familiar theme in the psychoanalytic literature (Lederer 1968, p. 153), and the term *lady* is a reassuringly "clean" and asexual one. Similarly, *lady* connotes an absence of aggressive impulses in the female sex. Ladies do not struggle with powerful hostile and destructive wishes, or at least they do not express them in a threatening (i.e., unladylike) fashion.

The term *girl* not only serves to avoid certain anxiety-arousing connotations inherent in the word *woman* regarding aggression, sexuality, and reproduction; it also serves to impart a tone of frivolousness and lack of seriousness to ambitious, intellectual, and competitive strivings that women may pursue. In a culture in which it is considered castrating or unfeminine for women to develop a vigorous, critical, and competitive intellectual style, it is not surprising that accomplished young women are referred to as girls. *Girl*, like *boy*, is a term that undoes any implications of status, authority, and true seriousness of purpose. (One can hardly imagine, for example, speaking of a girl or boy running for Congress, or a girl or boy winning a Nobel Prize.) Similarly, the term *lady* also imparts a tone of frivolity and lightness to the strivings and accomplishments of women. Linguists have commented that terms like *lady scientist* and *lady doctor* seem to minimize some of the anxiety that is associated with women who are successful and powerful in traditionally masculine competitive pursuits (Hage 1972). An exception to these linguistic preferences occurs in wartime, when we speak of our fighting men as boys (e.g., "the boys in Vietnam"). As with the term *girl*, the use of the diminutive term *boy* in this context may reflect an unconscious attempt to deny or minimize the destructiveness and sadism (in this case real rather than fantasied) associated with men at war.

LANGUAGE AS A REFLECTION OF SEX-ROLE PRESSURES

The preferred use of the term *girl* or *lady* reflects our current notions of femininity and female attractiveness. Women are indeed encouraged to remain girls and act like ladies. Of relevance is the accumulating literature documenting the intense pressures on women to inhibit direct and open expression of sexual and aggressive impulses; to relinquish serious intellectual, ambitious, and competitive strivings; and to develop adorable, childlike, dependent qualities, as well as "ladylike" virtues such as modesty, self-sacrifice, and service (Symonds 1971– 1972, Lerner 1974b).

The fact that men are not called boys (except to impart a tone of frivolousness of purpose, as in "going out with the boys") and are less frequently called gentlemen reflects the very different cultural pressures and expectations for their sex. While women have been encouraged to inhibit their sexuality (as in the glorification of naiveté or virginity), males are encouraged to make open displays of their sexual prowess (hence the difference between a loose or promiscuous woman and an experienced man). While females are encouraged to keep the peace, men learn that toughness and willingness to fight for their beliefs enhance their masculine attractiveness. While women are encouraged to "let the man win" or "play dumb," men are taught that intellectual prowess and seriousness of purpose enhance their masculinity. Whereas little-girl qualities are typically considered cute and lovable in women, childlike qualities are considered unmasculine or effeminate in men. In sum, we are comfortable with the term *man* because it is the cultural expectation that boys become men—an expectation that often involves unfortunate pressures to relinquish healthy expressions of fear, emotionality, and dependency needs. The avoidance of the term *woman* reflects the cultural expectation that females retain a self-experience of being girls or ladies, and behave accordingly. The pressure here is to inhibit healthy aggressive, independent, and self-assertive strivings and to relinquish any traits and qualities that might be construed as controlling, dominating, or in any way threatening to others.[2]

---

[2]The fact that feminists are called "women's libbers" and the women's movement is referred to as "Women's Lib" is another example of language reflecting unconscious anxiety about aggression and power in women. No other liberation movement in the history of the world has similarly been given a "cute" nickname that so undermines its spirit and seriousness of purpose. (One can hardly imagine referring to "the boys in the Black Lib," "National Lib Front," "Symbionese Libbers," etc.)

LANGUAGE AS A REFLECTION
OF INTRAPSYCHIC PRESSURES

The preferred use of the terms *lady* and *girl* reflects not only cultural values and expectations, but intrapsychic pressures as well. Of relevance are writings suggesting that pressures on adult females to remain girls (i.e., to cultivate adorable, innocent, childlike, dependent features) and behave like ladies (i.e., adhere to values of gentility, propriety, cleanliness, impulse control, and conformity to social norms) reflect deep-seated affects and anxieties that both sexes share about women's biologic function and fantasied destructive potential (Lederer 1968, Lerner 1974a).

There exists an impressive amount of psychological and anthropological evidence regarding the anxiety and terror (as well as envy and idealization) of women's reproductive functions (i.e., menstruation, childbirth, lactation) in cultures around the world (Lederer 1968). Similarly, the fear of the castrating vagina is a familiar one in the psychoanalytic literature, and I am in agreement with writers who have stressed that it is frequently the mother more than the father who is feared as castrator (Rheingold 1964, Lederer 1968). Whether the fear of the castrating and destructive woman has its origins in anatomic realities (i.e., the male having a penis that he fears to lose, the female having a vagina that engulfs, surrounds, and unconsciously threatens to castrate the penis) or whether the fear of women stems from the child's early experience with maternal sovereignty (Lerner 1974), is an issue that is beyond the scope of this chapter. Of importance is the fact that the fear of women is a powerful, if not universal, dynamic in both sexes—so much so that the basic feminine tactics of letting the man win, of pretending he's boss, and of de-skilling oneself in so-called masculine pursuits are all in the interest of "protecting a man's masculinity"—that is, of minimizing one's own castrating and fantasied destructive potential. It is especially those women who have difficulty successfully integrating and modulating aggressive impulses who frequently have a need to see themselves as the weaker sex and to maintain a self-experience of being ladies or "girls" long after they are mothers themselves. Clearly, ladies and girls need not be feared; they need only be protected.

IMPLICATIONS FOR TREATMENT

The word *woman* is so commonplace in our vocabularies that it may seem at first absurd to suggest that this term is associated with unconscious anxiety regarding reproduction, sexuality, aggression, and "destructiveness" in adult females. On the other hand, the avoidance of this generic term when the context does not specifically demand it is striking. In clinical settings, for example, I often hear the distinction made between the men and ladies in group treatment; and in individual case conferences, female patients in their 20s and 30s are only occasionally referred to as women. One wonders whether the preferred use of *girl* or *lady* reflects unconscious attitudes of the treater (does he or she need or wish to experience women as ladies/girls), and further, whether language perpetuates these attitudes.

When a clinical interviewer asks a woman how she relates to men, for example, and subsequently how she relates to "other ladies," is there not an unconscious communication that the patient ought to behave like a lady? Particularly in the case in which the patient has special difficulty with the direct expression and recognition of aggressive- and sexual-impulse life, the term *lady*, when it replaces the generic term *woman* in the therapist's vocabulary, may reinforce anxiety about "bad," destructive, or "dirty" aspects of one's self-experience. Similarly, if a young woman is deeply conflicted about intellectual, ambitious, and competitive strivings and has a defensive need not to take herself seriously in these areas, calling her a girl exacerbates guilt about serious achievement and the assumption of authority.

A patient's preferred use of *girl* or *lady* in reference to a therapist also has transference implications that can be made explicit and understood. For example, one patient, who early in treatment called me a girl, was able to understand this label as an expression of her suspicion that I was too young and inexperienced to be of any use to her. Another patient, an older man, unfailingly used the word *lady* in reference to the female sex, myself included. Exploring his discomfort with the term *woman* led to insight regarding aspects of his general distrust of women and his related need to keep distance between us.

Clearly, however, it is not the choice of language that is the critical issue, but rather the unconscious attitudes that underlie the choice. The intense cultural and intrapsychic pressures on women to maintain a self-experience of being girls or ladies has been widely acknowledged, and psychotherapists should take seriously the accusation that we frequently reinforce these pressures rather than help women overcome them (Chesler 1972). The fact that mental health professionals do experience adult female patients as girls or ladies suggests that we have indeed incorporated cultural definitions of femininity (implying childishness, dependency, conformity, purity, delicacy, nonaggressiveness, noncompetitiveness, etc.) into our thinking. When we no longer have a defensive need to see women in narrow, nonthreatening, or diminutive terms, our language will take care of itself.

REFERENCES

Chesler, P. (1972). *Women and Madness.* New York: Doubleday.

Hage, D. (1972). There's glory for you. *Aphra* 3:2–14.

Lakoff, R. (1974). You are what you say. *Ms. Magazine* 3:65–68.

Lederer, W. (1968). *The Fear of Women.* New York: Grune & Stratton.

Lerner, H. G. (1974a). Early origins of envy and devaluation of women: implications for sex role stereotypes. *Bulletin of the Menninger Clinic* 38:538–553.

—— (1974b). The hysterical personality: a "woman's disease." *Comprehensive Psychiatry* 15(2):157–164.

Random House Dictionary of the English Language (1967). New York: Random House.

Rheingold, J. C. (1972). *The Fear of Being a Woman.* New York: Grune & Stratton.

Symonds, A. (1971–1972). Discussion of Ruth Moulton's paper: psychoanalytic reflections on women's liberation. *Contemporary Psychoanalysis* 8:224–228.

Chapter 7

The Hysterical Personality

It is widely recognized that the diagnosis of hysteria is infrequently applied to male patients and very commonly to female ones.[1] A paper by Robins and colleagues (1952) suggests that hysteria in men is extremely rare, if indeed it occurs at all, and there is general agreement that an initial diagnosis of hysteria in males is somewhat of a clinical anomaly (Berger 1971). It should be noted that grave hysterical symptoms (e.g., conversion reactions, dissociative phenomena) have been observed in male patients, but these individuals tend not to manifest the type of cognitive and personality organization that is characteristic of the hysterical individual (Chodoff and Lyons 1958). It is especially in regard to the hysterical personality, character, or "style" that the male patient is a rarity, and it is in this sense that the word *hysteria* will be used in this chapter.

In explaining the preponderance of female hysterics, psychoanalytic theorists have focused on differences in preoedipal and oedipal developmental tasks that the two sexes must master (Zetzel 1968). It is my opinion, however, that theories of libidinal development offer only a partial explanation of the sex difference in hysteria and that social and cultural factors play a major role. Although the importance of such extrapsychic

---

[1]This chapter was first published in 1974 as "The Hysterical Personality: A 'Womans' Disease" in *Comprehensive Psychiatry* 15(2):157–164.

factors has not been fully appreciated, neither have these factors been entirely ignored. Marmor (1953), for example, has noted that the traits characteristic of the hysterical personality are feminine ones and are thus more acceptable in women than in men. Chodoff and Lyons (1958, p. 739) have commented that the hysterical personality "is a picture of women in the words of men and . . . what the description sounds like amounts to a caricature of femininity!" But beyond noting that the concept of hysteria involves a description of traditionally feminine qualities, the theoretical and diagnostic significance of this observation has not been explored.

This chapter will first review the diagnostic indications and behavioral characteristics of this patient group in order to outline with some specificity the criteria that will lead to a diagnosis of hysterical personality. Next it will be demonstrated how a girl's immediate social environment puts enormous pressure on her to develop a style of cognition and personality that will lend itself to this diagnosis on the clinical test battery or diagnostic interview. In this regard, it will be noted how the ego-constricting effects of a feminine socialization process may too readily be confused with the effects of massive repression. Finally, certain conceptual tangles that have resulted from the overlap between the hysterical character and the feminine character will be outlined.

DIAGNOSTIC INDICATIONS OF HYSTERIA

Although psychological tests and diagnostic interviews may be informative in determining the nature of psychosexual development, neuroses are diagnosed primarily in terms of their characteristic defense mechanisms and styles of adaptation (Rappaport, Gill, and Schafer 1968). The diagnosis of hysteria is frequently inferred from excessive use of repression, with only secondary concern for the hypothetical reconstruction of the fate of the Oedipus complex and the interplay of various drives (Schafer 1954, Rappaport, Gill, and Schafer 1968). Because a repressive style of defense has clearly defined effects on cognition and personality, the diagnostic assessment of hysteria should present no special problems. As Shapiro (1965, p. 108) points out, "In our current understanding of the operation of various neuroses . . . the picture of hysterical neurosis is relatively clear-cut . . . and, among neuroses, none has been more definitely or clearly associated with the operation of a specific defense mechanism than has hysteria with repression."

In regard to the diagnostic test indications of hysteria, Schafer has made the following summary statement:

> This diagnostic term [hysteria] covers those persons who rigidly and pervasively resort to the defense of repression in their efforts to cope with their impulses and the demands of the world about them. Excessive reliance on this defense appears to hamper the development of broad intellectual, cultural interests, to impair the ability for independent and creative thinking, and to make for striking emotional lability and naiveté. One or another of these characteristics will color a large part of the thought processes elicited by the test items. [1948, p. 32]

An example of a hysterical mode of responding on the Rorschach test is offered by Shapiro:

> Where the compulsive person may list and actively organize relations between varieties of botanical or marine specimens, the hysterical person says, "A beautiful bouquet" or "It's Paris! . . . like in the French Line posters." [1965, p. 112]

Purportedly as a result of pervasive reliance on repression, the cognitive style of the hysteric is a dramatically nonintellectual one characterized by a lack of concern with intellectual achievement, productivity, and mastery (Schafer 1948, Shapiro 1965). There is little investment in abstract and complex ideas, a flippant disregard for factual and technical information, and an inability to perform effectively on tasks demanding these skills. Independent and critical thinking is impaired, and the general mode of cognition is fuzzy, global, and undifferentiated. Hunch and intuition may replace active, effortful thought and concentration. Because intellectual activity and mastery are continuously avoided, the hysteric's thinking has been described as naive, egocentric, unreflective, affect-laden, and cliché-ridden.

In contrast to their lack of a technical-factual apprehension of the world, hysterical persons have a heightened involvement in interpersonal relationships and a direct and active engagement with the human world (Easser and Lesser 1965, Shapiro 1965). It is not unusual for these people to do superior work on a task of social judgment on the Wechsler intelligence test or to demonstrate an excellent understanding of conventional and proper social behavior. Similarly, hysterics are often vivid and likable social companions, and personality descriptions of them frequently include such adjectives as buoyant, sprightly, lively, colorful, and feminine (Easser and Lesser 1965).

At the same time, one sees dependent, demanding behavior and a heightened concern with receiving approval, admiration, and attention from others (Easser and Lesser 1965). Flirtatious, seductive behavior is frequently apparent, often accompanied by complaints of frigidity. Although Freud (1931) did not conceptualize a hysterical personality, he did suggest that the "erotic" type of person who is largely preoccupied with loving and being loved is predisposed to the development of hysteria. It should be noted that the romanticism of hysterics, although pervasive, is also shallow and superficial. Shapiro (1965) has described the Prince-Charming-will-come-and-everything-will-turn-out-all-right view of life that is characteristic of these individuals, and a naively romantic view of life is frequently conspicuous in thematic apperception test (TAT) productions.

Emotional lability is a term that is ubiquitous in descriptions of hysterical individuals, and it speaks to their inability to adequately modulate affective experience as well as to a stylistic tendency to utilize feelings rather than thought in dealing with crises and conflicts (Schafer 1954, Shapiro 1965). In keeping with an emotional and somewhat impulsive approach to life, childlike features are noteworthy. Easser and Lesser (1965) have described the little-girl qualities of a group of hysterical patients and noted that their families regarded these women as juvenile, dependent, cute, and lovable; one patient kept the nickname Baby until marriage. In regard to diagnostic testing, Schafer (1954) has noted that hysterics' childlike qualities make them appear like "babes in the woods" or "bunnies."

HYSTERICAL CHARACTER
VERSUS FEMININE CHARACTER

When I was teaching a graduate seminar in diagnostic testing, one student responded to the above summary with the confused protest, "But you're not describing a neurosis—you're just describing a woman!" There is, indeed, much truth to the observation that the diagnostic indicators of hysteria are very much in keeping with the media presentation of the female sex. We are all familiar with the stereotype of the giggling, blushing woman whose head is filled with Hollywood romance and trivia, who is unconcerned with technical or abstract intellectual problems, who prefers hunch and intuition to effortful concentration, who is childlike and dependent in the presence of men, who is emotional and impulsive in her behavior. In fact, many of the diagnostic indicators of hysteria are related to essential aspects of femininity and female attractiveness.

One might speculate that the female sex en masse suffers from a hysterical personality and that the media are merely portraying woman's true nature. Even if this were the case, a vicious cycle would be created by the fact that the role models for young girls are almost exclusively hysterical ones. (I cannot, for example, recall seeing a television program in which a group of women struggled effectively to solve a technical or scientific problem, while the men concerned themselves with social trivialities). But the problem is not simply one of role models, for if we examine societal notions of masculinity and femininity, we find that the pressures on women to adopt a

hysterical style are intense and continue throughout a lifetime. I wish to examine this point in greater detail.

It is widely believed that a woman should find her true
sense of fulfillment (and identity) in wifehood and motherhood
(Chesler 1972). From her earliest years, the young girl is
taught to spend her major efforts in preparation for these
roles, and the task of learning to be attractive to men, with the
hope of eventually finding a husband, frequently becomes con-
suming. There is little doubt that this state of affairs may be
conducive to the development of good social judgment and a
heightened sensitivity to pleasing (as well as manipulating)
other people. Colloquial language suggesting that women
catch, snare, or hook their men speaks to the notion that
highly developed social skills are an important asset for females. There is much truth to Firestone's statement that
"more real brilliance goes into a one-hour coed telephone dialogue about men than into that same coed's four years of
college study" (Firestone 1970, p. 21).

But if the cultivation of female attractiveness is conducive
to the development of social skills, it is inimical to intellectual
development. Females are taught in a variety of ways that an
independent and masterful intellectual style is unattractive,
and women who develop an aggressive and critical intellect are
often considered castrating or masculine. A growing body of
literature documents the remorseless stifling of a young girl's
creative intelligence as she learns to be feminine and attractive
to men (Lynn 1972, Lerner 1973). Since femininity is based on
a model of intellectual dependence and docility, it is not surprising that women tend to develop what appears to be a
hysterical mode of cognition. It is perhaps more surprising
that certain women escape it.

In this regard, an examination of popular teenage literature is especially enlightening. I have surveyed a wide selection
of books and magazines written for teenage girls on issues of
femininity and popularity, from which it is evident that girls
are encouraged to adopt a mode of personality and intellect in
keeping with the hysterical characteristics described earlier.
The recurring theme in this literature is that girls must be
clever enough to catch a man, but never to outsmart him, or as

Arlene Dahl (1965) puts it in her book *Always Ask a Man*, a woman must "never let her competence compete with her femininity." Young women are encouraged to be intellectually docile and to cultivate childlike, dependent qualities and social, manipulative skills. In many ways the "feminine character" and the "hysterical character" are synonymous. A comment by Kreps on the traditional female role is relevant:

> She is exhorted to play out the role of Cinderella, expecting fortune and happiness from some Prince Charming, rather than to venture out by herself. Be pretty, be pleasant, use mouthwash and deodorant, never have an intellectual thought, and Prince Charming will sweep you off to his castle where you will live happily ever after. [1970, p. 8]

In contrast, the qualities cherished in masculinity are not in keeping with the hysterical picture. For men, intellectual achievement, production, efficiency, and assertion are important values, and an interest in abstract and technical problems is encouraged. Male heroes chart the stars, cure diseases, create masterpieces, and actively build, shape, and destroy the world around them. Male children are encouraged to be logical (rather than intuitive), practical (rather than romantic), intellectually aggressive and forceful (rather than passive and conforming), self-reliant (rather than dependent and childlike) and intellectual (rather than emotional). Interpersonal sensitivity is not considered a priority for men, and a certain amount of social brutality, self-interest, and toughness may be considered attractive.

It seems then that the diagnostic indications of the hysterical character as presently conceptualized define a style of cognition and personality that runs dramatically counter to traditional notions of masculinity. Should a male begin to develop a hysterical style, he will be discouraged from giving expression to it. Our current notions of masculine attractiveness do not allow for expressions of childishness, naiveté, fearfulness, dependency, intellectual ineptness, or emotional (rather than intellectual) wisdom. For this reason, a diagnosis of hysteria in a male patient involves very serious difficulties in sexual identification. This has indeed been borne out by the clinical literature (Chodoff and Lyons 1958, Berger 1971).

HYSTERICAL PERSONALITY: REPRESSION OR ROLE PRESSURE

The literature regarding the hysterical personality is perhaps more replete with contradictions than any other (Easser and Lesser 1965), and the confusion between femininity and hysteria has undoubtedly contributed much to this state of affairs. For one thing, it has too readily been assumed that the style of personality and cognition described earlier results from defensive reliance on repression against the potential awareness of or expression of instinctual impulses and their derivatives. I suggest, however, that the same diagnostic indications may instead reflect a lifelong history of suppression (rather than repression) of intellectual skills and the adoption of a personality style that has been most linked to success in social situations. For certain women, it may indeed be anxiety-arousing to relinquish a flirtatious, childlike, sexualized style of interacting and assume instead a critical, independent, and intellectually "phallic" one. However, their anxiety may be related to a long socialization process regarding what is acceptable and desirable feminine behavior. When the diagnosis of hysteria reflects the effect of role pressures on women, the individuals so labeled will constitute a markedly heterogeneous group, for an exaggerated feminine style may exist with varying types and degrees of pathology. It is not surprising, then, that there are many clinical reports of women who initially "look hysterical" and later prove to be suffering from far more serious emotional disturbances (Easser and Lesser 1965, Zetzel 1968).

I also have some doubt regarding the widely held notion that women rely more heavily on the defensive use of repression than do men. Rather, an additional theory suggests that the socialization of women leads to a style of personality and cognition that in its observable outcome is not dissimilar to the effect of repression. A related point of considerable importance is that men who do in fact rely on a repressive style of defense will tend not to be diagnosed as hysterical, for our present stereotype of the hysterical character runs dramatically counter to the male socialization process and to acceptable masculine behavior. Of interest is Berger's (1971) statement that "the proclamation that hysteria can occur in males appears to be an attempt to appear objective. One gets the impression that a male hysteric is one who behaves 'like a woman' " (p. 279).

RECENT TRENDS IN DIAGNOSIS

Recent trends in diagnosis of the hysterical personality have gravely compounded the problems that are posed by the overlapping of the feminine character and the hysterical character. Certain diagnosticians are suggesting that we move away from psychodynamics and etiological speculations and confine ourselves to surface manifestations and observable behavior in diagnosing this particular character disorder (Chodoff and Lyons 1958, Lazare and Klerman 1968). This descriptive approach is epitomized by the work of Chodoff and Lyons (1958), who have consulted a representative group of publications and abstracted certain behavioral characteristics of hysterics that were agreed upon by most or all of the authors involved. They have suggested that six behavioral characteristics (e.g., vanity, sexual provocativeness, dependency) be generally agreed criteria for a diagnosis of hysterical personality and that underlying factors be ignored. Similarly, Lazare and Klerman (1968) state that hysteria can be defined and diagnosed only by searching the literature for clinical descriptions of these patients and abstracting out the common elements. These authors have defined hysteria by seven traits: egocentricity, exhibitionism, emotionalism, dependency, provocativeness, fear of sexuality, suggestibility.

If this descriptive approach is adopted, then we may do well to discard the diagnostic category of hysterical personality (with all its rich structural and dynamic implications) and simply speak of a feminine personality style that does not

purport to be more than a description of certain female characteristics in the eyes of male diagnosticians. It is puzzling to me
that Chodoff and Lyons, who champion this descriptive approach, have at the same time concluded their discussion of
the historical development of hysteria with the following comment:

> A situation analogous to the one described might be
> imagined if women psychiatrists spent some genera-
> tions coolly and rather inimically observing the less
> attractive foibles of males, and then put them together
> as the manifestations of a kind of personality charac-
> teristic of men! [1958, p. 734]

What is perhaps more puzzling is that psychiatry still remains
mystified over the sex difference in hysteria and has invoked
some rather esoteric theorizing in the service of partial explanation.

WHERE DO WE GO FROM HERE?

Berger (1971) has suggested that the hysterical personality
exists not in the patient, but rather in the observer. He states
that the best definition of hysteria is "behavior or symptoms
which arouse unconscious sexual feelings in the observer,"
(p. 283) and he argues that this clinical entity should be defined and understood in terms of its countertransference effect. While I do not support Berger's proposed conceptualization of hysteria, I do believe there is a danger that the
hysterical personality will be reduced to a description of a
particular type of feminine behavior that has a certain effect
on a male observer. To define hysteria in this manner, however,
seems like a singularly nihilistic approach that is hardly a step
forward from the descriptive method described earlier. Ideally,
we can adopt a more constructive approach and apply ourselves to untangling the confusions that presently exist between the hysterical character and the feminine character.
    Clearly this task is not a simple one, particularly in an

interview situation in which the diagnostician is male and the evaluation procedure is limited in time. For one must ask, Is the patient's dependent and childlike behavior the regressive defense against genital fears of the hysteric, or is it a learned aspect of feminine behavior? Is emotional lability a defensive operation reinforcing repression, or is it rather the patient's attempt to be a vivid and exciting companion? Are sexual provocativeness and flirtatiousness reflective of oedipal conflicts, or are they the behavior of a woman who feels she has little else to offer the male psychiatrist? These distinctions, which are not mutually exclusive, may be difficult ones to make in a brief diagnostic workup, and the stereotype of the hysterical female is so deeply ingrained that women are often carelessly and prematurely diagnosed.

In the midst of this conceptual muddle, it is easy to lose sight of the fact that a rather impressive body of clinical and theoretical literature has accumulated for this group of patients. Kernberg's (1967, 1970) summary of the hysterical personality, for example, is very much in keeping with the work of other psychoanalytic theorists who have noted that hysterical patients (as compared to those with lower-level character disorders) manifest better integration of ego and superego, a predominance of genital oedipal conflicts over oral and pregenital ones (although oral conflicts are often present), and a wider range of conflict-free ego functions and structures. Further, there is an absence of severe pathology of internalized object relations, and the hysterical individual is capable of fairly deep and stable relationships involving a variety of affective responses. Repression is the main defensive operation of the ego, and there is little instinctual infiltration into defensive character traits. We may note that none of the above diagnostic criteria are inherently feminine as opposed to masculine. The challenge for diagnosticians is to refine their ability to evaluate the above structural and genetic-dynamic considerations in a manner that will extricate them from the present confusion between hysteria and femininity. To do this we must put minimal diagnostic emphasis on the behavioral indices that overlap with traditional aspects of femininity, and we must also attempt to identify the observable effects of a repressive style of defense in men. In this regard, psychological testing can be an invaluable research and diagnostic tool, especially if clinical psychologists apply themselves to identifying formal test indications of hysteria that are independent of feminine and masculine role stereotypes.

In discussing the hysterical personality, I have not directed attention to the variety of clinical symptoms that have been associated with severe hysterical disorders, such as dissociative phenomena and disordered thinking. It seems evident that such symptomatology is not the result of cultural pressures, and in these cases the conceptual tangle posed by the overlapping of femininity and hysteria hardly seems relevant. In fact, such grave symptoms are by no means limited to female patients, and we at the Menninger Clinic have seen male patients in hysterical fits, complete with arching backs, Charcot-style. But the diagnosis of hysterical personality is very infrequently made on the basis of such symptomatology. Rather, it typically refers to the style of personality and cognitive organization described earlier, and it is here that the failure to account for social factors has led to a lack of conceptual clarity and diagnostic precision. It is hoped that clinicians will be encouraged to carefully reformulate the diagnostic criteria of the hysterical personality so that this entity does not in fact become what Chodoff and Lyons have labeled "a caricature of femininity."

AUTHOR'S NOTE

The term *histrionic personality disorder* (DSM-III) has now replaced *hysterical personality* (DSM-II). The same problems remain, however, and DSM-III notes that "in both sexes overt behavior is often a caricature of femininity." From my current perspective (1987), I would like to see this diagnostic category (by whatever name we call it) eliminated because it is inextricably interwoven with cultural pressures as well as unconscious biases and negative assumptions about women.

As I now see it, the tone of my own writing on this subject is problematic, reflecting my absorption of cultural norms that

devalue traditional feminine traits and behaviors and over-
value traditional masculine ones. We might just as well construct a "personality disorder" for those disturbed persons
who manifest a preference for ideas over people, work over love,
ambition over family responsibility, ideation over emotion, intellect over intuition, separateness over interdependency, distance over intimacy, competition over collaboration, and so
forth. Obviously, this disorder would occur predominantly in
men (see Kaplan 1983).

REFERENCES

Berger, D. M. (1971). Hysteria: in search of the animus.
Comprehensive Psychiatry 12:277.

Chesler, P. (1972). *Women and Madness.* New York: Doubleday.
Chodoff, P., and Lyons, H. (1958). Hysteria, the hysterical personality and hysterical conversion. *American Journal of
Psychiatry* 114:734.

Dahl, A. (1965). *Always Ask a Man.* Englewood Cliffs, N.J.:
Prentice-Hall.

Easser, B. R., and Lesser, S. R. (1965). Hysterical personality: A
reevaluation. *Psychoanalytic Quarterly* 34:390.

Firestone, S. (1970). Love. In *Notes From the Second Year:
Women's Liberation,* ed. S. Firestone. New York: Radical
Feminism.
Freud, S. (1931). Libidinal types. *Standard Edition* 21.

Kaplan, M. (1983). A woman's view of DSM-III. *American Psychologist* 38:756–792.
Kernberg, O. (1967). Borderline personality organization.
Journal of the American Psychoanalytic Association
15:641.
——— (1970). A psychoanalytic classification of character pa-

thology. *Journal of the American Psychoanalytic Association* 18:800.

Kreps, B. (1970). The new feminist analysis. In *Notes from the Second Year: Women's Liberation*, ed. S. Firestone. New York: Radical Feminism.

Lazare, A., and Klerman, G. L. (1968). Hysteria and depression: the frequency and significance of hysterical personality features in hospitalized depressed women. *American Journal of Psychiatry* 124:48.

Lerner, H. G. (1973). Women's liberation. *Menninger Perspective* 4:11–13, 20–21.

Lynn, D. B. (1972). Determinants of intellectual growth in women. *University of Chicago School Review* 80:161.

Marmor, J. (1953). Orality in the hysterical personality. *Journal of the American Psychoanalytic Association* 1:656.

Rappaport, D., Gill, M., and Schafer, R. (1968). *Diagnostic Psychological Testing*. New York: International Universities Press.

Robins, E., Purtell, J., Cohen, M., and Mandel, E. (1952). Hysteria in men. *New England Journal of Medicine* 246:677.

Schafer, R. (1948). *Clinical Application of Psychological Tests*. New York: International Universities Press.

—— (1954). *Psychoanalytic Interpretation in Rorschach Testing*. New York: Grune & Stratton.

Shapiro, D. (1965). *Neurotic Styles*. New York: Basic Books.

Zetzel, E. (1968). The so-called good hysteric. *International Journal of Psychoanalysis* 49:256.

Chapter 8

Special Issues for Women in Psychotherapy

In the late 1970s, the practice of psychotherapy came under heavy fire from feminist critics, who turned in large numbers to women's rap groups or feminist therapy as alternatives to more established modes of treatment (Chesler 1972).[1] Concern about widespread sexist practices in the treatment of women was also voiced by mental health professionals from traditional training programs and work settings (American Psychological Association 1975, 1978, Symonds 1978). This chapter explores the nature and legitimacy of such complaints and identifies issues of relevance to all women seeking psychotherapy.

Of the many criticisms leveled against traditional psychotherapies, a few may be summarized. First, traditional psychotherapy—and psychoanalysis in particular—tends to focus primarily, if not exclusively, on internal or intrapsychic conflicts rather than on the cultural context that has produced them. Such a therapeutic bias not only diverts energy from potential social and political change but may also foster in the woman a sense of uniqueness regarding her "pathology" rather than helping her to recognize that her symptoms, which may be ubiquitous among women, stem naturally from

---

[1]This chapter was first published in 1982 in *The Woman Patient: Medical and Psychological Interfaces*, vol. 3, ed. M. Notman and C. Nadelson, pp. 273–286. New York: Plenum.

patriarchal society's neglect and distortion of women's true intellectual, sexual, and social needs. Perhaps the most serious accusation against traditional psychotherapy is that, in subtle but powerful ways, it may lead women to conform to male-defined notions of femininity and may discourage rebellion from the "feminine role" by interpreting such rebellion as pathological.

For many therapists, however, such accusations do not ring true. As a staff psychologist in a traditional psychoanalytic institution, I can vouch for the good intentions of my colleagues. Well-trained psychoanalytic therapists do not strive to send their female patients back to the kitchen. Rather, the task of good psychotherapy, psychoanalytic or otherwise, is to provide women with the opportunity to overcome the barriers that interfere with the full utilization of their capacities. This, in theory, is to be done in an atmosphere of therapeutic neutrality in which a woman is free to find a comfortable and honest definition of her femininity, based neither on predominant stereotypes about women nor on rancor and rebellion against them.

With such purity of intention, most therapists do not view sexism in treatment as a serious problem. Feminist concerns may be written off as naive, outdated, or simply misguided. It is indeed difficult for therapists to examine openly and critically how their own unconscious biases and perceptions adversely affect and limit their treatment of female patients. Yet no longer can we close our eyes to the fact that every therapist has an implicit concept of normality for men and women that arises out of the cultural context in which she or he is embedded. As we will see in the following pages, a therapist's implicit (and often unconscious) absorption of cultural norms and values continuously affects the nature of the interventions that are made (or not made) in the course of the therapeutic process.

PSYCHOTHERAPY WITH WOMEN: DIFFERING IDEOLOGICAL PERSPECTIVES

Traditional therapists tend to view women's symptoms and dissatisfactions as an expression of individual psychopathology, to be analyzed and understood in light of the patient's unique individual history.[2] Even those therapists who are sympathetic toward feminist goals may not view cultural factors as the genuine or primary determinants that interfere with women's fulfillment. While cultural limitations on women may be superficially acknowledged, a patient's anger in response to these factors may be said to reflect an unhealthy sense of passive victimization that militates against constructive personal change. Thus a patient's sensitivity to the social and cultural roots of her difficulties may not be legitimized by the therapist as an important focus for treatment. Rather, feminist concerns may be interpreted as the patient's defensive attempt to avoid painful inner conflict by placing the blame for her unhappiness outside herself.

In contrast, those who identify themselves as feminist therapists view the social and cultural context of the patient's problems as a legitimate and important focus of treatment. Indeed, to deny or minimize these sources of conflict is seen "as inappropriate as attempts to treat black persons while denying that racism is an ugly reality that affects us all" (Bernardez-Bonesatti 1978a). The patient's capacity to identify and respond to ways in which women are depreciated, trivialized, scapegoated, or falsely defined in work and family is not viewed as peripheral to therapeutic work. Rather, the patient's expanded awareness of the false and constricting values, myths, and pressures that pervade the systems in which she operates is seen as crucial to the process of self-definition and growth. It is when a therapist fails to legitimize the patient's realistic anger and protest that the patient becomes further inhibited in her capacity for creative and free-ranging thought and action (Bernardez-Bonesatti 1978a).

Most sophisticated therapists, whether feminist or traditional, do not maintain a narrow, single-minded focus on

---

[2]By traditional therapists, I mean psychotherapists whose conceptualizations of their patients' difficulties and their own therapeutic goals or clinical techniques have not been significantly altered or influenced by the past two decades of feminism. My experience with traditional therapists is largely with colleagues whose individual or group work is psychoanalytically based.

either intrapsychic or sociocultural realities, which would, in either case, be akin to listening for the sound of one hand clapping. But therapists differ, if not in conscious beliefs, then in the nature of their interventions and their approach to women's struggles during this period of social change. There still exists much controversy about whether women who angrily protest societal definitions of femininity and the feminine role are themselves expressing neurotic conflicts, or whether, on the other hand, it is our very definitions of femininity and the feminine role that are the pathogenesis of female symptomatology. This is not simply a matter of theoretical interest, for a therapist's position regarding this controversy (whether conscious and explicit or unexamined and unconsciously held) determines the very course and process of treatment, despite that therapist's very best intentions to "help patients make their own choices" in an atmosphere that is "value-free" (Lerner 1978a). To illustrate this point, let us consider the following hypothetical case.

Clinical Example

Janet, a 34-year-old homemaker, has two healthy children and an ambitious, successful, and concerned husband. Janet tells herself that she "has everything," yet she seeks psychotherapy because of feelings of depression and malaise as well as a growing anger and resentment toward her children and husband. From her own perspective, her dissatisfaction is entirely irrational, and she begins her first therapy hour by telling her therapist, "I have nothing to be angry and depressed about." Her goal for treatment, as she initially states it, is to be a better and more satisfied wife and mother. Let us examine how two different therapists, Therapist A (traditional) and Therapist B (feminist), might conceptualize and work with Janet's problems.

Therapist A

Therapist A views Janet's anger and depression as a symptom reflecting unconscious conflicts that interfere with her capacity to nurture and care for others. Therapist A might explore with Janet deep-rooted feelings of neglect and deprivation from her own childhood, which now make it difficult for her to provide for her children without resentment and hostility. If Janet's anger at her husband is associated with the envious wish that she, too, would like to achieve and compete in the world outside the home, these "masculine strivings" might be interpreted in light of Janet's neurotic discomfort with her own feminine role.

Therapist A might also reassure Janet that a mother's job is a difficult one, particularly in her children's early years, and that her anger and ambivalence are to some degree a natural part of the difficult and challenging career of motherhood. In addition, Janet might be encouraged to find some time away from the children that is hers alone, or perhaps to take up some independent hobby or activity. In a supportive and nonjudgmental context, therapist and patient may together explore a range of early conflicts and relationship paradigms with the goal (as Janet herself has stated it) of helping the patient to become a better and more satisfied wife and mother.

Therapist B

Therapist B might agree that Janet (like every human being) has neurotic conflicts that prevent her from parenting her children more competently and comfortably. However, these conflicts might not be viewed as a primary, or even an important, focus of treatment. Indeed, Therapist B may consider Janet's anger and depression healthy, legitimate, and realistic, despite Janet's own protests that it is irrational. This therapist might first choose to explore with Janet the internal pressures and the external realities that caused her to lose sight of her own hopes, aspirations, and dreams for herself, and to choose instead to live vicariously through her husband and her children. Expressions of anger, competitiveness, or envy in regard to her husband, or men in general, might be interpreted as healthy strivings for mastery, success, and self-sufficiency, which are frightening for Janet to acknowledge. Historical and intrapsychic determinants may be explored at length—not, however, with the goal of making Janet a better wife and mother in the conventional sense. Rather, this therapist might use her or his skills to analyze the unconscious anxiety and guilt that prevent Janet from acknowledging and expressing more autonomous, self-seeking strivings for mastery and success.

In addition, Therapist B will help Janet to identify the familial and institutional realities that interfere with her potential fulfillment in both parenting and work pursuits. Therapist B may question Janet's assumption that the "good mother" (in singular contrast to the "good father") always puts the needs of her young children before her own growth and creative development. Although Therapist B will recognize that Janet has her own private neurosis, it is not this neurosis that the therapist believes to be at the core of the problem. Rather, Janet's difficulties are seen as a symptom of the institution of motherhood and family (as it has been defined by male "experts"), which has excused the male sex from the day-to-day task of child rearing, while demanding that a mother's growth and development be exchanged for the growth and development of the child she has borne.

The striking difference in focus between these two therapists illustrates the fact that we are living in a time of considerable controversy regarding our basic understanding of women's pleasures and problems. The following pages will continue to demonstrate how psychotherapy invariably reflects the cultural context in which it is embedded. Every therapist, whether feminist or "Freudian," will express, in the course of treatment, her or his own values and visions for women. There is no "value-free" psychotherapy.

THE MASCULINE–FEMININE DICHOTOMY:
IMPLICATIONS FOR THERAPEUTIC PRACTICE

Many therapists have absorbed culturally defined notions of masculinity and femininity and consciously or unconsciously view these concepts as reflecting what is healthy or "natural" for men and women. Therapists who explicitly label, or even privately conceptualize, certain of women's wishes, strivings, and behaviors as being unfeminine may unwittingly exacerbate their patients' inhibitions rather than increasing their options (Kronsky 1971). In certain cases, women may become further constricted in treatment as their aggressive strivings for dominance and power (which may indeed have certain pathological aspects) are labeled as masculine or phallic by the therapist, often without acknowledgment of the healthy and adaptive components of such behaviors. While purportedly providing insight, therapeutic interpretation may subtly be aimed at encouraging the patient to stop her aggressive, controlling, or competitive behaviors (Bernardez-Bonesatti 1976). With men, however, the therapeutic goal would more typically be to help the patient achieve a healthier and more comfortable, conflict-free integration and expression of these same qualities or behaviors.

Failure to Analyze Conformity
to Traditional Feminine Scripts

It is important to recognize that most good therapists do not consciously hold to narrow, stereotypical ideas about women; rather, they respect the patient's right to pursue treatment goals that may be out of keeping with the traditional feminine role. However, a subtle, serious, and more pervasive problem arises for the patient who does indeed fit the cultural stereotype, but for the wrong reasons (e.g., the traditionally feminine woman who opts for full-time motherhood out of neurotic anxieties about competition, success, and intellectual achievement). In these cases, many therapists fail to analyze the conflicts and anxieties that keep the woman in her role and restrict her choices (GAP 1975, Lerner 1978a). I have noted that unhealthy degrees of self-sacrifice, dependency, and under-achievement in women (except in their extreme and most con-spicuous "masochistic" forms) are often not recognized or questioned by the therapist since these may strike one as quite natural characteristics of the female sex. The failure of psycho-dynamic therapists to analyze sufficiently the defensive and maladaptive determinants underlying a patient's choice to con-form to culturally prescribed notions of femininity is a common phenomenon in psychotherapy. This problem occurs with ther-apists operating from a family systems perspective as well.

Clinical Example

Dr. B. worked with Mr. and Mrs. Porter for seven months before requesting consultation on this case.[3] Mr. Porter was a middle management executive, and Mrs. Porter was a homemaker with a college degree. Both were in their early forties and had three daugh-ters, aged 6, 12, and 14. Dr. B. described a marital situation seen commonly in clinical work: The wife angrily blamed her husband for her unhappiness, yet she implicitly complied with his demands and did not make moves to effectively challenge the status quo. In addition, she was excessively reactive to her husband's work problems, and according to Dr. B., she placed her husband in a "double bind." If Mr. Porter did not pro-vide his wife with a full report on what was happening at work, she felt angry and rejected. When he did fill her in she would either move in quickly to advise or fix things, or she would criticize his management of, or reactions to, a particular situation. When stress was high, Mr. Porter occasionally threatened divorce.

Dr. B., who was learning to work from a Bowen Family Systems framework, sought my help because

---

[3]This chapter was first published in 1987 as "Is Family Systems Theory Really Systemic? A Feminist Communication" in *Journal of Psychotherapy and the Family* 3(4):41–56.

he felt unsuccessful in helping the wife assume a calmer, more objective, and less blaming perspective in the marriage. In addition, he found himself blaming the blamer, (i.e., Mrs. Porter) despite his own attempts to remain neutral. While Dr. B. was aware that Mrs. Porter overfunctioned enormously on the domestic scene at her own expense, he nonetheless felt put off by what he labeled as manipulative and passive-aggressive behavior. For example, Mrs. Porter reported feeling resentful about her husband's practice of giving her an "allowance" and asking her to account for her personal expenses; but rather than taking a firm and non-negotiable stand that this was not acceptable to her, Mrs. Porter "manipulated" her husband into giving her extra money which she then spent irresponsibly and impulsively.

Using the genograms that he had constructed during initial meetings, Dr. B. had questioned Mr. and Mrs. Porter about the history of marriages in the previous generations, including questions about how marital partners got along, how money was managed, how differences were navigated, and so forth. Dr. B's stated goal was to help Mrs. Porter separate or differentiate from her "masochistic" mother, which he hoped, in turn, would allow her to move out of her angry, dependent position in the marriage.

Dr. B. had ignored entirely, however, the impact of the wife's economic dependency on this marriage, and he failed to attend to the fact that she had no life plan or personal goals for herself. This "traditional" family structure was simply the norm for Dr. B. and did not, in itself, suggest any particular arena for questioning.

During our consultation, Dr. B. requested that we focus on Mrs. Porter, who was the source of his distress. To this end, I asked him to think about a number of questions:

• Was there a connection between Mrs. Porter's over-involvement with her husband's work problems and

her own lack of participation in the work world outside the home?
- Did she believe her husband's work was more valuable than her own?
- If so, was this a factor in her "wishy-washy" approach to asking him to take on more housework
and child-care tasks?
- What was the connection, if any, between
Mrs. Porter's irresponsible and manipulative behavior concerning her "allowance" and her actual financial dependence?
- Which women in Mrs. Porter's nuclear and extended
family had clarified personal and work goals for
themselves and which women had not?
- For those women in previous generations who had
put their energy into their own life goals, what impact did this have on their marriages?
- How did Mrs. Porter's sister, mother, and grandmother balance responsibility for family with responsibility for self?
- Had Mrs. Porter ever talked with these women about
their personal goals and aspirations or the lack of
them?
- Did Mrs. Porter think about long-term goals for self?
- How could we understand the fact that Mrs. Porter
whined and complained about her circumstances,
but did not effectively clarify a bottom-line position
with her husband on any major emotional issue?
(For example, "This allowance business is not acceptable to me. I also work, albeit in the home, and I
want the same access to our finances that you
have.")
- What specifically did she think would happen in this
marriage if she began to operate from a position of
greater strength and assertiveness?
- Did Mrs. Porter believe she had to choose between
having a marriage and having a self?
- If her marriage ended in divorce (as do almost 50 percent of marriages), what was Mrs. Porter's life plan?

- Was she familiar with the statistics regarding the economic status of women with dependent children following divorce?
- Did Mrs. Porter equate divorce not only with the loss of her primary relationship, but also with the loss of status, identity, esteem, and financial support?
- If Mrs. B believed that she could not survive economically without her marriage, how did this effect her ability to navigate clearly and assertively within it?
- Is it possible to assume a truly differentiated position in a marital or work system if one is convinced that one cannot live without it?
- Did Mrs. Porter view her gender as having some relevance to her current problems and unhappiness?
- Did she see other women (both on her genogram and outside the family) struggling with issues similar to her own?
- Had she connected with any of these persons to share perspectives on common problems and to learn how other women had attempted to solve similar dilemmas?
- In what way had the feminist movement influenced, or not influenced, her thinking about herself and her family?

Dr. B. had not considered most of those questions, and he pondered them with interest. Yet, he reacted negatively to the idea that we might think together about opening up related lines of questioning within the marital sessions, while staying relevant to the couples presenting problems. Dr. B. had chosen to consult with me, in part, because of my knowledge of women's issues; yet he now feared his therapeutic neutrality was at stake. He said to me, "I think any questions along these lines would convey that Mrs. Porter should get a job or become more liberated. I'm just not comfortable imposing values on clients." Dr. B. told me

that the consultation had nonetheless been very helpful to him because his angry reactions toward
Mrs. Porter were replaced by more empathic ones, as
my questions led him to consider the context of her life
more thoughtfully. Yet, he could not see his way clear
to translate what he had gained from this consultation
into his practice.

Like Dr. B., I do not view it as a therapist's job to
encourage a client to seek employment, embrace feminism, or the like. Questioning within a Bowen framework is used to lower intensity, to broaden a client's
perspective and sense of connectedness to her own
family and cultural context, to encourage thinking and
the gathering of facts, and to help her view as many
options as possible with the greatest degree of clarity
and objectivity. Surely women have enough "experts"
telling them what to do. What was interesting about
Dr. B.'s position, however, was his assumption that
not opening up certain areas for questioning and
failing to focus on certain aspects of context represented a neutral or objective stance. From my perspective, Dr. B.'s absorption of patriarchal values regarding
"traditional" family structure stood in the way of his
becoming a more skilled questioner and ultimately a
more helpful therapist to this couple.

These errors of omission affect great numbers of female
patients, for most women entering treatment are themselves
unable to consciously acknowledge wishes or longings that are
out of keeping with traditional feminine scripts. Indeed, many
women who seemingly choose to relinquish self-seeking professional or autonomous strivings do so because they cannot
freely, and without guilt and anxiety, fulfill themselves through
personal achievement (Chasseguet-Smirgel 1970). In my experience, it is not uncommon for a bored, exhausted, intellectually impoverished, and isolated mother of small children to
begin treatment with the following goal: Make me a better wife
and mother to my husband and children. She may, quite literally, have no other vision for herself that feels acceptable, and

the only form of protest she can voice is her symptoms, which frequently take the form of an unconscious wildcat strike against her "sacred calling" (Rich 1976); she may complain, "I am too depressed/fatigued/confused to run the household and care for my children."

Traditional therapists, especially those who believe that small children need their mothers continually at home, often fail to skillfully explore with the patient other alternatives and options (GAP 1975). Further, they may not help her to clarify the nature of her legitimate anger and complaints against her prescribed role, which the patient dare not herself express, except through her symptoms.

THE FEMALE PATIENT–MALE THERAPIST DYAD: REPLICATING PATRIARCHAL ARRANGEMENTS

Some feminist critics have warned that psychotherapy for women may entail a potential reenactment of male–female relationship paradigms as they exist in the culture at large (Chesler 1972). It is indeed true that many women in psychotherapy become intensely dependent on an idealized male therapist, who may become the center of their fantasy life. If the relationship is eroticized, it may, much like an affair, dilute and eclipse other important relationships and pursuits in the patient's life and serve as a resistance to change. It may be so gratifying for a woman to receive support and empathic understanding from a warm, nurturant male authority (and so gratifying for a male therapist to be able to comfortably express and be appreciated for these "maternal" qualities) that the therapeutic relationship itself may foster dependency without facilitating autonomous solutions.

Women have a long history of experiencing unegalitarian relationships with males as natural, and of compliantly following leaders and "experts." Cultural pressures on women to "please men" are so profound that the woman's desire to be attractive and admired by her therapist may override a more honest process of self-definition and self-determination. Women's attempts to fit themselves to definitions of femininity that

are implicitly communicated by their therapists are often unconscious and subtle and may thus go unrecognized by both
therapist and patient. I have spoken to a number of women
who have participated in both individual treatment and feminist consciousness-raising groups, and who have stated in
retrospect that the latter allowed them a greater opportunity to
explore personal issues with real honesty and depth. Some of
these women saw the limitations of their psychotherapy as
stemming from their own deep-seated and often unconscious
need to please the male therapist and to remain unthreaten-
ing. Others reported that their dependent, nonthreatening
behaviors were induced, or at least unconsciously rewarded,
by the therapist himself. Experienced supervisors do indeed
report that male therapists may covertly and unwittingly encourage compliant behaviors and discourage a challenging,
independent stance in female patients (Bernardez-Bonesatti
1976).

Although female therapists are hardly immune from
adopting such attitudes, it is my observation that the problem
occurs most intensely and with least conscious recognition in
the male therapist–female patient dyad. Of significance is the
fact that the feminine socialization process teaches females to
protect the male ego at all costs by inhibiting any traits, qualities, and behaviors that may be threatening to men. Cultural
pressures to play dumb, let the man win, or pretend he's boss
are all crude, if not comic, expressions of a more subtle but
powerful cultural injunction that states that in intimate male–
female dyads, the man should be (or at least should feel like)
the more capable, successful, and dominant partner. For the
many couples who deviate from this arrangement, psychiatry
has designed such terms as role reversal, role confusion, or
matriarchal family, all of which are mildly pejorative terms
suggesting that things are not in their natural place. Indeed,
women who dare to compete openly with men on issues of
competence and power may be labeled castrating or unfeminine and have their very attractiveness and love of humankind
brought into question. As many authors have noted (Lerner
1974, 1977, Dinnerstein 1976, Bernardez-Bonesatti 1978a),
this patriarchal arrangement reflects, in part, men's persistent

irrational anxieties about the dreadful effects of female aggression and dominance, as well as women's related irrational fears of their own destructive, castrating potential. These shared fears of female destructiveness date back to our long years of helpless dependency on women (our mothers and other female caretakers) and are rarely consciously recognized by either sex. Rather, these anxieties are contained and held in check by social arrangements that allow men to maintain power and control over women, who are discouraged from expressing aggression and dominance except in indirect, covert, or manipulative ways.

Given such intrapsychic and cultural pressures, it is hardly surprising that male therapists, in particular, may encourage a patient to be self-assertive and autonomous in her family and work life but may subtly encourage her to have a "nice relationship" (i.e., to follow his advice and to accept and value his interpretations) within the therapeutic hour. The paradox of therapeutic interpretations that are purportedly in the service of fostering the patient's independence, while subtly patronizing her or undermining her autonomy within the therapeutic relationship, may go unnoticed by both therapist and supervisor ("No matter how much I interpret or try to push her, she still won't be assertive with her husband!"). Further, the woman's healthy expressions of anger, criticalness, or competitiveness directed toward the therapist may be felt by him as an unhealthy display of aggression or an attempt to control. If the woman is, in fact, hostile and controlling, he may accurately interpret the pathogenic components of such behavior, but without recognizing the positive and adaptive aspects of what the patient is attempting to communicate or accomplish. Bernardez-Bonesatti (1976) has commented on the especially strong feelings of revulsion and disapproval that male therapists may feel when confronted with openly hostile and domineering behavior in their women patients. Because women themselves have enormous unconscious fears regarding their own destructiveness and the related fragility of the male ego, both patient and therapist may fail to recognize the subtle ways in which the woman is being "a good patient" at the expense of her own autonomy and growth.

Bernardez-Bonesatti (1976) has noted that women therapists may also be prone to excessive disapproval of their female patient's anger or competitiveness, especially if the target of the patient's hostility is a male. Not only is a protectiveness for males aroused, but the female therapist who unconsciously fears that her own unrestrained anger may be hurtful to men is threatened by her identification with a female patient whom she perceives as destructive or castrating. I have also been impressed by the need of female therapists to avoid identifying with women who are angry at men, even if they perceive them as having a legitimate cause.

SEX OF THERAPIST

Advantages of Female Therapist

A significant number of factors go into the making of a good psychotherapist that far outweigh the matter of one's sex. It is my opinion, however, that other things being equal (level of skill, experience, quality of training, etc.), female patients may have much to gain in working with a woman therapist. At the risk of offering somewhat oversimplified generalizations, I would briefly outline some of the advantages as follows:

1. Many women find it difficult to be open with a male therapist. For example, their frankness and specificity regarding sexual experiences may be limited. In general, a more honest exploration of self may be facilitated by work with a same-sex therapist. With a female therapist, the patient is less pulled to unconsciously fulfill stereotypical feminine behavior (e.g., "protectiveness" of the male therapist's ego and sense of importance, avoidance of direct confrontation and competition) that will block more creative, free-ranging work.

   In intimate dyadic relationships, men have very little experience relating to women in a truly egalitarian manner, although many men may consider themselves exceptions to this rule. As noted earlier, men are more likely than women to overlook subtle aspects of female compliance, dependency, deskilling, and so on, since these are the expectable and familiar ways that women relate to men in close dyadic relationships.

2. With a female therapist, sexualization of the relationship, which may serve as a major resistance against learning, is characteristically avoided. While homosexual feelings and fantasies may emerge with a same-sex therapist, these are usually not used defensively and seductively in the service of warding off anxiety and the threat of confrontation.

3. The opportunity to identify with a female therapist's professional skills and competence is extremely helpful for many women, particularly in instances in which there is deep guilt and anxiety over issues of achievement and autonomous functioning. Some patients are better able to consciously acknowledge and express jealous and competitive feelings toward a therapist of their own sex, without having to feel castrating or unfeminine.

4. The firsthand experience of women therapists with specifically female emotional, physical, sexual, and spiritual experiences may facilitate a greater depth and intensity of clinical work. Women have incorporated a great number of male-defined myths regarding the "feminine experience," which can best be explored with a female therapist who has herself taken seriously the task of her own consciousness-raising.

5. Women's conflicts and inhibitions often have their roots in unresolved issues of autonomy and separation from the mother, although these conflicts may be masked by the girl/woman's transfer of dependency onto male authority figures and a premature flight into heterosexual relationships (Bernardez-Bonesatti 1978b, Lerner 1978b). A female therapist may allow for a richer and deeper exploration of the mother–daughter relationship and may facilitate an affective reexperiencing of the profoundly complex and ambivalent nature of this bond.

6. Affirmation by a same-sex therapist has especially significant meanings for certain women. To be accepted by
another woman in the context of a close relationship characterized by trust and mutual respect may be more "validating" of one's worth and self-esteem than working with a
cross-sex therapist. This is especially the case for narcissistic women with poor self-esteem who unconsciously experience male therapists (or men in general) as relatively more
seducible, easily flattered, or fooled by appearances than are
women.

7. A same-sex therapist offers greater opportunities for identification. While this is an advantage for all patients, it may be
especially critical for more disturbed individuals, who have
not consolidated a stable and coherent sense of gender
identity.

Paradoxically, the potential advantages of same-sex therapy
are also associated with unconscious threats that may lead
certain women to seek out male therapists. For example, a
woman who is involved in an intense, unresolved struggle to
separate from her own mother may experience considerable
anxiety in anticipating dependency on the female therapist.
Women who lack a stable and coherent sense of identity and
fear themselves to be without substance and depth usually
have consolidated a repertoire of cross-sex behaviors that make
it easier to begin treatment with a male therapist, with whom
these behaviors may help to control the anxieties inherent in
beginning a therapy relationship. Women with unconscious
conflicted wishes to achieve and succeed in the world outside
the home may wish to avoid a relationship with a professional
woman in which these conflicts will inevitably be stirred. In
sum, many women consider a male therapist "safer" than a
female therapist, although this feeling may not be their conscious experience. Rather, unconscious fears of women may be
defensively masked by an experience of female professionals as
less capable or authoritative than their male counterparts.

Prospective psychotherapy patients who voice a strong
preference for male therapists may do so for adaptive, con-

structive reasons; for example, a woman whose family life has included a psychologically or physically absent father may need to experience male nurturance. It is my opinion that when a woman feels strongly that she wishes to see a therapist of a particular sex, her choice should be respected. Although such preferences invariably include both adaptive and defensive components, the patient's anxieties should not be overriden or prematurely interpreted, and the wisdom of the patient's unconscious should not be ignored.

As is true of all generalizations, those stated here tell us nothing about the advantages or disadvantages of a particular therapist or the unique needs of an individual patient. Surely being male does not condemn one to tunnel vision or to a rigid and unexamined adherence to patriarchal attitudes. Nor does being female guarantee one's freedom from unconscious biases and prejudices against women. As Alonso and Rutan (1978) pointed out, there are female therapists who are male-identified, who look on their female patients with some measure of scorn, or who may lack empathy for women who have struggled less successfully than they have. Certainly not all women therapists, by virtue of their femaleness, have enhanced empathic understanding of women. Some, for example, may be vulnerable to greater distortion through overidentification and a reliance on projection, which may lead to a false assumption of sameness or understanding where it does not exist.

Similarly, a therapist's being a feminist tells us little about her professional expertise. While some feminist therapists have had excellent training, others have not, perhaps because they have avoided traditional, male-dominated institutions at a time when there are few alternative programs available that offer the opportunity for intensive, high-level clinical training. Certain feminist therapists, following an egalitarian treatment model that stresses demystification of the therapist's expertise, may engage in nontherapeutic openness and self-disclosure that blur the appropriate boundaries and fail to provide for the patient the optimal conditions for free-ranging fantasy and exploration. Feminist therapists, like traditional therapists, may be competent or not.

In light of the individual differences between psychotherapists and the many important factors that go into the making
of a skilled professional other than his or her sex, it may be
tempting to deny real differences between female and male
therapists in the treatment of women. As Alonso and Rutan
(1978) noted, it is difficult for all of us to come to terms with
the limitations of our own capacity to empathize and identify
with patients whose experience we cannot enter. In discussing
such limitations of empathy, these authors have reminded us
of the painful experience that white liberals had during the
racial tensions of the 1960s, and I recall vividly my own defensive reaction to being informed that blacks could not deal
effectively with issues of power and self-definition in groups
that included white members, and especially white "experts."
Women, like blacks, have learned in the past decades of feminism that there is a certain development of consciousness and
self-definition that can be achieved only in all-female groups.
Along these lines, Bernardez-Bonesatti (1978b) has described
the special advantages and benefits that an all-women's therapy group can provide for its members. Yet, perhaps because of
unconscious fears about hurting or excluding men and incurring their anger and disapproval, even female mental health
professionals may deny or minimize the potentially powerful
therapeutic benefits of same-sex therapy.

In sum, psychotherapy can be a creative, expanding process of
unfolding from the center, or it may reinforce conformity to
constricted and externally defined notions of femininity. Similarly, the therapeutic process may free a woman to identify
more clearly the sociocultural context of her difficulties, or it
may "cool the mark" by encouraging her to cultivate her personal neurosis like a flower garden, while minimizing the
pathogenic effects of the system in which she is operating. To
write off the more unhappy of these outcomes as isolated
instances of "bad therapy" is tempting, for it allows therapists
to avoid taking seriously the difficult task of critically evaluating their work with female patients. As I have tried to show
here, good intentions and dedication to helping women become all they can be hardly ensure nonsexist work. It is only

through a deeply felt commitment to one's own consciousness-raising that therapists can even begin to gain freedom from the unconscious biases and assumptions that adversely affect the treatment of women.

REFERENCES

Alonso, A., and Rutan, J. S. (1978). Cross-sex supervision for cross-sex therapy. *American Journal of Psychiatry* 135(8):929–931.

American Psychological Association (1975). Report of the task force on sex bias and sex-role stereotyping in psychotherapeutic practice. *American Psychologist* 30:1169–1175.

—— (1978). Report of the task force on sex bias and sex-role stereotyping in psychotherapeutic practice, guidelines for therapy with women. 33:1122–1123.

Bernardez-Bonesatti, T. (1976). Unconscious beliefs about women affecting psychotherapy. *North Carolina Journal of Mental Health* 7(5):63–66.

—— (1978a). Women and anger: conflicts with aggression in contemporary women. *Journal of the American Medical Women's Association* 33(5):215–219.

—— (1978b). Women's groups: a feminist perspective on the treatment of women. In *Changing Approaches to the Psychotherapies*, ed. H. Grayson and C. Loew, pp. 55–68, New York: Spectrum.

Chasseguet-Smirgel, J. (1970). Feminine guilt and the Oedipus complex. In *Female Sexuality: New Psychoanalytic Views.* ed. J. Chasseguet-Smirgel et al. Ann Arbor: University of Michigan Press.

Chesler, P. (1972). *Women and Madness.* Garden City, N.Y.: Doubleday.

Dinnerstein, D. (1976). *The Mermaid and the Minotaur: Sexual Arrangements and Human Malaise.* New York: Harper & Row.

Group for the Advancement of Psychiatry, Committee on the College Student (1975). *The Educated Woman: Prospects and Problems*, GAP Report 92. New York: GAP.

Kronsky, B. (1971). Feminism and psychotherapy. *Journal of Contemporary Psychotherapy* 3(2):89–98.

Lerner, H. G. (1974). Early origins of envy and devaluation of women: implications for sex-role stereotypes. *Bulletin of the Menninger Clinic* 38:538–553.

—— (1977). Taboos against female anger. *Menninger Perspective* 8(4):4–11.

—— (1978a). Adaptive and pathogenic aspects of sex-role stereotypes: implications for parenting and psychotherapy. *American Journal of Psychiatry* 135(1):48–52.

—— (1978b). On the comfort of patriarchal solutions: some reflections on Brown's paper. *Journal of Personality and Social Systems* 1(3):47–50.

—— (1987). Is family systems theory really systemic?: a feminist communication. *Journal of Psychotherapy and the Family* 3(4):41–56.

Rich, A. (1976). *Of Woman Born.* New York: W. W. Norton.

Symonds, A. (1978). Psychoanalysis and women's liberation. *Journal of the American Academy of Psychoanalysis* 6(4):429–431.

Chapter 9

The "Giving" Therapist and the Female Patient

It is a truism in family process that "the solution becomes the problem," and so it is in psychotherapy as well.[1] In an attempt to be helpful to female patients, therapists may unwittingly apply solutions that block growth, or they may participate in patterns that maintain the very symptomatology and dysfunction for which the patient seeks help. This chapter will describe, through use of clinical example, a problematic countertransference paradigm that commonly occurs with female patients. The topic that will be discussed here is only a piece of a much larger picture in which our current gender arrangements, which are inextricably interwoven with the therapist's own unresolved family-of-origin issues, serve to negatively affect the treatment of women.

COUNTERTHERAPEUTIC EFFECTS OF THE "GIVING" THERAPIST

Over the course of intensive psychotherapy, patients will invariably test a therapist's capacity to set limits and to define a clear position regarding such key boundary issues as the

---

[1]This chapter is adopted from a paper co-authored with Sally Davis entitled "Negotiating Requests to Alter Treatment Parameters: An Opportunity for Professional Growth." It was first published in 1987 in *The Clinical Supervisor* 5(1): 73–87.

management of fees and the scheduling of appointments. Patients will similarly test the degree to which their therapists will assume an overresponsible, rescuing, or "fix-it" position in response to the patients' expressions of anxiety or underfunctioning. While this can occur with any patient, irrespective of gender, (Lerner and Davis 1987) special countertransference issues may arise in work with female patients.

Clinical Example

Dr. B., a third-year resident in psychiatry, was seeing Ms. J., a depressed homemaker, for an initial interview. Mid-session, as she was describing the dire straits of her life, she suddenly burst into tears and asked Dr. B. if he would continue to see her if she became unable to pay for her sessions. Dr. B., feeling anxious and flustered, proceeded to explore the reason for the question. The attempt at exploration led nowhere, and when at the end of the hour Ms. J. again pressed him for a reply, he said, "Well, we need to look further into the underlying meanings of your request, but it could be arranged." Ms. J. did not return for her next scheduled appointment or thereafter.

During a later supervisory exploration of Dr. B.'s countertransference feelings, he related that it felt uncaring, if not hurtful, to clarify that psychotherapy is a professional service for which he expected payment. He also anticipated that the initial therapeutic alliance would be strengthened by his "giving" stance and threatened by the rejection that might be implied by a firm clarification of his expectation of payment. In fact, such a clarification might well have been affirming and reassuring to Ms. J., whose central problem, as she described it in the preadmission material, was her own inability to set limits with family members and friends. In a self-administered test packet that the patient filled out prior to her first appointment, she referred to herself as a "one-person American Red Cross" who feared "hurting" others by failing to honor their requests and demands. Put somewhat differently, the presenting problem that brought Ms. J. into therapy might be stated as follows: How can I proceed to do what I need to do for myself when important others, in response, act hurt or disapproving? Perhaps, in attempting to obtain help with her dilemma, she was unconsciously testing how her new therapist would himself handle a parallel situation, as part of an unconscious attempt to assess whether this therapeutic relationship would be a place in which she could constructively struggle with her own problem.[2] In this instance, Dr. B. did not model the more autonomous stance that Ms. J. felt forbidden to assume in her own life, nor did he provide the conditions for the growth-enhancing relationship that she unconsciously sought.

In Dr. B.'s clinical work, he tended to assume the role of "rescuer" to depressed female patients, whom he experienced as helpless damsels in distress. He failed to appreciate the potential of these women to solve their own problems and manage their own pain, and he moved in quickly and intensely when his female patients presented a picture of vulnerability, offering the "special" help (additional sessions, telephone access during his vacations, etc.) he deemed necessary. When the absence of clear limits and boundaries led to an escalation of his patient's demands, he blamed these women (implicitly, via interpretation) for being excessively needy, manipulative, or infantile. In his own family of origin, Dr. B., a first-born son, was in an overfunctioning or rescuing position in

---

[2]The concept of "unconscious test" was first introduced by Weiss (1971) and later elaborated by Weiss and Sampson (1986), who suggest that patients entering treatment are primarily motivated to solve (rather than simply reenact) their conflicts. Their unconscious plans to solve their problems involve repeated tests designed to assess the conditions of safety in the treatment relationship. From this perspective, a patient who invites the therapist to reenact an early dysfunctional relationship paradigm is unconsciously wishing that the therapist will pass the test by *not* behaving as the parent did, thus providing the new conditions that will allow the patient to master old conflicts and move ahead.

a key family triangle in which his father would call him about his mother's drinking and Dr. B. would spend long hours on the telephone diagnosing his mother's behavior and engaging in repetitive unsuccessful efforts to persuade his mother to enter psychotherapy.

The following case illustrates the problem of the giving therapist in detail, this time with a female therapist.

Clinical Example

Dr. T. was home on the last lap of a three-month maternity leave when she received a telephone call from Ms. S., a 25-year-old woman in long-term, psychoanalytically oriented therapy. Ms. S., who had been hospitalized the year before for an immobilizing depression, began the call by recognizing that Dr. T. was not due back for another week; nevertheless, she (Ms. S.) was "cracking up" and in need of an emergency appointment. The crisis, as she described it, involved her father, who was visiting for three weeks and purportedly driving her crazy by criticizing her homemaking and offering endless unsolicited advice about parenting. Ms. S. appeared to be upset, but functioning well.

Dr. T., who was nursing her baby at the time of the call and was struggling with loyalty conflicts of her own regarding work and family, wanted to say, "I appreciate that you're having a hard time, but we'll talk about it next week at our scheduled appointment." Instead, she agreed to meet with Ms. S. the following day. During the session, Ms. S. complained about her situation but showed no genuine motivation to change or challenge the status quo with her father. Dr. T. noted this and explored the patient's reactions in response to both requesting and receiving the additional hour. Ms. S. discussed her feelings of discomfort as well as her "gratitude" for the additional time, and dutifully explored the many meanings that the additional session had for her. At the same time, she remained stuck and resistant to making use of Dr. T.'s help.

A central theme in Ms. S.'s treatment concerned her reluctance to set limits with her father to protect her relationship with her husband and daughter from what she viewed as her father's intrusive, patronizing attitudes and behaviors. Earlier psychodynamic exploration had revealed that Ms. S. feared that her firmness and clarity on such issues would devastate her father and result in his feeling intolerably excluded by the patient and her new family. This fear, at first unconscious, resulted in part from a projection of her accumulated rage stemming from her long-standing pattern of silent submission to her father's perceived needs. It was also an externalization of her own separation anxiety, which was evoked by maintaining a clear "I" position with her father and experiencing herself as separate and alone in this relationship. Her fear of "hurting" her father and her resistance to change were also rooted in the realities of the family system; there was evidence that any move on Ms. S.'s part to assume a more differentiated stance or to clarify her primary commitment to her new family was followed by her father's depression and withdrawal, and the subsequent reinstatement of the old pattern by Ms. S.

In helping Ms. S. to struggle with her dilemma, Dr. T. had made any number of accurate and well-timed interpretations. The implicit message from Dr. T. to the patient might be summarized as follows: It is all right for you to clarify your priorities, your preferences, and your primary commitment to your new family, even if your father, in response, becomes depressed or angry. Your relationship with your father is very important, but it is not your job to protect him from depression by sacrificing your own development. And yet, a nontherapeutic double bind was invoked by Dr. T.'s own guilt and anxiety about clarifying treatment boundaries that "excluded" the patient. In the example just discussed and in many others, Dr. T. was reluctant to refuse the patient's requests for extra sessions or evening phone calls, although she would attempt to explore the meaning of such requests. When Ms. S. tested her further by failing to comply with an agreed-upon plan for paying off her large outstanding balance, Dr. T. made this a continuing topic of therapeutic exploration but did not take a clear position regarding her continuing the work in the face of Ms. S.'s failure to make her agreed-upon payments.

Viewed from one perspective, Dr. T. was failing Ms. S.'s unconscious tests regarding the degree of separateness, self-assertion, and limit-setting that was permissible in the patient's life. In addition, granting Ms. S.'s requests for a "special" hour or phone call implicitly communicated that Dr. T. neither expected nor encouraged Ms. S. to use her own competence to manage her life between scheduled appointments. Dr. T.'s anxiety about the patient's relapsing into another immobilizing depression paralleled and subtly encouraged the patient's sense of responsibility and overconcern for her "fragile" father, who she unconsciously believed needed protection from the realities of her adult life. It also paralleled the father's protective and overconcerned stance with Ms. S., his little girl whose potential competence and maturity he feared recognizing.

A turning point in the treatment occurred when Dr. T. was able to use supervision to shift her therapeutic stance and warmly but firmly hold fast to the agreed-upon boundaries of therapy. For example, when Ms. S. called her at home at 7:00 in the morning to cancel her afternoon appointment for that day, Dr. T. told her during the following session, "When you call me to cancel a session, I would like you to do so during working hours." When the patient argued that she could not pay her bill because she was too depressed to seek employment, Dr. T. responded, "I appreciate that you are feeling depressed, but it is necessary that you find a way to meet your payments in order for your therapy to continue." In regard to telephone calls, she told Ms. S., "I've been thinking about our work together, and from now on I prefer that you do not call me at home. I think our work belongs here, in our scheduled sessions. I find I am most able to be helpful in this way."

Dr. T. was able to firmly clarify limits and boundaries without lengthy explanations (which would have implicitly conveyed discomfort or guilt) and without negatively interpreting the motives for the patient's requests. That is, Dr. T.'s comments and interventions in no way suggested that Ms. S.'s requests were reflective of excessive dependency, demandingness, or other pathological underpinnings. Equally as important, Dr. T. was able to calmly and empathically "sit still" through the patient's displays of hurt, withdrawal, and anger while maintaining the therapeutic boundaries. What followed was Ms. S.'s own slow but steady moves toward assuming a more differentiated stance in her own life. She more clearly defined her own thoughts and feelings on important issues, even when this brought anger and disapproval from significant others. She began to take less responsibility for others' feelings and more responsibility for ensuring the quality and direction of her own life. When her moves toward greater autonomy and independence predictably evoked strong resistance in others, she did react with a moderately severe depressive episode. However, when Dr. T. maintained a calm, nonreactive position and continued to keep the work within the boundaries of the two scheduled weekly hours (despite the patient's requests for additional sessions) Ms. S. rather quickly worked through her depression and continued to move ahead.

Dr. T.'s initial difficulty maintaining treatment parameters and clarifying appropriate limits had multiple sources. First, she had an exaggerated sense of guilt about the negative impact of her pregnancy and leave of absence on her patients (complicated by her

own conflicted wish to be rid of professional responsibilities entirely), and she responded with attempts to
be all-giving and available. Second, Dr. T.'s own sibling
position as a youngest child, combined with her gender and sex-role socialization, contributed to her considerable discomfort with exercising authority. Adding
to this problem was the absence of a clear theoretical
framework that would allow her to question her giving
stance. Throughout her training, Dr. T. (who was one
of the two women in her training program) had been
praised by teachers and supervisors for her "maternal," intuitive, and caring capacities, as if these traditionally feminine qualities were sufficient to facilitate
change and could not be exercised to excess. Finally,
Dr. T., like Dr. B., easily became anxious about her
female patient's perceived vulnerabilities and failed to
recognize that even the most severely disturbed individuals need a therapist who can model appropriate
self-seeking and self-assertive behaviors, maintain
treatment boundaries, and resist assuming an anxious, over-responsible and overfunctioning position.

Both male and female patients will test the therapist's ability
to exercise authority, set limits, protect treatment boundaries,
and resist overfunctioning and excessive concern. For women
in particular, however, it is important that the therapist model
the autonomous, authoritative, and differentiated behaviors
that have been discouraged or covertly forbidden for women.
As the previous case illustrates, the therapist's style of navigating such issues provides powerful messages about what is
permissible for the patient in her own life.

Irrespective of diagnostic category and severity of pathology, women often learn to protect relationships at the expense
of the self, to take responsibility for the feelings and behaviors
of others rather than putting their primary energy into identifying their own personal goals and directions, and to feel selfish and uncaring if they are anything less than an emotional
service station to others. Some women rebel against this legacy
by emotionally disengaging or by identifying with men who

pursue work goals at the expense of intimate relatedness and family responsibility, but the legacy affects them no less deeply. Underfunctioning for the self while overfunctioning for others is a prescribed way of operating for women. The therapist's management of his or her own tendency to overfunction for the patient is a crucial treatment variable. With women patients in particular, therapists may need help learning *not* to assume the role of emotional rescuer and to comfortably set limits and maintain boundaries in the face of the patient's invitations to do otherwise. Here it is the therapists' behaviors (and not their interpretations) that permit the female patient to initiate and hold fast to more assertive and differentiated behaviors in the face of countermoves and "change back!" maneuvers from significant others.

Because gender and sex-role socialization is a major (although relatively ignored) variable shaping countertransference reactions (Kaplan 1979), male and female therapists may experience a somewhat different internal press toward a nontherapeutic overfunctioning or overly giving stance. As in Dr. B.'s case, the male therapist may be readily poised to see himself as the rescuer or problem solver for the female in distress, confusing the woman's vulnerable and helpless self-presentation with her actual and potential capabilties and strengths. As doers, experts, and overfunctioners in the instrumental realm, men may have greater difficulty assuming a less active stance which would allow the woman more space to assume responsibility for solving her own problems and managing her own pain. Male therapists in particular may fail to recognize the ways in which female displays of vulnerability, helplessness, and dependency are part of a complex, gender-related interactional process in which female underfunctioning reflects an unconscious attempt to bolster and protect the male therapist and to safeguard the "closeness" of the patient–therapist relationship through the sacrifice of self (Lerner 1983). In a different vein, female therapists, like Dr. T., typically experience anxiety and guilt about the exercise of authority and may feel uncomfortable taking a firm stand on such crucial treatment parameters as scheduling appointments and collecting fees (Kaplan 1979). Further, their training may have overemphasized their reliance on traditional female traits (e.g., caring, empathy, and intuition) at the expense of equally crucial instrumental skills that have typically been viewed as masculine. Female therapists are also likely to be struggling with the same unconscious dilemmas as their female patients and may operate from a position of overresponsibility for other people's feelings and behaviors and underresponsibility for protecting the self and the boundaries of their own lives.

Any number of variables interact with gender to contribute to a therapist's overfunctioning position. These include such factors as the therapist's sibling position, role in the family of origin, level of professional experience and expertise, level of differentiation of self and associated clarity regarding the boundaries of individual responsibility, and characteristic style of negotiating relationships under stress. In addition, psychotherapy training and supervision, when influenced by the traditional male-established medical model, fosters the paradigm of the passive patient and the expert doctor who is accountable for curing his case (Lerner 1979). Ultimately, however, whatever the pressures to the contrary, it is the therapist's ability to be competent and emotionally connected without overfunctioning that allows the female patient to become the very best expert on her own self.

References

Kaplan, A. G. (1979). Toward an analysis of sex-role-related issues in the therapeutic relationship. *Psychiatry* 42(5):112–120. Also in *The Gender Gap in Psychotherapy*, ed. P. R. Rieker and E. Carmen, pp. 349–359. New York: Plenum, 1984.

Lerner, H. G. (1983). Female dependency in context. *American Journal of Orthopsychiatry* 53(4):697–705. Also in *The Gender Gap in Psychotherapy*, ed. P. R. Rieker and E. Carmen, pp. 125–133. New York: Plenum, 1984.

Lerner, H. G., and Davis, S. (1987). Negotiating requests to alter treatment parameters: an opportunity for professional growth. *The Clinical Supervisor* 5(1):73–87.

Lerner, S. (1979). The excessive need to treat. *Bulletin of the Menninger Clinic* 43(5):463–471.

Weiss, J. (1971). The emergence of new themes: a contribution to the psychoanalytic theory of therapy. *International Journal of Psychoanalysis* 52:459–467.

Weiss, J., and Sampson, H. (1986). *Psychoanalytic Process: Theory, Clinical Observations, and Empirical Research.* New York: Guilford.

Chapter 10

Effects of the Nursing Mother–Infant Dyad on the Family

Breast-feeding, when it is a relatively conflict-free experience, is a profoundly gratifying act for mother and child.[1] In addition, breast-fed babies are reported to have clear immunological, metabolic, and nutritional advantages over their bottle-fed brethren (Raphael 1973, Newton 1971). While breast-feeding and bottle-feeding are thought by some to be interchangeable phenomena, other experts consider artificial feeding to be a physiologically curious, if not bizarre aberration of the Western world (Newton 1978). Newton, an active researcher in this field, believes that lactation provides the psychohormonal component to the love relationship between mother and infant and has stated that, "Beginning the mother–baby relationship without lactation is like beginning the marriage without coitus" (1978). While there exists no convincing evidence that babies who are bottle-fed with love and affection suffer later psychological costs, many experts agree that breast-feeding is the very "essence" of mothering (Rich 1976). Certainly breast-feeding offers the unique opportunity for unmatched emotional and physical closeness between mother and infant.

It is perhaps surprising, then, that this pleasurable and

---

[1]This chapter is based on a May 1978 presentation at the annual meeting of the American Psychiatric Association in Atlanta, Georgia. It was first published in 1979 in the *American Journal of Orthopsychiatry* 49(2):339–348.

mutually beneficial experience is disavowed by a large percentage of American women. Approximately 25 percent of all women begin to breast-feed their babies, and as many as 62 percent give it up after only a brief trial (Pryor 1977). In part, this low percentage reflects the realities of institutions, many of which lack adequate child care facilities and do not have flexible work schedules that would allow mothers to combine nursing with part-time employment. In addition, intrapsychic and familial conflicts also lead women to wean prematurely or to avoid breast-feeding entirely. It is through our understanding of societal, familial, and intrapsychic factors that mental health professionals, as well as obstetricians, pediatricians, and public health nurses, can offer parents help in facilitating successful breast-feeding.

Intrapsychic factors underlying women's difficulties with breast-feeding have been considered at length in the psychoanalytic literature. Middlemore (1941) has discussed the mother's conflicts with breast-feeding in terms of the unconscious oral-sadistic fantasies remaining from her own infantile experience. Deutsch (1945) has associated disavowal of breast-feeding with fears of losing one's attractiveness, freedom, comfort, and vocational achievement, as well as with feelings of shame, guilt, and anxiety over the erotic stimulation involved. The focus of psychoanalytic writings is typically on the early life experience of the mother and the degree to which she has resolved critical developmental crises.

What is striking about the voluminous literature on breast-feeding is the dramatic neglect of any mention of the father. He may be mentioned perfunctorily, or ignored entirely, but little serious attention is directed to the fact that the nursing couple is part of a larger family system in which the father's reactions to the infant and to the infant–mother dyad will have a profound effect on all involved. Yet women's difficulties with nursing cannot be understood apart from the familial context in which they exist. Indeed, careful research on breast-feeding suggests that a nonsupportive atmosphere for the nursing mother is a central precipitating factor in an anxiety–milk loss–failure syndrome (Raphael 1973). Clearly, attempts to analyze the infant–mother dyad as if it existed on an isolated pink (or black) cloud will surely leave us with a partial, if not inaccurate, understanding.

While the professional literature is just beginning to examine fathers' reactions to the nursing mother–infant dyad, the popular literature is characterized by no such neglect. From Spock (1968) to more recent advisers of new mothers, one theme emerges clearly and repeatedly—that husbands, in addition to feeling proud and gratified by the nursing relationship, may also feel superfluous, inadequate, envious, and excluded. These authors note that he may respond with defensive hostility, withdrawal, or nonsupport, and that surely he will need special help from his wife to feel included and integrated into the newly enlarged family (Pryor 1977). While the psychoanalytic literature has tended to maintain a "dignified fraternal silence" (Lederer 1968) on these matters, the popular literature speaks clearly to the fact that every grown man was once a nursing infant at his mother's breast, or received in her arms its symbolic equivalent, the bottle, and that the nursing infant–mother dyad will reactivate a wealth of affects, anxieties, and fantasies in the new father.

This chapter will focus on the father's conflictual reactions to the nursing mother–infant dyad and the effects that these reactions may have on the mother. In particular, I am interested in how the nursing mother–infant dyad may disrupt a previous marital adjustment and how the couple may adopt dysfunctional "solutions" in the service of returning the marital relationship to its prior equilibrium. It is my conviction that women's difficulties with breast-feeding, as well as women's difficulties integrating breast-feeding with other aspects of their lives (especially professional activity), can be understood only within the broader familial and societal context.

Positive, nonconflictual paternal reactions to breast-feeding are not the focus here, although clearly, many fathers experience creative surges of pride and gratification in response to their nursing wives, leading to increased maturity and a deepening of family commitment. Such responses have not only been widely acknowledged and appreciated, but have generally been emphasized as the norm. Negative male reactions are often treated as comic, idiosyncratic, or pathological and, as such, are invalidated as being part of the expectable experiential world of the new father. Waletzky (1979), one of the few psychiatrists to focus attention on husbands' conflictual reactions to breast-feeding, has noted that our skewed emphasis on the positive has prevented parents from becoming aware of the expectable stresses that accompany breast-feeding. Men may be left feeling guilty and alone with their conflictual reactions, while women may angrily feel that they are unique in having a nonsupportive husband. Both partners may be prevented from coping patiently and creatively with the stresses that accompany breast-feeding.

MALE ENVY AND FEAR

Male envy of female reproductive capacities is a pervasive, if not universal, dynamic about which conspicuously little appears in the professional literature (Lederer 1968, Lerner 1974). Perhaps the only act of great significance that can be carried out by one sex only is the capacity to produce new life and sustain its growth with milk from one's own body. Many boys and men are consciously in touch with envious feelings during their mother's or wife's experience of pregnancy, childbirth, and lactation. In other males, envy is apparent only in the form of its denial or in a defensive devaluation of all other aspects of female creativity (Ribble 1965).

The myth of Genesis may be one reflection of male envy of female reproductive powers. Here, man is born of God, an idealized male figure, and woman is born from man's body, thus making Adam the first mother. This denial and reversal of the facts of creation is expressed not only in the Judeo-Christian tradition, but in a wide range of mythology (Lederer 1968). The universal exclusion of women from positions of authority and power may have partial roots in men's defensive handling of their own exclusion from the emotionally and physically powerful act of bringing forth new life (Ribble 1965). Psychoanalytic writers, who have reduced women's pleasure in pregnancy and childbirth to a displaced wish for a penis, may also be expressing their envy of female reproductive capacities—through a defensive and distorted emphasis on women as creatures who wish (even through their pride in their procreative powers) first to be men.

Male envy of the lactating breast cannot be understood in concrete anatomical terms alone. Rather, the breast is a symbol of "women's magic" and may symbolize the infant's and child's experience of the mother as an omnipotently powerful figure who possesses boundless nurturance as well as limitless powers for good and evil. While this early experience of mother is often defended against by seeing women as the weaker or castrated sex, my own clinical experience is in keeping with Chasseguet-Smirgel's (1970)   observation that images of women as deficient or castrated are a denial for both sexes of the imagoes of the primitive mother (i.e., the good omnipotent mother symbolized by the generous breast, fruitful womb, wholeness, and abundance, and the bad omnipotent mother symbolized by frustration, invasion, intrusion, and evil).

Lederer (1968) provided impressive anthropological data that, in regard to female reproductive capacities, men struggle also with intense feelings of fear and disgust. The theme of the pregnant or lactating woman as unclean or untouchable is a common one in many cultures, in which nursing women may remain taboo for many months following childbirth. In our society, such primitive fears operate largely unconsciously and are reflected in defensive idealized notions of feminine purity and daintiness or, alternately, in an overemphasis on the sexual aspects of women. In regard to the latter, Raphael (1973) found that a common male response to questions about breast-feeding was to switch the topic to the erotic aspect of the breast and even in some instances to tell dirty jokes. Among well-educated males, fears of female reproductive capacities may be contained and held in check by an intellectual appreciation of the processes involved as well as by the control of reproduction that men exercise through the medical profession, where, until the recent upsurge of the women's health movements, men typically "delivered" babies, with the woman in a passive, childlike, and often drugged position. Again, primitive anxieties and affects that men share regarding pregnancy, childbirth, and lactation cannot be conceptualized entirely in terms of anatomical differences. Rather, they may reflect persistent infantile fantasies regarding the mother's perceived magical powers to bring forth and sustain life and, by association, to take it away.

MALE REACTIONS TO THE MOTHER–INFANT DYAD

The husband's reactions to his wife's lactating breast, per se, are secondary to the crisis he faces with the birth of a first child, whereby a family of two—in one sudden and irreversible movement—is transformed into a family of three.[2] Within this new triad, the nursing mother–infant couple forms an interdependent subsystem that may appear to the husband to be complete unto itself. The husband, who until this time may have experienced himself as his wife's protector, as well as the sole recipient of her nurturance and attention, may suddenly find himself feeling like an "outsider" in a threesome. The popular literature on breast-feeding takes note of this trauma to the father and advises the new mother to reassure her husband that she still needs him:

> You may seem so capable in carrying out your maternal responsibilities and, as a nursing mother, so self-sufficient, that he underestimates your need for him. . . . He needs your assurance that he has not slipped to second place in your life. [Pryor 1977, p. 143]

Nursing mothers are also warned that their husbands may feel that they have no meaningful way to take care of the baby and that the male experience may be that of being a peripheral

---

[2]Arthur Mandelbaum (personal communication) has noted that a family never consists of two members, but is rather always a triadic subsystem consisting of wife–husband and their own families of origin. The new triad of wife–husband–child confirms, supports, and threatens further distance of the wife and husband from their families of origin, causing a need for a new adaptation to a newly formed subsystem. The separation of the wife from her family of origin shifts even more sharply. In former times, this shift was eased by the assistance the new mother received from her own mother, now often made impossible by geographical distance.

spectator, observing an intimate and often sensuous relationship of unmatched closeness between mother and child (Pryor 1977). Striking in certain of the popular literature is the mildly infantilizing attitude toward the husband, who is described much like a displaced child who needs continuing reassurance that he is, indeed, an important family member. This emphasis is interesting since such paternalistic attitudes, more typically directed toward women, point up a significant psychological truth that I have observed clinically. The birth of a first baby, particularly when it is breast-fed, may disrupt and even reverse the dynamic equillibrium between husband and wife. More specifically, I have noticed that the introduction of the nursing infant–mother dyad may seriously disrupt the way that each spouse has previously used the marriage to manage his or her own conflicts between dependency needs and autonomous strivings. This matter will be examined in greater detail, and a clinical example will illustrate the pathological means to which a couple may turn in an attempt to restore the previous homeostatic balance of their relationship.

AUTONOMY CONFLICTS

Every individual struggles with the conflict between passive-dependent longings and more active autonomous strivings. We wish (at least unconsciously) to remain our mother's child as well as to declare our independence from her. The universal conflict between infantile-dependent longings and more mature strivings toward autonomous functioning is never completely resolved. Rather, it is worked on in a variety of interpersonal contexts throughout a lifetime (Karpel 1976).

It is relatively common for married couples to manage this conflict through defensive splitting and projective identification. Rather than the partners in the marital relationship containing or "owning" the complicated, conflictual, although internally more whole, experience of integrating bipolarities within themselves (e.g., dependence-independence, passivity-activity, submission-dominance), husband and wife may unconsciously contract to each contain and express one side of the conflict. Although there are many exceptions to the rule, intrapsychic and cultural factors often combine to predispose the wife to become the container for passive-dependent longings and for the husband to contain strivings toward autonomy and independence. By assuming the role of the helpless, needy, dependent child, the wife helps her husband to disown his own dependency wishes and feelings of neediness. His experience may be one of self-reliance and independence marred only by his having to contend with a clinging, insecure, child-wife. Similarly, the husband protects his wife from experiencing the dangers of competence and autonomy. She may not have to come in touch with feelings of anxiety and loss that may be associated with the experience of achieving a greater degree of separation and individuation from her own husband and mother.

While this use of defensive splitting and projective identification may have certain psychological costs, it allows each partner to avoid experiencing both sides of his or her own conflict. In many instances it may provide for an uneasy but predictable, fairly stable, and workable marital relationship which is, nevertheless, vulnerable to change and stress. But this "solution" may be especially vulnerable to the introduction of the nursing mother–infant dyad into the marriage.

Shifts in the Marital Equilibrium

The experience of pregnancy, childbirth, and lactation may provide for a woman an enormous sense of physical prowess and strength. (Men who watch their wives in the delivery room often express awesome respect: "I could never do that.")[3] In addition, the new mother, who can vicariously enjoy her own infant's passive dependency, may now be in touch with previously denied feelings of power and mastery. With the new baby entirely dependent on her for its nurturance and very life,

---

[3]Another male reaction to observing childbirth is that of guilt. Hemingway wrote a famous short story of a husband who commits suicide after watching the difficult labor of his wife.

her role in the nursing couple may parallel the one her husband previously had with her. (She is the strong, life-sustaining force for one more helpless than herself.) Forming such a dyad with her dependent infant, and experiencing the intense fulfillment of the intimate nursing relationship, the wife may no longer express childlike dependency or neediness in her interaction with her husband. This is not to imply that she does, in fact, form a self-sufficient unit with her infant. Indeed, as Raphael's (1973) work has indicated, the nursing mother is herself in special need of nurturant and supportive caretakers in her environment. But her need for nurturance may be associated with an experience of competence and inner power, rather than stemming from weakness, inferiority, or helplessness.

With his wife no longer containing and expressing the incompetence or childlike dependency in the relationship, the husband may be confronted with the surfacing of such feelings of his own. In addition, the husband's passive-dependent oral longings and regressive strivings may be further stirred by his identification with the nursing baby, while his new experience of his wife as a "mother" may reactivate unresolved oral-dependent issues with his own mother. Conflictual wishes to return to a state of blissful symbiosis, and his anger about his own unmet oral-dependent needs, will be difficult for him to deny with a defensive or exaggerated masculinity, at a time when the nursing infant–mother dyad may leave him feeling peripheral, incompetent, and without a more helpless family member who is primarily dependent upon him. Particularly to the extent that infantile and narcissistic features predominate, the husband may, indeed, feel traumatized and react with anger, depression, or withdrawal. Even the most resilient husband is faced with special difficulty by a situation that stirs up his own dependency needs precisely at a time when his wife may be least available to meet those needs and when she and her infant may appear to form a complete unit unto themselves. If the husband undergoes sufficient stress, the marital relationship will be threatened and it may then become the wife's move to make an unconscious attempt to restore the earlier homeostatic balance.

THE WIFE'S REACTION

When the husband responds to the nursing mother–infant dyad with depression, defensive hostility, or withdrawal, the wife may in turn react with anxiety and guilt. Two nursing mothers I have seen in intensive individual therapy both took their husband's reactions as a threatened loss of the relationship between them, and responded by attempting to make an unconscious "sacrifice" to the husband. One woman's sacrifice involved relinquishing nursing, as well as experiencing her new infant as far less pleasurable than she might have otherwise. For the second woman (whose treatment will be described here), the sacrifice took the form of becoming depressed and planning to relinquish her valued career. Both women had mothers who were experienced as possessive and unfulfilled women who had difficulty tolerating their daughter's successes and felt excluded or jealous of the daughter's other dyadic relationship (daughter and father, daughter and husband). These patients' heightened vulnerability to experiencing anxiety and guilt about "excluding" their husbands from the mother–infant dyad stemmed both from the realities of the current family dynamics and from their earlier relationship with mother. The following case example is illustrative.

Clinical Example

When Karen entered psychotherapy at age 29 (with complaints of anxiety attacks at work), her professional career as a lawyer was well underway. Because she had long-standing plans to combine motherhood with a legal career, it was at first surprising to hear her speak during her pregnancy of tentative plans to drop her work entirely for a year or two despite her own reports that this action would have serious professional costs for her. Karen brought to her therapy hours the "encouraging" reactions of her co-workers when she verbalized her wish to be a full-time mother. For example, when she shared with her secretary her thoughts of staying home full time following the birth of her child, this woman responded enthusiastically and warmly, "That's wonderful! I always knew you would be a good mother!"

In response to such comments, Karen reported feeling guilty about that part of her that wished to have both a baby and a career. Her guilt, as she first understood it, reflected her concern that as a professional woman she would provide her baby with a less-than-optimal mothering experience. After further therapeutic exploration, it became evident that her guilt was associated with the experience of having "too much" and with her anxiety that by having both a baby and a profession, she would incur the envy and anger of other women, who might then wish to sabotage and spoil what she had. In the course of treatment, Karen's heightened sensitivity to other people's envy emerged as salient. Her unconscious (and later conscious) reactions to other women or men who so quickly encouraged her to relinquish her work were that they were trying to "keep her down" and take something away from her. In the face of real or perceived envy or competitiveness from others, she tended to make some apology—in this case, by strengthening her resolve that she would, indeed, relinquish her valued career.

Karen's experience of her mother as a jealous and unsatisfied woman, who might withdraw her love if her daughter received too much pleasure without her, was reflected in the transference shortly following the birth of her daughter. Assuming that I was without children, Karen came into the session complaining at length about the displeasure of breast-feeding, the constant draining demands of her infant, her sore nipples, and so on. Her initial inability to experience and acknowledge the pleasure in breast-feeding related to her guilt and anxiety about having something that did not include me and, further, that I might want for myself. My interpreting her readiness to relinquish pleasure in nursing to protect me from feeling hurt, jealous, or excluded allowed her to shift quickly to an experience of breast-feeding as pleasurable as well as erotic.

With continuing therapeutic work, Karen chose to return to her job part time while nursing her infant. Her ability to combine a pleasurable nursing experience with the gratification of her career was impressive. Indeed, she radiated a sense of inner strength and attractiveness. An earlier childlike, dependent stance that she had displayed in her relationships both with her husband and with me lessened dramatically. While I later learned that there was a growing tension and distance in her relationship with her husband at this time, she did not bring this into the treatment, nor did it seem to affect her at first. All was going apparently well until a particular incident occurred at work which affected her profoundly. The "traumatic" incident was as follows:

One day Karen brought her baby to the office and nursed her there before collecting some papers to bring home in her briefcase. As she was leaving, a female graduate student who shared the office commented, "Wow! A nursing baby in one arm and a briefcase in the other—what a sight!" Whether the comment was expressed critically or admiringly was unclear to me. But irrespective of the reality, the effect on Karen was dramatic. She at once became depressed, and her depression persisted. She soon announced that she was seriously considering stopping her work because the combined demands of nursing and having a career were "too much of a hassle" for her and her family. Further, she claimed that her depression left her with little investment in pursuing anything.

Therapeutic exploration revealed that Karen heard the student's comment as a mocking, hostile, and competitive attack on her "having so much." Rather than react competitively in return, Karen unconsciously attempted to apologize by again making plans to sacrifice her work. Her readiness to perceive the student's comment as one of hostile envy, her anxiety and guilt associated with her fear of losing a relationship, and her "solution" to react with depression and a vow to sacrifice a valued aspect of her life all had roots both in her earlier relationship with her mother and in her current relationship with her husband.

Karen's mother was a college graduate with considerable intellectual gifts and a clever, caustic wit. She herself had relinquished valued professional aspirations in order to further her husband's career and to be a "good mother." She was now understandably resentful about the fact that many women, including her three daughters, were finding such sacrifices unnecessary. Following the birth of Karen's baby, her mother communicated in passing that she was receiving antidepressant medication from the family physician; although details were neither given nor requested, Karen assumed that the depression was a consequence of her becoming a mother. According to Karen, her mother's letters contained subtle encouragement to her daughter to stop working while breast-feeding, while at the same time discouraging her from continuing breast-feeding as well. Her mother tended throughout Karen's lifetime to push her toward higher achievement and then subsequently to ignore or undermine her successes. Karen's father was described as a kind but distant man who would have known better how to relate to sons. His stance was one of not wanting to interfere with the relationships between "mother and the girls" and he was generally unavailable. Karen's unconscious experience of her mother was that her mother would become jealous, depressed, or retaliative if Karen were either to exclude her or to have too much without her. Karen's readiness to sacrifice her work and become depressed was her unconscious attempt to protect her mother from jealousy and depression and to preserve a threatened bond between them.

In her relationship with her husband, Bob, Karen

also struggled with unconscious anxiety and guilt about excluding him through her own independent pleasures and gratifications. Bob, a bright and ambitious man, had recently suffered a serious professional disappointment and seemed to be binding his anger by a harsh and unrealistic questioning of his own worth. In addition to this narcissistic blow, the nursing infant–mother couple seemed to strengthen his wished-for, but feared, infantile-dependent longings, which he had managed up until the birth of the baby to project onto his wife. From Karen's reports, it was probable that unresolved issues of sibling rivalry with his sister, one and a half years his junior, were also revived.

While I did not see the husband in treatment, there was considerable indication that his feeling excluded from the nursing couple, combined with the surfacing of his own conflicted dependency needs at a time when his wife was feeling especially independent and fulfilled, precipitated his assuming a withdrawn, critical stance in the marital relationship. When she nursed the baby, for example, he abruptly moved into a different room. His sexual interest in her diminished dramatically and he told her that her breasts, expelling milk during sexual excitement, disgusted him and made him feel that he was sleeping with "a mother." His depressed, withdrawn, critical, and rejecting stance was in contrast to the affectionate and mutually supportive relationship that the couple had shared during the pregnancy and prior to the birth of their child.

Karen's depression, as well as her readiness to relinquish her career, was not merely an enactment of an intrapsychic drama with a jealous, unfulfilled internalized maternal imago; her "sacrifice" also served as an unconscious attempt to restore an actual threatened relationship with her husband. This unconscious strategy was indeed successful, for in the face of her depression and tentative plans to stop working, the marital relationship improved conspicuously. Bob rose quickly to the call of caring for his now-dependent wife and child and was clearly bolstered by his family's need to have him in the role of the masterful leader. His renewed sense of being the "strong one" on whom others depended allowed him to become again loving and appreciative of his wife. Because he possessed considerable psychological strengths, he was also able to encourage Karen to stay with her work, which he valued a great deal when his own self-esteem was not threatened. Despite real strengths in the marital relationship, Karen continued to fear that her own pleasures and successes would stir envy and hurt in others and lead to the eventual dissolution of some important relationship (e.g., that with her mother or husband). It took continuing therapeutic work before Karen was comfortably and competently able to derive pleasure from both her baby and her career.

The past decade has witnessed a growing awareness of the need to become more familiar with the origin and manifestations of paternity (Coleman and Coleman 1971). In regard to breast-feeding, Waletzky (1979) has noted that a failure to help both partners understand and master their complex reactions to nursing may turn the perinatal period into what has aptly been labeled "a breeding ground for marital and parental maladjustment" (Pittenger and Pittenger 1977). Waletzky has described a variety of exciting new programs and workshops that sensitize both husbands and wives to expectable stresses accompanying the experience of parenthood.

An exclusive focus on the mother–infant dyad is characteristic not only of the literature on breast-feeding but of the voluminous literature on infancy and childhood as well (Brody 1956). This narrow focus is surprising in view of our knowledge that the birth of a first child produces a temporary crisis in the lives of both parents, who must make major psychological adjustments in order to shift successfully from a subsystem of two to a subsystem of three. In that almost magical, transitional moment when daughter becomes mother, son becomes father, and parents become grandparents, a man and woman are called upon to make profound and complex psychological adjustments and shifts in identifications (Minuchin 1974). Clearly, the mother–child relationship cannot be studied and understood apart from the marital interaction, the profound roots of husband and wife in their families of origin, and the complex and changing culture in which the family is embedded.

REFERENCES

Brody, S. (1956). *Patterns of Mothering.* New York: International Universities Press.

Chasseguet-Smirgel, J. (1970). Feminine guilt and the Oedipus complex. In *Female Sexuality: New Psychoanalytic Views*, ed. J. Chassequet-Smirgel et al., pp. 94–134. Ann Arbor: University of Michigan Press.

Coleman, A., and Coleman, L. (1971). *Pregnancy: The Psychological Experience.* New York: Herder and Herder.

Deutsch, H. (1945). *The Psychology of Women*, vol. 2. New York: Grune & Stratton.

Karpel, M. (1976). Individuation: From fusion to dialogue. *Family Process* 15(1):65–82.

Lederer, W. (1968). *The Fear of Women.* New York: Grune & Stratton.

Lerner, H. G. (1974). Early origins of envy and devaluation of women: implications for sex-role stereotypes. *Bulletin of the Menninger Clinic* 38:538–553.

Middlemore, M. (1941). *The Nursing Couple.* London: Hamish Hamilton.

Minuchin, S. (1974). *Families and Family Therapy.* Cambridge, Mass.: Harvard University Press.

Newton, N. (1971). Psychologic differences between breast- and bottle-feeding. *American Journal of Clinical Nutrition* 24:993–1004.

Newton, N. (1978). Completing the female sexual cycle: intercourse, childbirth, and breast-feeding. *Sexual Medicine Today* 2(5):34–40.

Pittenger, J., and Pittenger, J. (1977). The perinatal period: a breeding ground for marital and parental maladjustment. *Keep Abreast Journal* 18.

Pryor, K. (1977). *Nursing Your Baby*. New York: Simon and Schuster.

Raphael, D. (1973). *Breast-Feeding: The Tender Gift*. Englewood Cliffs, N.J.: Prentice-Hall.

Ribble, M. (1965) *The Rights of Infants*. New York: Columbia University Press.

Rich, A. (1976). *Of Woman Born*. New York: W. W. Norton.

Spock, B. (1968). *Baby and Child Care*. New York: Hawthorne.

Waletzky, L. (1979) Husbands' problems with breast-feeding. *American Journal of Orthopsychiatry* 49(2):349–352.

Chapter 11

Female Dependency

Dependency needs are a universal aspect of human experience.[1] The struggle to achieve a healthy integration of passive-dependent longings and active autonomous strivings constitutes a life-long developmental task for both men and women. Yet despite such universality, the very word *dependency* is more frequently associated with the female sex. Indeed, dependency, like passivity, has been considered the very hallmark of femininity.

It is true enough that women show dependent behavior more openly than do men. On the adaptive side, women tend to be more affiliative and self-disclosing, and better able to acknowledge and express realistic fears, vulnerability, and wishes to be cared for (Pleck and Sawyer 1974, Miller 1976). On the maladaptive side, women more frequently display pathological dependency (Miller 1976); such women do not take action to solve their own problems, do not clearly state their opinions and preferences out of fear of conflict or disapproval, turn fearfully away from the challenges of the outside world, and avoid successful and autonomous functioning at all costs.

---

[1]This chapter is based on a May 1982 presentation at the annual meeting of the American Psychiatric Association in Toronto, Canada. It was first published in 1983 as "Female Dependency in Context: Some Theoretical and Technical Considerations" in the *American Journal of Orthopsychiatry* 53(4):697–705.

Although the ability to acknowledge and express realistic dependency is an essential aspect of healthy psychological functioning, it is the pathological apsects of dependency that have loomed largest in the literature on female psychology.

Although certain psychoanalytic writings have invoked anatomy-is-destiny theories to account for the association of femininity with passive-dependent behavior, the more recent literature emphasizes familial and cultural determinants (Miller 1973). More than a decade of research by feminist scholars and mental health professionals has indicated that females are often trained in pathological dependency from birth (Bardwick 1971, Women 1972). While etiological factors remain controversial, there nonetheless seems to be wide agreement that women are, in fact, the more dependent sex. Certainly we hear a great deal more about the dependency needs of women than of men—as if women, by nature or nurture, were possessed of more of a bad thing. Much of the professional literature, as well as popular books such as *The Cinderella Complex* (Dowling 1981), speaks clearly to the ubiquity of this belief.

Part of the reason for spurious generalizations about excessive female dependency is that the structural or contextual factors that evoke women's dependent behavior have not been taken seriously enough by mental health professionals. For example, the professional literature has noted that even active and self-reliant women often become excessively dependent, if not phobic, following marriage (Symonds 1971). Little attention, however, has been given to the ways in which the structure of traditional marriage facilitates an increasing sense of economic and psychological dependence in women, their individual strengths notwithstanding. In addition, the popular and professional literature has tended to ignore the obvious fact that men also have dependency needs, the fulfilling of which has been a role assigned to women.

Unlike men, who go from mother to mother again, in the form of wife, women often relinquish their mothers in order to do the mothering. By traditional standards, a "good wife" cleans, cooks, comforts, nurtures, soothes, admires, encourages, listens, sympathizes, and supports—although she is less frequently on the receiving end of such nurturing and caretaking. Through the process of providing for the dependency needs of others (including husband and children), a woman may consciously or unconsciously anticipate that her own needs will be met; when her needs are left unmet, she may manifest behavior that appears to be excessively dependent or demanding. Little attention, however, may be given to the fact that the woman's dependency needs are not being adequately met by important others, or that she is unable actively to pursue self-directed, self-seeking activities that would allow her to provide for her own wants. From this perspective, women are not the excessively dependent sex. A more accurate generalization might be to say that women are not dependent enough. Most women are far more expert at worrying about the needs of others than at identifying and assertively claiming their own needs.

Spurious generalizations about female dependency stem from an additional conceptual failure. Many theorists and practitioners fail to distinguish between the passive-dependent behavior that women so frequently display, if not actively cultivate, and the actual level of autonomy or differentiation of self that women have, in fact, achieved. As a group, women may behave in a more passive-dependent fashion than do men, but women are not more dependent than men if we consider the actual level of autonomy or differentiation of self that an individual achieves. To understand the distinction between a woman's passive-dependent behavior and her actual level of differentiation, it is important to appreciate that women's displays of passive-dependency frequently have a protective and systems-maintaining function for significant others. This point will be examined in greater detail.

THE PROTECTIVE ASPECTS
OF FEMALE DEPENDENCY

Research in marital systems has indicated that both partners tend to be at the same level of psychological differentiation or independence (Bowen 1978). There is generally little difference between spouses in the actual level of autonomous functioning or clarity of self that each has achieved in the family of origin. Often it may appear dramatically otherwise, as when a high-powered businessman brings his symptomatic, infantile-dependent wife into a psychiatric hospital. The reason for this apparent discrepancy is that the underfunctioning of one spouse allows for the overfunctioning of the other. In Bowen's (1978) terms, if one person "de-selfs" herself or himself, the other gains in "pseudo-self." Like a seesaw, the helpless-dependent stance of one partner has an adaptive, ego-bolstering effect on the other. When the "underfunctioner" moves in the direction of more autonomous functioning, the "overfunctioner" starts to do worse and will predictably make any number of "countermoves" to restore the relationship to its prior equilibrium.

In my clinical work, I have noted how frequently the passive-dependent stance that characterizes so many women is inextricably interwoven with the prescribed underfunctioning role that women assume in order to protect and stabilize the systems in which they operate. Put somewhat differently, women's dysfunctional passive-dependent behavior is, in part, derived from the unconscious "rules" that guide certain relational systems. Women are rarely as dependent as they learn to appear; rather, women learn to display passive-dependent behavior in order to protect others (including the therapist) and maintain the delicate homeostatic balance of systems in which any move away from a dependent stance is responded to by important others as a hurtful and aggressive act; it is disloyalty, a betrayal. Maintaining a dependent self-experience in order to protect and bolster others is a dynamic that has its roots in the family of origin. It is also culturally prescribed and spelled out most clearly in women's adult relationships with men.

Protecting Men

Before the current wave of feminism, girls and women were explicitly encouraged to offer males narcissistic protection by cultivating passive-dependent behavior and by feigning weakness and incompetence if these did not come naturally. As one expert in female popularity advised in the mid-1960s:

> If you smoke, don't carry matches. In a restaurant, let your mate or date do the ordering . . . you may know more about vintage wine than the wine steward, but if you are smart, you'll let your man do the choosing and be ecstatic over his selection, even if it tastes like shampoo . . . the successful female never lets her competence compete with her femininity. [Dahl 1965, p. 8]

This bit of advice is characteristic of the majority of guide books for women written before the 1970s, which explicitly prescribed male dominance while implicitly warning women that men were weak. In one popular book, *Help Your Husband Stay Alive* (Lees 1957), the author went so far as to insist that men are physically incapable of surviving unless women assume a dependent and subordinate role. Underlying her prescription to underfunction, the author wrote:

> What is humiliating about being under a man— whether in business, in government, or any role of life . . . if it is clear to you that he is only on top because you are holding him up? [p. 14]

The paradoxical notion that women must strengthen men by relinquishing their own strength is widespread even today. An explicit example of this philosophy can be found in *Fascinating Womanhood*, a best-selling book based on the same principles as Marabelle Morgan's *Total Woman*. In a 1980 edition, Andelin provided the reader with detailed instructions on how to cultivate a childlike, dependent stance, with the explicit goal of protecting the marital bond. One assignment, for example, instructed the reader to carefully observe and copy the behavior and mannerisms of little girls, while other chapters suggested ways to suppress tendencies to appear competent or self-reliant in "masculine," independent pursuits.

Our time-honored fairy tales also contain the paradoxical

prescription that females should protect men by letting men protect women. These stories teach that passive-dependent behavior is the hallmark of successful femininity, as well as the vehicle that permits and encourages masculine independence and activity (Bettelheim 1976). It is the damsel in distress who provides her brave rescuer with the opportunity to slay dragons, solve riddles, or otherwise be heroic. The male hunter could not have rescued Little Red Riding Hood were it not for the fact that she was utterly helpless in the teeth of the wolf and lacked even the intellectual resourcefulness to distinguish her grandmother from a wolf in a nightcap. Little Red Riding Hood is just one of many fairy tale heroines who does not solve her own problems, but rather provides men with the opportunity to act on her pathetic behalf.

It is tempting to view the dictates of popular culture as outdated cliches that have little relevance to current clinical practice or to the real-life experience of contemporary women. Certainly, most women who enter our consulting rooms today do not willfully or effortfully practice childlike dependence in order to bolster the male ego and thus ensure the predictable security of their relationships. Nonetheless, the behavior occurs unconsciously, without awareness or intent. Underlying the passive-dependent stance of many women is the unconscious motivation to bolster and protect another person as well as the unconscious conviction that one must remain in a position of relative weakness for one's most important relationships to survive. Even intellectually liberated women unconsciously feel frightened and guilty about "hurting" others, especially men, when fully exercising their capacity for independent thinking and action. In reality, women who do begin to define more clearly the terms of their own lives are frequently accused of diminishing men, hurting children, or in some way being destructive to others. These reactions, which occur in response to the anxiety that is stirred when a woman behaves more autonomously, represent a powerful counterforce to change.

Our gender arrangements as well as our very definitions of femininity contain an important metacommunication which remains an unconscious guiding rule for many women. The message is that *the weaker sex must protect the stronger sex from recognizing the strength of the weaker sex lest the stronger sex feel weakened by the strength of the weaker sex.* This message persists despite changing times and new egalitarian beliefs; women are still encouraged to protect men by containing and expressing the very passivity and dependency that men fear in themselves (Miller 1976, Lerner 1978). Because women do learn that being an autonomous, self-directed person is hurtful to others, especially men, their dependent behavior is often an unconscious "gift" or sacrifice to those they love; it is the gift of giving up self so that the other may gain self.

Needless to say, not all women succumb to pressures to assume a dependent role with men, and not all heterosexual relationships are based on such complementarity. In couples that operate at a relatively high level of differentiation, there is less reliance on splitting and projective identification; each spouse is able to tolerate the complicated and conflictual experience of integrating bipolarities (e.g., activity-passivity and dependence-independence) within one's own self. Each partner is able to feel competent and to view the other as competent, with no need either to minimize or exaggerate dependency, vulnerability, or helplessness. Nonetheless, large numbers of women who appear in our consulting rooms do unconsciously protect men by cultivating a passive-dependent stance. This dysfunctional position reflects, in part, powerful cultural injunctions to underfunction which are fueled by irrational fantasies about female power and male vulnerability (Lerner 1974, 1978); however, it also has its roots in the family of origin, where separation–individuation issues are first negotiated. It is there that the growing girl may learn to inhibit her strivings toward more autonomous functioning in order to protect the family system or to solve some problem in her parents' relationship.

In families in which the marital relationship is weak, and the mother herself has been blocked from proceeding with her own growth, daughters frequently learn to cling to passive-dependent behavior as an unconscious "oath of fidelity" to remain the mother's child, as if the daughter's own moves

toward greater separateness and autonomy constitute disloyalty and betrayal. Later this drama is continued in adult heterosexual relationships and is reinforced by warnings to
women that men must be protected from women's full
strength and abilities. I believe that girls and women are especially vulnerable to anxiety and guilt in regard to making their
own declaration of independence from their first family
(Lerner 1978, 1980). Many psychotherapists fail to appreciate
the degree to which female anxiety and guilt about autonomy
and separateness reflect, in part, the patient's accurate perception that her most important relationships have little flexibility to tolerate her continuing growth and independence and
that, further, her passive-dependent stance serves a protective
function for other family members. Paradoxically, a patient
may become free to relinquish a dependent position when her
therapist can identify and respect the adaptive functions that
are served by her maintaining a dependent stance, and appreciate with her the actual risks and potential losses that she
and others face if she permits herself to behave in a more
autonomous and self-directed fashion.

IMPLICATIONS FOR TREATMENT

In my supervisory work, I have noted that a woman's dependent self-experience and behavior frequently elicit negatively
toned interpretations implying that her dependency needs are
weak, childish, or excessive. In addition to exacerbating the
patient's feelings of guilt or inadequacy, such interventions
seriously miss the point. A patient may, indeed, present herself
as a needy child, motivated by the infantile wish to be passively
nurtured by, or symbiotically fused with, an all-providing
mother; however, this is less than half the story. All human
beings, irrespective of sex and diagnostic category, strive for
autonomy and competence. The internal press toward growth
is always more powerful than the wish to remain a dysfunctional child; therapeutic interventions that imply that the patient does not want to grow up fail to recognize that the costs
of growing up may be quite high, including the outbreak of

symptomatology in other family members and the threat of dissolution of important relationships.

The oral rage that characterizes severely dependent women stems not from the fact that their excessive dependency needs are being frustrated; rather, their rage is associated with their unconscious conviction that they must continue to thwart their own growth for the sake of protecting family ties and fulfilling family loyalties and obligations. Family systems theory has elegantly demonstrated how a patient's resistance to change must be understood in the context of the powerful pressures against change exerted by the multigenerational, rule-governed family and cultural systems in which the patient operates (Keeney 1979). This focus is especially crucial in regard to the therapeutic management of female dependency.

While the feminist movement has helped therapists become more aware of their failure to confront passive-dependent behavior in women, the focus here will be on a therapeutic error of a different order. Therapists frequently encourage their women patients to be more assertive or independent without first analyzing the adaptive function being served, or the family problem being solved, by the patient's dependent stance. The nontherapeutic outcome is frequently a resistant impasse in which the patient feels caught between the therapist who is pushing for change, and family communications that press for homeostasis and sameness. At this point, the treatment may go from bad to worse, as the therapist begins to confer a strong negative connotation not only on the patient's dependency, but also on her resistance to change, as if this resistance is simply a countertherapeutic force or a negative transference reaction to be abolished through interpretation. The resistance impasse may be broken when the therapist is able to assess carefully the family system's tolerance for change and appreciate the function served by the patient's dependent stance in this context. This requires, among other things, the ability to track carefully the actual reactions of other family members when a situation of systems disequilibrium arises as a result of the patient's tentative moves toward greater independence. It also requires a phenomenological shift on the part of the therapist to allow for a truly neutral, respectful, and emotionally unreactive position regarding the patient's choice to change or not to change.

In regard to transference-countertransference issues, another point deserves attention. The same therapist who prematurely encourages female patients to be more assertive and independent in their family and work relationships may unwittingly foster dependency in the therapeutic relationship (Bernardez-Bonesatti 1976, Lerner 1982). The exasperated therapist who complained, "No matter how much I interpret, or try to push her, she still won't be assertive with her husband" failed to recognize the double-bind situation evoked by his injunction to the patient to assert herself outside the hour and by his disqualifying message that she should be a "good patient" within the therapeutic relationship and dutifully value and follow his advice. He accurately interpreted the maladaptive aspects of the patient's refusal to make use of his help; yet he failed to appreciate the adaptive components of what the patient was trying to accomplish by asserting her wish to not assert herself. As a result of the therapist's interventions, the patient shifted from a defiant to a compliant stance in which she inhibited expressions of differences and unconsciously attempted to make the therapist feel useful and important. While the therapist saw this shift as an "improvement," the patient was actually placating him and protecting his narcissism, while she remained as stuck as ever in her own life. When the therapist was able to view positively the patient's ability to disagree with him, and when he was able to relinquish his sense of responsibility for the patient's own decision regarding how dependently or independently she would behave in her marriage, the patient felt safer to assume a more differentiated stance with both her therapist and her husband.

It may be especially difficult for male therapists to appreciate the degree to which female patients, like our fairy tale heroines, underfunction in the therapeutic hour as an unconscious attempt to help the therapist feel bolstered and protected (Lerner 1982). The patient may cultivate a needy, dependent stance for the therapist's sake, or otherwise pull for excessive worry and concern, because to do otherwise may feel like a violation of an unconscious allegiance, obligation, or contract to remain "close" through underfunctioning. While unconsciously associating autonomy and separateness with disloyalty, betrayal, and potential loss, the female patient will repeatedly test in the transference the degree to which the therapist will choose to see her as dependent and dysfunctional and the degree to which the therapist is comfortable with the patient's competence and autonomy. The unconscious tests may take an infinite variety of forms. Sometimes they consist of the patient's requesting or demanding something that, in fact, she is quite capable of doing without. The "something" may be an additional hour, a telephone call at home, extra time at the end of the session, or a request to see another professional during the therapist's absence. It is easy for therapists to "fail" the tests by going along with the patient's requests and replicating a dysfunctional family picture of excessive protectiveness, overconcern, and overresponsibility, which translates to a prescription or injunction to underfunction for the identified patient. Therapists commonly encourage female patients to be assertive with their spouses, while covertly prescribing compliant behavior and discouraging a challenging, independent stance which includes the expression of anger and competitiveness within the patient–therapist dyad. The incongruent nature of such therapeutic interventions often goes unidentified by patient, therapist, and supervisor.

Rather than attempt a comprehensive overview of the multifaceted and complex subject of female dependency, this paper has focused on a point that can significantly alter the direction and tone of a particular treatment. Women who are "stuck" in a dysfunctional passive-dependent stance frequently elicit negatively toned interventions which only heighten the patient's resistance to change and lead to a negative therapeutic outcome. In the midst of such an impasse, it may be especially difficult for therapists to recognize that a woman's passive-dependent self-experience and behavior are essentially a sacrifice. This sacrifice of competence, clarity, and growth cannot be understood in terms of its secondary gains or gratifications (although these may be present), nor can it be successfully analyzed solely in light of the patient's projections, infantile wishes, irrational anxieties, early deprivations, and distorted internalized object representations. It is important that the patient's behavior be analyzed and understood in terms of the family systems pressure for homeostasis as well as its flexibility to tolerate change; a systemic conceptualization of the patient's dependent posture allows for an appreciation of the loyal and adaptive aspects of what the patient is trying to accomplish and the ways in which her dependent posture plays an important role in the self-regulatory needs of the family system as a whole. Appreciating the systemic meaning of the patient's ongoing sacrifice of personal growth is effective when it occurs in the context of a therapeutic relationship that encourages the patient's autonomy and that does not foster or collude with patient–therapist "closeness" based on the patient's underfunctioning position.

REFERENCES

Andelin, H. (1980). *Fascinating Womanhood.* New York: Bantam.

Bardwick, J. (1971). *Psychology of Women.* New York: Harper and Row.

Bernardez-Bonesatti, T. (1976). Unconscious beliefs about women affecting psychotherapy. *North Carolina Journal of Mental Health* 7(5):63–66.

Bettelheim, B. (1976). *The Uses of Enchantment.* New York: Knopf.

Bowen, M. (1978). *Family Therapy in Clinical Practice.* New York: Jason Aronson.

Dahl, A. (1965). *Always Ask a Man.* Englewood Cliffs, N.J.: Prentice-Hall.

Dowling, C. (1981). *The Cinderella Complex.* New York: Simon and Schuster.

Keeney, B. (1979). Ecosystemic epistemology: an alternative paradigm for diagnosis. *Family Process* 18:117–129.

Lees, H. (1957) *Help Your Husband Stay Alive.* New York: Appleton-Century-Crofts.

Lerner, H. G. (1974) Early origins of envy and devaluation of women: implications for sex-role stereotypes. *Bulletin of the Menninger Clinic* 38(6):538–553.

—— (1980). Internal prohibitions against female anger. *American Journal of Psychoanalysis* 40(2):137–148.

—— (1978). On the comfort of patriarchal solutions: some reflections on Brown's paper. *Journal of Personality and Social Systems* 1(3):47–50.

—— (1982). Special issues for women in psychotherapy. In *The Woman Patient: Medical and Psychological Interfaces*, vol. 3, ed. M. Notman and C. Nadelson, pp. 273–286. New York: Plenum.

Miller, H. (1973). *Psychoanalysis and Women.* New York: Brunner/Mazel.

Miller, J. (1976). *Toward A New Psychology of Women.* Boston: Beacon.

Pleck, J., and Sawyer, J. (1974). *Men and Masculinity.* Englewood Cliffs, N.J.: Prentice-Hall.

Symonds, A. (1971). Phobias after marriage: women's declaration of dependence. *American Journal of Psychoanalysis* 31(2):144–152.

Women On Words And Images. (1972). *Dick and Jane as Victims.* Princeton, N.J.: Carolingian.

Chapter 12

Work and Success Inhibitions

F emale anxiety and guilt about ambitious strivings and the exercise of competence are so ubiquitous that the "fear of success" syndrome has become a household word (Horner 1972). Women do indeed fear that they will pay dearly for their accomplishments. They frequently equate success, or the very wish for it, with loss—loss of femininity and attractiveness, loss of significant relationships, loss of health, or even loss of life (Person 1982). The following is illustrative:

> Ms. B., 38 years old, was unable to progress with her doctoral dissertation.[1] For more than a week she wrote and rewrote her introductory section, without success. One morning, however, she awoke with a new idea and began reorganizing her material, proceeding with clarity and ease. She was excited about the dissertation and about exercising her own competence, and for the first time she saw herself as capable of making a valuable contribution in her field.

---

[1]The case presented in this chapter was discussed in "Can a Feminist Still Like Murray Bowen?" in *The Family Therapy Networker* 9(6):36–39, 1985, as well as in "The Challenge of Change," in *Everywoman's Emotional Well-being*, ed. C. Tavris, pp. 375–392. New York: Doubleday, 1986. This chapter was first published in 1987 as "Work and Success Inhibitions in Women: Family Systems Level Interventions in Psychodynamic Treatment" in the *Bulletin of the Menninger Clinic* 51(4):338–360.

Later that afternoon she experienced chest pains and feared that she was about to have a heart attack. When I saw her the following day in therapy, she reported, "I know this sounds crazy, but I was convinced it was all over. And I said to myself, 'Well, that's what you get. That's your punishment. That's what's coming to you for trying to get a PhD'."

Although Ms. B. consciously feared paying penance for her "sin" of ambition, one more frequently sees the unconscious in action. Feelings of depression and anxiety, as well as self-sacrificing and self-sabotaging behaviors, are common ways that women apologize for their competence and success on the one hand, or ensure the lack of it on the other.

Psychoanalytically oriented therapists have a questionable track record for helping women identify the internal barriers and external obstacles that block them from higher achievement. Indeed, therapists often unwittingly exacerbate female anxiety and guilt through questions and interpretations that imply negative connotations to ambitious and competitive wishes in women, or they view these wishes as representing masculine strivings. Even feminist therapists commit errors of omission, neglecting to identify and analyze work inhibitions in female patients who fail to identify such inhibition as a problem.

It is beyond the scope of this chapter to summarize the multiplicity of factors that contribute to women's problems with work. The beginnings of such a summary would include intrapsychic and psychodynamic formulations (Applegarth 1976, Nadelson, Notman, and Bennett 1978, Person 1982, Stiver 1983, Krueger 1984, Moulton 1985); the negative impact of sex-role stereotypes (Lerner 1983, Krueger 1984); the realities of discrimination and lack of opportunity (GAP 1975); the impact of situational and contextual factors that affect women in male-defined and male-dominated work settings (Kanter 1977, Stiver 1983); the structure and division of parenting responsibilities (GAP 1975); and much more. A multiplicity of factors—intrapsychic, familial, institutional, and sociocultural—all combine to make the road to professional fulfillment an especially difficult one for women.

To provide a partial theoretical formulation for work inhibitions in women, I will focus on a single clinical case, highlighting the usefulness of systems-level interventions in individual psychodynamic treatment. I will also emphasize the clinical interventions that are pivotal in the process of change and that are specifically linked to relational dynamics in the marital system, the nuclear family system, and the multigenerational family system.

Clinical Example

Ms. J. was 30 years old and married, with a financially successful husband and a 2-year-old daughter. The complaint that led her to seek therapy was persistent depression, which had begun after the birth of her daughter. While Ms. J. initially did not define her problem as difficulty moving ahead with her career, this subject had long been a focus of her personal distress and marital tension.

During our initial meeting, Ms. J. tearfully told me that her life was "going nowhere." She explained that she was bored and exhausted with substitute teaching and that she frequently thought about returning to graduate school to increase both her income and her career options. During the initial stage of treatment, however, Ms. J. saw the locus of her dilemma as existing entirely within her husband who, according to her own report, refused to grant her permission to work until their daughter was in kindergarten. Ms. J. described him as a "brilliant workaholic" who engaged in repetitive cycles of distancing and dominating the family.

Therapeutic exploration revealed that Ms. J.'s description of her husband as a powerful tyrant barely masked her underlying fear that he was a narcissistically fragile man who would have difficulty tolerating her competence or even her enthusiastic involvement in work activities that excluded him. In keeping with the dictates of culture, the prescribed complementarity of marriage, and the patterns in the patient's own family of origin, Ms. J. dutifully underfunctioned, putting aside her ambitions to bolster her husband and preserve relationship harmony.

This dynamic, which I have discussed elsewhere (Lerner 1979, 1983, 1985), is ubiquitous among women and is often partially rooted in aspects of mother–daughter fusion and related father–daughter distancing, as well as in the actual flexibility of the marital, family, and cultural systems to tolerate change. I will briefly discuss the marital dyad before moving on to earlier determinants of Ms. J.'s work inhibitions as they related to her family of origin.

THE MARITAL SYSTEM

During the initial stage of treatment, I was able to help Ms. J. move out of her entrenched blaming stance toward her husband by systemic questioning, which allowed Ms. J. to identify how her own lack of action on the graduate school issue functioned to protect her husband and to preserve togetherness (albeit a conflictual togetherness) in their marriage. Although space does not permit a description of interpretive work derived from a systemic framework (Lerner and Lerner 1983), the following excerpts from the therapy are examples of questioning that helped Ms. J. assume responsibility for her own problem so that she was able to think consciously about the impact of her professional growth on her marriage. From an intrapsychic perspective, a focus on relationship systems might reinforce resistance by further deflecting the patient from an exploration of the "real" internal difficulties, but this is not the case in actual practice. Rather, when the therapist can carefully identify the adaptive systems-maintaining function of the patient's "stuckness," resistance is considerably lessened, allowing rapid moves toward greater self-exploration (Lerner and Lerner 1983). Further, women's fears that their own growth and self-seeking strivings will lead to the disruption, if not the dissolution, of a relationship is grounded not only in fantasy and projection, but also in the actual rules and roles of their relationship systems (Lerner 1979, 1983, 1985).

Clinical Example

Session 3

Patient: No matter how much I fight with Jonathan (Mr. J.) about graduate school, he won't change his mind. (Patient goes on to criticize her husband's domineering style and chauvinistic attitude.)

Therapist: How do you understand his strong feelings on the subject?

Patient: He just feels strongly about Cara (the daughter) having a mother at home . . .

Therapist: Putting Cara aside for a moment, what effect would your returning to graduate school and becoming involved in developing a career have on your relationship with Jonathan?

Patient: What do you mean?

Therapist: Well, would the two of you be closer or more distant? Would you fight more or less? Would your husband be pleased or threatened? (Silence.) How would it influence the way the two of you are together?

Patient: Oh, I don't know; it probably wouldn't make any difference. (She laughs nervously.) He would probably like it because I wouldn't be on his back nagging and complaining all the time.

Therapist: What about the other men in Jonathan's family? Which men have wives who have careers and which men have wives who don't have careers?

Patient:	Well . . . his mother stayed at home. There's no way she would have worked.
Therapist:	And Jonathan's brothers?
Patient:	Well, the younger one is married to Claire, who does bookkeeping for their shop. But it's more like she "helps out." The middle brother was married to someone who went to law school but that didn't work out. They got divorced last year.
Therapist:	So in your husband's family, the only marriage where both partners had a career hasn't worked out?
Patient:	That's right.

Session 5

Ms. J. begins the session with a long, detailed description of yet another escalating battle about the graduate school issue, inviting me to join her in criticizing Jonathan, who is portrayed as unreasonable and obnoxious.

Therapist:	My goodness, the two of you sure are good at banging your heads together. It sounds like "Godzilla meets Tyrannosaurus Rex." (Patient laughs and relaxes.) Let me ask you a question. What do you think would happen if you stopped fighting with your husband and calmly told him that it was important for you to return to graduate school and . . .
Patient:	He'd give me a hundred reasons why I couldn't.
Therapist:	What if you didn't argue with him, since you know from experience that fighting goes nowhere? (Patient laughs.) What if you were able to tell him, without fighting or criticizing him, that you appreciate his concern for Cara but that graduate school is very important to you—that you have

been struggling with the issue for a long
time and have many mixed feelings yourself, but that your decision is to move
ahead with it? (Silence.) What if you explained to Jonathan that you didn't expect
him to like your decision or approve of it,
but that you needed to do what you think
is best for you at this time?

Patient: I would never, ever do that. You don't know
my husband!

Therapist: That's absolutely right. And I am not suggesting that you should do this. I'm asking
these questions not to suggest action, but
because I want to get a clearer perspective
on your husband—how he might react to
changes you make, and how you react to
his reactions. (Silence.) So, what specifically would Jonathan say or do if you made
such a declaration and stood behind it
warmly—even lovingly—without getting
drawn back into the old fights?

Patient: Well, I don't know. (Pause.) I think he'd
faint.

Therapist: (Therapist laughs.) How's that?

Patient: Oh, I guess because it would be so different. I wouldn't be the same old predictable,
nagging wife. (Patient laughs.) Anyway, I
would never do that.

Therapist: And what would Jonathan do after he was
done fainting? He'd pick himself up off the
floor—and then what?

Patient: I don't know; I really can't think about it. I
guess he'd argue a lot and give me reasons
why I couldn't do it.

Therapist: And if you didn't participate in the old
fights? What if you respected his concerns
but stood behind your decision?

Patient: Well—I guess then he'd withdraw. He does

| | that when he gets depressed and angry. He'd just get distant and sullen, and he might go around the house sulking. |

Therapist: What do *you* do when your husband sulks?

Patient: I sulk back and then I usually go after him to try to discuss it. I try to make him talk about it, and then he gets more furious at me for not leaving him alone.

Therapist: If you gave your husband some space to sulk without getting hostile or fighting with him, how long would you predict he would stay depressed and sulky?

Patient: I really couldn't say.

Therapist: A week? Two months? Three years?

Patient: Well, I'd say maybe a couple of weeks. I mean I don't think he'd get really seriously depressed.

Therapist: Has Jonathan ever been seriously depressed?

Patient: Once, before we were married, he was engaged to this other woman and she broke off the engagement, like a month before they were supposed to get married. He got really depressed then because he went into the student hospital for I think about a week. But then he was okay and I really don't know that much about it.

Therapist: Would you say that Jonathan has a pretty intense reaction to loss? That loss or separation is a tough issue for him?

Patient: Yes, very. He's had a lot of losses in his life. People dying and things.

Therapist: If you were to return to graduate school now and moved ahead with your career, would that be a loss? Might that feel like another loss to Jonathan?

Patient: Well, I don't know. (Silence.) It would certainly be a loss of the old bitchy, nagging me! (Patient laughs.) Well, I guess ... I mean, I'm sure he could handle it. I don't think he'd really fall apart. I mean, I certainly don't think we'd end up divorced or anything.

The foregoing fragments of dialogue are illustrative of the early clinical process in which I elicited Ms. J.'s beliefs and observations about how her moves toward and away from graduate school would affect her husband and the marital relationship. Partly as a consequence of such questioning, Ms. J.'s rigid externalizing stance gradually softened.

Session 15

Patient: You know, last night I found myself fighting again with Jonathan and I just got a totally helpless—or maybe hopeless—feeling like this could go on forever. I mean, by the time Cara is in school we'll probably have another baby on the way and it will be the same thing. And I'll just be there yelling at him, saying the same old lines, and be just as stuck as ever. (Ms. J.'s labeling herself as "stuck" represents a significant shift from her initial blaming position.)

Therapist: Well, you surely have a very difficult dilemma on your hands—a dilemma that has no easy or painless solution.

Patient: How do you mean?

Therapist: I suspect that if you move ahead with graduate school, you may, as a consequence, feel quite guilty and uncertain. Such an act might make you feel disloyal to your husband, and you might worry about how Jonathan would react to such a big change. We've seen how sensitive you are to Jonathan's ups and downs and how you fight with him when you get concerned about his potential for depression. (This interpretation was based on data collected in additional sessions and was later linked to the patient's role in her own family of origin as the rescuer of her mother.) On the other hand, if you continue to sacrifice your own ambitions and goals, you may keep the marital boat calm, but you may pay the price of feeling bitter, resentful, and depressed.

Patient: (Silence.) Well, yes, I know that. That's nothing new. That's what got me in here to begin with. (Silence.) I know that hundreds of other women have the same problem. I mean, it's really a common problem.

Therapist: I guess it's safe to say that you're not the first woman in the twentieth century to struggle with such a dilemma. (Patient laughs.) Does knowing that you're not alone, and that you have good reason to be struggling with this problem, help you feel better about your situation?

Patient: Yes, it really does. But I still don't know what to do. I feel like I'm damned if I do and damned if I don't.

Therapist: Well, what kind of damnation do you prefer? Do you prefer putting yourself first and feeling selfish and guilty? Or do you prefer sacrificing your personal goals and priorities and feeling bitter and depressed?

Patient: (Patient smiles.) Definitely the second one. Oh, well, I don't know. I mean the second one is more familiar. (Silence.) But what I'm thinking about is what if I went ahead with graduate school and I didn't like it, or maybe I wouldn't do that well . . .

Therapist: Well, I suppose one advantage of continuing the old fights with Jonathan is that you'll never have the chance to test yourself out there. Going back to school would put you to the test, wouldn't it?

Patient: I've always done well in school. I have nothing to be worried about. But it's been a while. (Silence.) Sometimes I worry that all this time at home with Cara may have turned my brains into mush—like that saying, "If you don't use it, you lose it." (Patient continues to talk about her self-doubts and anxieties about studying for a higher degree.)

The foregoing sequence of events is predictable; that is, if the therapist can help a female patient bring to consciousness and articulate concerns about the impact of her growth on her marriage (and other important relationships), the patient herself will begin to broaden her perspective and examine her own anxiety about change. On the other hand, an interpretation that casts a negative connotation on the patient's focus on external obstacles might heighten resistance and preclude mutual appreciation of the powerful covert injunctions against change that characterize the systems in which many women operate. *When faced with the choice (in fantasy or reality) of sacrificing the self to preserve a relationship, or strengthening the self at the risk of threatening a relationship, women often choose the former.* In Ms. J.'s case, her husband did become depressed and symptomatic when she stopped fighting and moved full-speed ahead with her career plans. Predictably, a new level of marital conflict emerged as Ms. J. moved out of her role of the nagging and bitchy, yet accommodating, partner and began to operate from a higher level of assertiveness and differentiation. Ms. J. was able to manage well in the marital arena following therapeutic work that focused on her family of origin.

THE MOTHER–DAUGHTER DYAD IN CONTEXT

Initial inquiry regarding how family members had responded to the patient's ambitions and achievements elicited an almost exclusive focus on Ms. J.'s widowed mother, Lillie. According to the patient, Lillie's contradictory messages about her daughter's achievements were captured by the following folk poem Ms. J. carried in her wallet.

Mother, may I go out to swim?
Yes, my darling daughter.
Hang your clothes on a hickory limb
And don't go near the water.

According to Ms. J. her mother's ambivalent attitudes were readily identifiable. "Be independent!" her mother would say—but then, "Be like me!" or even, "Be for me!" was the contradictory message. "Be successful!" was one communication, but then Lillie would subtly ignore or undermine her daughter's successes. As Ms. J. explained, "When I graduated from college with honors, my mother got a migraine headache and missed the ceremony. When I told her I was thinking about getting my master's degree, she told me about a friend's daughter who just got into medical school. Now I tell her nothing. She really doesn't want to hear it."

The theme is a familiar, if not a universal, one. A mother who has been blocked from her own self-development and growth may ignore or devalue her daughter's competence, or she may do the opposite and encourage her daughter to be a "special" or "gifted" child whose successes the mother will vicariously enjoy. During the initial stage of treatment, Ms. J. was unable to reflect on her relationship with her mother with any degree of psychological mindedness because of the intensity of her emotional reactivity. The patient was locked into a rigid, blaming position toward her mother that was similar to her stance with her husband. This entrenched position served to hold the clock still and to maintain a fused, hostile-dependent tie between mother and daughter. Because the level of differentiation in a marital relationship is the same as that achieved in one's family of origin, the striking parallels between the patient's relationship with her mother and that with her husband were hardly surprising. Ms. J.'s marital pattern of alternating blame and accommodation mirrored aspects of her relationship with her mother, who she simultaneously fought with and protected through the sacrifice of her own personal growth.

If left to her own devices, Ms. J. would have spent countless therapeutic hours reciting her mother's crime sheet, thus inviting me to form a triangle in which patient–therapist closeness would operate at the mother's expense, with Lillie (like Jonathan) in the role of the outsider or the one to blame. Ms. J. also resisted examining her own part in maintaining these interactions, and she clung to the perception that her mother (again, like her husband) had "caused" her pains and problems (a perspective which, unfortunately, countless therapists share). As in her marriage, the patient's rage was partially an outgrowth of the sacrifices she herself made to preserve the fusion with her mother and thus to protect her mother from experiencing envious and competitive feelings. Ms. J. feared that not only her husband but also her mother would be hurt and threatened by her success. In addition, Ms. J.'s experience of her mother (at first unconscious) was that of a jealous, unfulfilled individual who would be further depleted and depressed if her daughter moved toward greater autonomy and professional growth.

Like many women, Ms. J. adopted a compromise solution to the difficult challenge of differentiation by transferring dependency from her mother to her husband. The financial and psychological "separateness" which Ms. J. associated with a more serious work commitment frightened her because it challenged the old mother–daughter enmeshment and stirred unconscious fears about the loss of this important bond. In earlier papers (Lerner 1979, 1980) I have elaborated on this theme, describing the special difficulties the daughter may encounter in expressing her separateness and difference from her mother. Such difficulties should not be reified as a "natural" or inherent aspect of the mother–daughter relationship, for what is seen clinically are distortions of this bond, stemming from dysfunctional family and cultural patterns. Also of significance are the special difficulties faced by Ms. J.'s generation of adult women as they strive to become more ambitious and self-seeking, thus challenging a long tradition of female selflessness, self-sacrifice, and service (Chernin 1985).

Profound anxiety and guilt are the legacy of women who strive to have for themselves what the previous generations of women could not; such reactions deserve the most careful therapeutic exploration. Psychodynamic work that narrowly focuses on transference phenomena and on interpretation of the internalized drama with the preoedipal or oedipal mother is neither sufficient nor effective enough to help women identify and overcome the enormous guilt (often obscured by anger and blame) that blocks them from conflict-free participation in their careers. In the following pages, I will focus selectively on areas of clinical intervention that relate to a phenomenon I call *multigenerational guilt*, paying particular attention to helping patients address important emotional issues at their source— that is, with members of the patient's own nuclear and extended family.

MULTIGENERATIONAL GUILT

Underlying Ms. J.'s chronic complaints about her mother was a deep well of guilt and a strong sense of family loyalty that blocked the patient's path to professional self-fulfillment. This guilt, not consciously available early in treatment nor analyzable in the usual psychoanalytic terms, was associated with the patient's vague sense of the hardship, deprivation, and unfulfilled longing of the previous generations of women in her family. Multigenerational guilt is particularly intense in situations in which the parents or grandparents have immigrated—a traumatic event that involves the massive loss of relationships and the disruption of emotional ties, which are organizing factors in women's identities and lives.

Contemporary women who strive to enter what was, for their mothers, a man's world are, not surprisingly, having difficulty breaking away from old patterns. Embracing privileges and challenges that separate them from the female traditions of the past is not easy or without conflict for these women. What merits special therapeutic attention, however, is how to help women gather the facts of their own multigenerational histories so they may begin formulating a clearer perspective about their anxiety and guilt toward work in this context. This requires slow and careful therapeutic work, because of the patients' intense resistance to reconnecting with their family members in order to gather data about their lives; the degree of anxiety is in direct proportion to the amount of fusion (or its flip side, distance and disengagement) in the family relationships.

Using questioning techniques from Bowen family systems theory (Bowen 1978, Kerr 1981), I asked Ms. J. about her family, gradually allowing her to step out of a linear blaming stance toward her mother and to adopt a more thoughtful approach about the context in which the subject of achievement and career had become a "hot issue" between them. During the first year of psychotherapy, the patient had a virtual allergy to her own family history. The following is illustrative:

Session 20

Patient: My mother is just amazing . . . I mean she just has never given me credit for anything. Last week I substituted in a class and I just got inspired. Kids usually hate substitute teachers, but I designed a game to teach them grammar, and they just loved it. (Patient goes on to describe a highly creative and innovative approach.) Anyway, that night my mother called and I told her about it. I mentioned that if I went back to graduate school maybe I could do a thesis on this subject and really develop the ideas. So, do you know what she did? She changed the subject. She immediately began to talk about how my sister is depressed again.

Therapist: What did you say to her then?

Patient: I dropped it. It's impossible. I'm not going to set myself up to be insulted.

Therapist: Is that the typical pattern when this subject comes up? Does your mother react by distancing and then you distance as well?

Patient:	I learned a long time ago to just forget it. (Patient elaborates at length on mother's insensitivity and critical nature.)
Therapist:	What's your perspective on your mother's reaction? (Silence.) How do you understand that sharing your excitement about your work is not a calm, neutral subject?
Patient:	I don't know. I have no idea.
Therapist:	What do you know about your mother's own family that might give you some perspective on her reaction?
Patient:	Well, I just don't know. She's just critical of me. She's never treated me as if I had very much in the brains department. (Patient points to her head.)
Therapist:	How did your granny (patient's maternal grandmother) react to your mom's achievements and to her competence and skills?
Patient:	Who knows? I only know they fought a lot.
Therapist:	Does your mother think she has much in the brains department, in her mother's and father's eyes?
Patient:	I don't know—only her brothers went to college, not the girls. I don't really know anything about it or about how granny saw my mother, in terms of brains and stuff.
Therapist:	Would your mother have wanted more education, if that had been possible for her?
Patient:	I doubt it. I don't know. We don't talk about things like that. And I wouldn't talk to her about it either. We don't discuss things. You don't know my mother.

In fact, Ms. J. herself did not know her mother. Only slowly, over time, did the patient begin to experience Lillie as a separate individual whose behavior and reactions could be understood in the context of her own family. This occurred through the use of a genogram (see Diagram 1) and by continued questioning about the extended family according to Bowen's well-developed family systems theory (Bowen 1978, Kerr 1981).

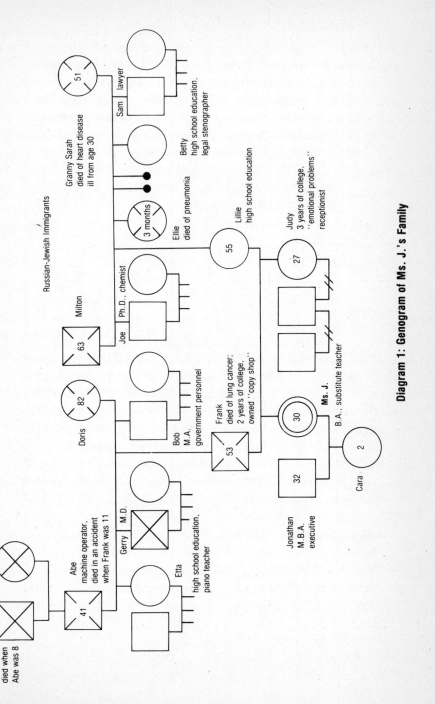

Diagram 1: Genogram of Ms. J.'s Family

MOTHER'S FAMILY

Ms. J.'s mother was the second child and first daughter of Russian-Jewish immigrant parents for whom the education of sons was the highest priority. Lillie's entrance into the family was followed by the loss of an infant girl from pneumonia and two subsequent miscarriages, before the birth of the two surviving siblings. When Ms. J. mobilized the courage to talk with her mother rather than just react to her, she learned not only about the impact of these losses, but also that as the oldest female child, Lillie's considerable competence and sense of responsibility were channeled into caring for her brothers and sister. Lillie did an enormous amount of mothering while she was growing up and she reported that she did so willingly and without protest, partly filling in for her own mother, who was in poor health for much of her adult life. Although Lillie graduated second in her high school class, financial resources were scarce and only the boys were able to go to college, with the help of Lillie, who contributed to her brothers' education from her own wages.

As Ms. J. began to view her relationship with her mother through a wide-angle lens, she became more thoughtful about her work dilemma and her available options. After ten months of psychotherapy, Ms. J. was calmer and more assertive in her marriage, and she had enthusiastically filled out an application to graduate school. Once accepted by the school, however, her anxiety skyrocketed and she temporarily reinstated the old patterns of nonproductive fighting with her husband and cold withdrawal from her mother, both of whom were also reacting with anxiety to Ms. J.'s new decision and to the higher level of assertiveness she was manifesting. According to her report, her husband became more preoccupied with work at the expense of their family, and her mother increased her worried focus on Ms. J.'s younger sister. At this point, I asked Ms. J. about the pros and cons of talking openly and directly with her mother concerning the patient's own fears about graduate school. In my clinical experience, such a dialogue serves to detoxify an underlying conflict within the relationship system, where it is more intensely colored by mutual projections. Predictably, the patient's reaction was negative.

Session 46

Patient: I would never tell my mother my problems. There's no point to it. My mother won't change.

Therapist: I would surely agree that there would be no point in trying to change your mother. I've been in this business a long time and I've never been able to change anyone's mother. (Patient laughs.) I'm talking about what it would be like for you to be able to be clear with her about an important problem that you are struggling with.

Patient: What problem?

Therapist: That with graduate school, part of you says "go!" and another part says "no!" That when it comes to the question of career, you've felt pretty stuck for a long time.

Patient: If I told her, she would get defensive and feel like I was blaming her for doing something wrong.

Therapist: That's a good point. What if you clearly told her that this was your problem—that you are sharing it to let her know something important about yourself, and perhaps to get her perspective on it?

Patient: She'd tell me what to do, like she does with Judy (Ms. J.'s younger sister). She'd play therapist, and one therapist is more than enough. (Therapist laughs.)

Therapist: So your mother is a fix-it person? (Patient smiles and nods affirmatively.) When you have a problem she gets anxious and rushes in to rescue or give advice?

Patient: That's right. And the last thing I need is advice, or her worrying over what I'm worrying about.

Therapist: And then you would worry about her worrying over what you're worrying about? (Patient laughs.) So it's like when one of you itches, the other scratches. . . . (Patient interrupts to give examples of her mother's intrusiveness.)

Therapist:	What if you could say to your mother that you aren't asking for advice—not even good advice—but that you are more interested in learning her perspective about how other women in the family have struggled with similar dilemmas, or how others in the family, herself included, struggle with balancing family responsibilities with their own personal goals?
Patient:	It's just something I would never do.

Over the next several months of psychotherapy, I did not encourage the patient to act, but I did continue to explore and analyze aspects of mother–daughter fusion as well as the related issue of Ms. J.'s internal prohibitions against sharing with her mother her vulnerable, dependent, or underfunctioning side. Later I tentatively suggested that there might be some advantages for the patient if she could more clearly define herself within her family of origin and could openly share important emotional issues in her life. Because the patient now had a less reactive and more thoughtful attitude toward relating to her mother, I also shared my own thoughts (derived from clinical findings of family systems theory) about how she might approach her mother. My use of Bowen coaching within psychodynamic work derives from my conviction that projections and distorted internal object representations are not fully resolved through the transference relationship; instead, resolving such issues requires considerable direct work within the family system, including helping the patient to gather family facts that relate to salient conflicts and later to reconnect with family members around emotionally important issues.

Although the patient's new behavior with her mother proved to be one of several important turning points in the therapy, certain interactions could not have occurred early in the treatment. Only after the patient had gained sufficient insight into family patterns and her own part in them was it possible for Ms. J. to approach her mother in a calm manner that did not further escalate the already high level of anxiety between them.

With the help of therapy, Ms. J. engaged her mother for the first time in a discussion of her work problem, validating Lillie as a woman who could help her daughter by sharing more about herself. Ms. J. said, "You know, mother, I've been fighting with Jonathan about the graduate school business, but I'm beginning to recognize that I have mixed feelings about it myself. I want to go ahead and have the best career possible, but I think I'm also scared to death. I'm not asking you for answers or advice, because I have to make my own decision in the end. But it would be very helpful to me to hear more about your perspective and experience." The patient asked her mother whether she had ever experienced a similar problem, how other women in the family had balanced work and family, and whether her mother had any thoughts about Ms. J.'s problem.

In later conversations, Ms. J. asked additional questions about her mother's family in order to learn more about important themes regarding women and work in the previous generations.

- How did your mother and father react to your talents and achievements?
- Were you seen as smart in your family?
- What about your sister?
- Did you ever think about going to college?
- What was your parents' attitude about that?
- If you had started a career early in life, what would have been your first choice?
- Do you think you would have been successful at it?
- What might have stood in your way?
- How was it decided that your brothers were able to go to college and your weren't?
- What are your feelings about that?
- What was it like for you to have so much responsibility in your family as you were growing up?
- Did Granny have any special talents or ambitions?

Ms. J. was surprised by her mother's growing eagerness to talk about her past. In my experience, family members, including the most dysfunctional of parents, usually do want to share their experiences if the patient first shares a current struggle and expresses a sincere wish to learn more about how other members of the family have experienced and managed similar problems. Lillie revealed to her daughter that she once had her heart set on being an English teacher, but this goal was eclipsed by her responsibility for others in her first family, and later in her second. She also told the patient that her mother, Granny Sarah, had been a skilled dressmaker who had dreamed until her death of opening a small shop, although she recognized the impossibility of this dream. Granny did sell a few items from her home, and Lillie had several pieces of Granny's handiwork that she showed to her daughter for the first time. Ms. J. also learned that she (Ms. J.) was the only married woman on her mother's side of the family (cousins included) who was trying to achieve an advanced degree.

I believe that the patient sensed all of this information in a vague, preconscious way, but the impact of openly discussing these facts with her mother was a pivotal point in the process of change. First Ms. J. gained a reality-oriented and empathic understanding of her mother's ambivalent attitude toward Ms. J.'s ambitions and achievements, which reminded her mother of what she and her own mother (Sarah) could not have. This understanding was not merely an intellectual task but rather an anxiety-provoking move toward greater differentiation, as Ms. J. began to experience Lillie as a separate and different "other" with a personal history of her own. Ms. J. then began to experience a previously unacknowledged guilt and "funny depression" associated with her personal ambitions and self-seeking strivings as key women on her family tree became real persons to her, whose lives, far more difficult than her own, she was just beginning to imagine. She also gained a better understanding of how stressful it is to be a pioneer. A year and a half into therapy, Ms. J. commented, "No one here (pointing to her mother's side of the genogram) has had both a family and a real career for several hundred years. Why should I be the first one?" I agreed with her that it was difficult to be a pioneer without making apologies to the important women who came before her.

At this point in treatment, Ms. J. was starting her first year of graduate school. She was, however, having difficulty allowing herself to enjoy the program. Following a meeting with a teacher who told Ms. J. that her thought-provoking term paper would be distributed to her classmates, Ms. J. engaged in an episode of potentially serious acting out (speeding through a red light). I interpreted this self-sabotaging act as a reflection of Ms. J.'s guilt (and her related unconscious fear of incurring the envy of others) and as an effort to apologize to the previous generations of women. I tentatively suggested that she share her conflict with her mother, and I explained that openly sharing a problem at its source, rather than unconsciously acting it out, might help her proceed more clearly and thoughtfully with her dilemma. I also helped her clarify her thoughts about how to share her own problem with her mother without communicating that she was holding Lillie responsible for it.

Perhaps Ms. J.'s most courageous moment during our three years of working together came when she was able to detoxify the issue of mother–daughter competition in a direct yet nonblaming fashion. According to the patient's report, she said, "You know, Mother, this may sound kind of crazy, but as I learn more about myself in therapy, I realize that I'm scared and guilty about being successful. There is a part of me that feels guilty or worried about having opportunities that bright and competent women like you and your own mother were not able to have. You've shared that you are satisfied with your choices and that you like your life as it is. But I still feel funny about allowing myself to have what my own mother and grandmother could not have—even if you had wanted it. And you're so bright and competent that sometimes I can't help but think what a fantastic teacher you would have been if you had gone in that direction."

In response to Ms. J.'s self-disclosure, Lillie looked puzzled. She shook her head and said, "Well, that doesn't make much sense to me." Then she changed the subject. A week later, however, her mother phoned to announce that she had just signed up for a college course and was wondering whether to audit it or take it for credit. "Goodness knows why I'm doing something like this at my age!" Lillie said. When Ms. J. got off the phone, she felt an unexpected surge of love for her mother, and burst into tears without knowing why.

Although Lillie predictably made changes in response to her daughter's new ability to move differently in their relationship, her flexibility for change is not a significant aspect of this case. Of importance was Ms. J.'s own ability to learn about multigenerational patterns, to define herself clearly with her mother (and eventually with others in the family as well) around work issues, and to unearth underlying conflicts to allow for the correction of primitive projections and distortions at their emotional source. These accomplishments detoxified much of the anxiety surrounding career issues and allowed for a lessening of fusion and emotional intensity in the mother–daughter dyad.

The Father-Daughter Dyad in Context

A year after Ms. J.'s marriage to Jonathan, her father died. The patient minimized the emotional impact of this loss by focusing on the long-standing distance and disinterest that had characterized their relationship and which had become especially pronounced when she was 11 years old. Although communication had rarely been openly intense or conflictual, Ms. J. blamed her father for his emotional unavailability, and she initially viewed him as unilaterally causing the distance between them.

Within this context of emotionally distant relatedness, the patient's father, Frank, had quietly encouraged Ms. J.'s intellectual development and school performance. During the process of therapy, Ms. J. recalled her father's high standards for grades ("Nothing less than an A would do") and the many times he encouraged her to higher achievements. When Ms. J. was 9 years old, for example, she watched with interest a television program about surgery. Following the show her father said, "You can be a surgeon if you really want to be one," and several days later he brought her a library book for young readers describing various specialties of medicine. That evening her mother angrily criticized him for choosing a book that was too difficult for someone their daughter's age. An escalating fight ensued, followed by a bitter withdrawal of both spouses. At this time Ms. J. retreated to her room; she never opened the book.

Both parents conveyed considerable anxiety about father and daughter navigating a person-to-person relationship without the mother in the middle. Further, Ms. J. felt puzzled and anxious by her father's communications that she should "be someone" when he obviously did not have similar aspirations for his wife. "He wanted me to really use everything that I had, but if my mother had taken a job at Burger King, that would have been fine with him. I remember many times when he put her down intellectually in front of other people, and I used to get angry at her that she would just take it."

For Ms. J., intellectual and professional strivings were unconsciously equated with a move toward, and closer identification with, her father. This, in itself, would not have been problematic, except for Ms. J.'s unconscious conviction that such a move would threaten the crucial mother–daughter bond. While multiple factors evoked and maintained this paradigm, I want to stress that oedipal issues are only one piece of the complex nature of triangles and covert coalitions in human systems. The mutually reinforcing reciprocal pattern of overly intense mothering and overly distant fathering that, over time, becomes increasingly entrenched is a natural outgrowth of structural aspects of the traditional nuclear family. As the patient herself once said, "My father had his work and his children but my mother had only her two girls." Even as a young child, Ms. J. sensed that her mother would feel threatened and betrayed if Ms. J. moved closer to her father and that her father would feel anxious and at a loss.

While mutual distancing between father and daughter diminished family anxiety, this solution blocked Ms. J. from achieving a comfortable and conflict-free integration of career-related strivings, which she unconsciously viewed as masculine. Female patients often must deal with intrapsychic, familial, and cultural factors that combine to reinforce the conviction that serious work is something "men do." At the same time, family roles and rules over several generations have often fostered a triangle in which men in general, and fathers in particular, are distant and shadowy figures—larger than life, yet emotionally incompetent and taboo as objects for emotional relatedness and identification.

FATHER'S FAMILY

Ms. J. resisted constructing a genogram for her father's side of the family because it challenged her to think about him as a person rather than as a figure defined by family myths and the patient's own unconscious anxieties, wishes, and projections. At the same time, the multigenerational perspective helped Ms. J. view her father with greater clarity, objectivity, and caring. For example, gathering family facts provided Ms. J. with a new context in which to understand her father's retreat from parenting. During preadolescence, Frank had lost his own father in an accident, a loss connected with Frank's withdrawal from his daughter when she reached age 11. Ms. J. also learned that at the age of 8, her grandfather had lost his father. Knowing that two generations of sons had lost their fathers helped Ms. J. understand that her father's distance from her was an expression of anxiety rather than a lack of love.

Therapeutic questioning and intervention helped Ms. J. identify how all family members played a part in maintaining her father's distance and helped her examine her own deep-seated anxiety and guilt about navigating an emotionally closer relationship with him. Helping the patient reexamine this relationship and reconnect with her father's side of the family was a crucial aspect of treatment because Ms. J.'s work inhibitions were partially fueled by an incomplete and unresolved mourning process, and by a key family triangle in which she and her mother had an intense (albeit conflictual) relationship, with her father in a distant, outside position with both women.

A critical point in the treatment occurred when Ms. J. was able to open up the lines of communication with her father's two surviving siblings to gather information on the subject of work and career in the previous generations and, more specifically, to inquire about her father's own work history and experience. Through letters and visits, Ms. J. shared a bit about her own struggles and asked Frank's siblings (Ms. J.'s aunt and uncle) many questions that allowed her grandfather, her father, and his siblings, to further emerge as real persons whose struggles with work and career were both similar to and different from her own.

Before this time, the patient had manifested a number of work-related symptoms, frequently viewed in the psychoanalytic literature as expressions of penis envy. These symptoms included a fear of being discovered as fraudulent; uncertainty about her accomplishments despite considerable proven ability; the conviction that she was lacking an element essential to securing her success; and a sense of inferiority to men, whom she saw as magically free of the work-related anxieties and conflicts that troubled her. These symptoms, all of which were partially derived from the patient's mystification and masculinization of work-related pursuits, lessened dramatically as Ms. J. persisted in establishing an emotional connection with her father's side of the family, replaced fantasy with more factual data about the legacy of work and career in the male line, and made small but significant moves to challenge a long-standing multigenerational pattern of emotional distancing in the father–daughter relationship.

Not surprisingly, Ms. J. experienced a reactivation of painful affects surrounding her father's death that had been held in check by the emotional cut-off from her father's family. Her father's family had always been "of lesser importance," as Ms. J. put it, and her ties to these relatives had been superficial at best and almost nonexistent since her father's funeral. The act of talking about her father within the context of his own family stirred in her feelings of missing him, and also evoked a deep sadness about the lost opportunity to know him better. It also brought to consciousness a previously inarticulated sense of guilt that she was hurting her mother by openly acknowledging her father's importance and by independently moving toward establishing her own relationships with members of his family. Thus, previously unconscious mental contents emerged full force and became accessible for further therapeutic work.

Women's difficulties with work and career have their roots in early relationship paradigms as well as in the roles, rules, and structures of the current family and work systems in which women operate (Ulrich and Dunne, 1986). As noted earlier, I have not attempted to summarize the multiplicity of factors that combine to make the road to intellectual and professional fulfillment an especially difficult one for women, nor is it possible here to convey the complexity of clinical theory and technique derived from a family systems perspective. Rather, the treatment fragments described in this chapter illustrate my psychodynamic understanding of female work inhibitions in a particular patient, and reflect my conviction that unconscious conflicts and distorted internalized object representations derived from dysfunctional patterns at any developmental stage cannot be fully resolved unless they are renegotiated within the intense emotional field of actual family relationships.

REFERENCES

Applegarth, A. (1976). Some observations on work inhibitions in women. *Journal of the American Psychoanalytic Association* 24(Suppl.): 251–268.

Bowen, M. (1978). *Family Therapy in Clinical Practice.* New York: Jason Aronson.

Chernin, K. (1985). *The Hungry Self: Women, Eating and Identity.* New York: Harper & Row.

GAP, Committee on the College Student (1975). *The Educated Woman: Prospects and Problems* 9(92).

Horner, M. (1972). The motive to avoid success and changing aspirations of college women. In *Readings on the Psychology of Women,* ed. J. Bardwick, pp. 62–67. New York: Harper & Row.

Kanter, R. M. (1977). *Men and Women of the Corporation.* New York: Basic Books.

Kerr, M. E. (1981). Family systems theory and therapy. In *Handbook of Family Therapy*, ed. A. S. Gurman and D. P. Kniskern, pp. 226–264. New York: Brunner/Mazel.

Krueger, D. W. (1984). *Success and the Fear of Success in Women*. New York: The Free Press.

Lerner, H. G. (1979). Effects of the nursing mother–infant dyad on the family. *American Journal of Orthopsychiatry* 49:339–348.

—— (1980). Internal prohibitions against female anger. *American Journal of Psychoanalysis* 40:137–148.

—— (1983). Female dependency in context: some theoretical and technical considerations. *American Journal of Orthopsychiatry* 53:697–705.

—— (1985). *The Dance of Anger: A Woman's Guide to Changing the Patterns of Intimate Relationships*. New York: Harper & Row.

Lerner, S., and Lerner, H. G. (1983). A systemic approach to resistance: theoretical and technical considerations. *American Journal of Psychotherapy* 37:387–399.

Moulton, R. (1985). The effect of the mother on the success of the daughter. *Contemporary Psychoanalysis* 21:266–283.

Nadelson, C. C., Notman, M. T., and Bennett, M. B. (1978). Success or failure: psychotherapeutic considerations for women in conflict. *American Journal of Psychiatry* 135:1092–1096.

Person, E. S. (1982). Women working: Fears of failure, deviance, and success. *Journal of the American Academy of Psychoanalysis* 10:67–84.

Stiver, I. P. (1983). *Work Inhibitions in Women*. Wellesley, Mass.: Stone Center for Developmental Services and Studies.

Ulrich, D. N., and Dunne, H. P. (1986). *To Love and Work: A Systemic Interlocking of Family, Workplace, and Career*. New York: Brunner/Mazel.

Chapter 13
Depression

Depression is one form of emotional reactivity associated with loss.[1] This chapter will address female depression as it relates to a particular aspect of loss that occurs as women betray or sacrifice the self in order to preserve relationship harmony. In attempting to navigate the delicate balance between the "I" and the "we," women frequently sacrifice the "I" in the service of togetherness, thus assuming a de-selfed position in relationships. Depression may result from the sacrifice of self and the concomitant loss of self-esteem which accompanies the unconscious awareness of self-betrayal.

Excessive self-sacrifice, or de-selfing, occurs when one participates in relationship patterns that block one's own growth or when too much of the self (one's beliefs, values, wants, priorities, ambitions) becomes negotiable under relationship pressures. The de-selfing process begins in the family of origin and is continued most conspicuously in women's relationships with men. In previous work, I have illustrated the complex pressures on women to assume such a position in adult heterosexual relationships and the powerful intrapsychic, familial, and cultural forces that mitigate against change (Lerner 1983, 1985).

---

[1]This chapter was first published in 1987 as "Female Depression: Self-sacrifice and Self-betrayal in Relationships" in *Women and Depression: A Lifespan Perspective*, ed. A. Gurian and P. Formanek, pp. 220–221. New York: Springer.

The following clinical example depicts how female depression is inextricably interwoven with the sacrifice of self that occurs in key relationships and the related fear of object loss. The conceptual links among depression, anger, and women's "relationship orientation" will also be clarified.

A CASE HISTORY: MS. R.

Ms. R., a 35-year-old homemaker with 10-year-old twin girls and a 4-year-old son, sought psychotherapy for depression and marital unhappiness. She had deliberately selected a therapist with a feminist orientation, and she arrived at her first session complaining of her husband's chauvinist attitudes and outrageous deeds. Her own part in the marital drama was a common one for women: She complained about her husband and blamed him for her unhappiness, but nonetheless accommodated to his demands and remained profoundly resistant to examining and modifying her own position in the relationship.

Ms. R.'s symptomatic depression was associated with her experience of being caught in a very narrow space in which she could not move. The circumstances of her marriage were so intolerable to her that she could no longer continue in the old ways; yet she would not even consider the possibility that she wanted out. She was not ready to face the risk of putting her husband and herself to the test of whether change was possible and she had already convinced herself that the relationship could not tolerate much change. She was unable to say to herself, "I am choosing to stay in this unhappy marriage," nor could she clarify her bottom line and say, "If these things do not change, I will leave."

Ms. R.'s depression placed her in the role of the "sick one" and obscured the marital issues, yet it also served as an indictment of the system in which she was operating, drawing attention to its unworkable nature. It paradoxically served to both protect and protest the status quo, forcing change while holding the clock still. For example, the severity of her symptom undermined her competence to manage her home and children, and thus allowed her to go on strike against her "sacred calling," which she was unable to protest more directly. Her husband, who had formerly avoided all family responsibility, now put the children to bed at night and occasionally made their breakfast in the morning, because otherwise these tasks would not be done. He did so, however, to fill in for his dysfunctional wife, and not because Ms. R. had openly challenged the old rules of the relationship by clarifying her own needs and redefining what she would and would not do.

For many women, depression serves to bind anger and obscure its sources, allowing these women to deny marital difficulties entirely and maintain a singleminded focus on the question "What's wrong with me?" In Ms. R.'s case, however, her depression did not block her from experiencing and expressing rage at her spouse. Yet she protected both of them from the threat of serious dialogue by venting her anger in a manner that would invite him to ignore her or write her off as irrational, hysterical, or sick. For example, Ms. R. was furious with her husband for his condescending and patronizing treatment of her. When she finally addressed this issue with him, she "lost control" of herself and began yelling hysterically, thus confirming that she was, indeed, the weak and irrational child he needed her to be. Her husband listened coolly to her outburst and then sympathetically asked her whether she had taken her medication that day. Therapeutic exploration revealed that Ms. R. was afraid to state her position in a way that would ensure that she could not so easily be written off. She preferred to be in the one-down position, rather than to put her husband on the spot by identifying her dissatisfaction in a firm, calm, and articulate manner and insisting on real dialogue. She was unconsciously convinced that her husband could tolerate only an accommodating child-wife, and she was correct. When, later in treatment, Ms. R. began to function at a higher level of self-assertion and maturity, her husband distanced, had an affair, and threatened to dissolve the marriage.

For Ms. R., as for many women, remaining the sick one or the depressed one was easier than clarifying the sources of her dissatisfaction and moving out of a de-selfed position. This is not because she gained masochistic gratification from being in a victimized or abused position, but because she was unconsciously convinced that her most important relationship could survive only if she continued to maintain the status quo. To become clearer, to act stronger, to be more separate, assertive, and self-directed were all equated with a castrating, destructive act that would diminish and threaten her partner, who might then retaliate or leave. This unconscious belief is common, if not universal, for women (Lerner 1980, 1983, 1985).

Although she had not consciously articulated her dilemma for herself, Ms. R. was convinced that she had to choose between having a marriage and having a self. Rather than encourage her in a particular direction, therapeutic work on the marital relationship involved systemic questioning, which helped Ms. R. to identify the systems-maintaining function of her depressed stance and the positive, protective function that it served for both herself and her husband. The actual and fantasized risks of moving out of a de-selfed position were explored as carefully as were the costs of maintaining sameness.

During the early phase of therapeutic work, it was crucial that I appreciated the fact that making waves in her marriage was not an option for Ms. R., as she equated aloneness with psychological and even physical death. This high level of anxiety had its roots in her difficulty in achieving separateness and autonomy from her first family, as well as in problems evoked and maintained by the institution of marriage. Ms. R. had spent years cloistered in the home and had no marketable skills, few support systems, and little confidence that she could provide for herself and her children in the case of divorce. The loss of her husband threatened her not only with a loss of identity but also with the actual loss of economic security and social status. Although she possessed considerable internal strengths and resources, they were obscured from her experience, in part, by entrenched dysfunctional marital patterns in which she occupied an underfunctioning position. Only after Ms. R. was confident that she could survive without her marriage was she able to move differently within it.

Self-sacrifice in the Family of Origin

To help Ms. R. more clearly define herself in her marriage and give voice to previously denied aspects of self, considerable therapeutic time was spent exploring her depression and patterns of self-sacrifice within the context of her first family. In previous work (Lerner 1979, 1980), I have suggested that a woman's de-selfed position in adult relationships is associated with an earlier de-selfing with mother; that is, daughters frequently thwart their own autonomy and growth, and sacrifice valued aspects of the self (e.g., ambition, sexuality, creativity, and zest) in order to protect a special bond with their mothers, who are unconsciously perceived as unable to tolerate the daughters' moves toward separateness and success. I have also stressed that such difficulties (which leave the woman vulnerable not only to depression but also to other symptoms and dysfunctional behaviors) are not an inherent or "natural" aspect of the mother–daughter relationship, but rather reflect larger systems issues, including the structuring of gender roles over many generations and women's subordinate status (Lerner 1978, 1987).

From my current perspective, however, this narrow theoretical and clinical focus on mothers (even when the role of culture is acknowledged) is problematic. On the one hand, the mother–daughter dyad is often the most intense and conflictual in the family. At the same time, this relationship cannot be isolated or understood apart from other family relationships or from multigenerational patterns that give shape and form to the family. Although many psychotherapists appreciate this systemic view in theory, they are often at a loss to put it into practice, especially when the patient's own focus on her mother is intense and other family members are presented as shadowy or unimportant. In my clinical experience, the use of the genogram and a multigenerational perspective helps clinicians put mothers and daughters back in context and mitigates against the tendency to overfocus on this dyad at the expense of exploring other interlocking family relationships. It is from this perspective that I will discuss historical facts and family patterns that were linked to Ms. R.'s self-sacrificing behaviors in her own family and ultimately to her de-selfed and depressed position in her marriage.

Ms. R.'s Family of Origin

Diagram 1 is a partial genogram of Mr. R.'s family of origin, collected during our initial meetings. The limited amount of family information included highlights key relationships, dates, and patterns associated with Ms. R.'s depression. Readers unfamiliar with the construction of a genogram should see S. Lerner (1984) and McGoldrick and Gerson (1985).[2]

As the genogram illustrates, Ms. R.'s entrance into the family was colored by loss. At the time of her birth, her mother (Mary) was still under the emotional sway of a second-trimester miscarriage that had occurred 15 months earlier. Ms. R.'s father's mother (Katherine) died from a protracted illness only weeks before Ms. R. was born, and her mother's father (Andrew) was killed in a car accident shortly after her first birthday. These three significant losses—a miscarriage and the deaths of two grandparents occurring around the time of Ms. R.'s birth and first year of life—influenced family relationships and intensified key family triangles linked to Ms. R.'s vulnerability to depression.

Ms. R.'s father, John, managed the powerful affects generated by his mother's death, coinciding in time with the arrival of his first child, by distancing from both his wife and new daughter. In addition to intensifying work-related pursuits, he became increasingly preoccupied with the well-being of his widowed father Joe, and his relationship with his oldest sister, Lois, became increasingly conflictual as they argued about issues surrounding their mother's death and their father's financial situation. The growing marital distance compounded Mary's sense of loss, and she became increasingly focused on,

---

[2]In a genogram, squares indicate males and circles, females. The horizontal line connecting a square and circle indicates a marriage. Children are drawn on vertical lines descending from the marriage line, in chronological order, beginning with the oldest on the left. An X inside a circle or square indicates that the person has died.

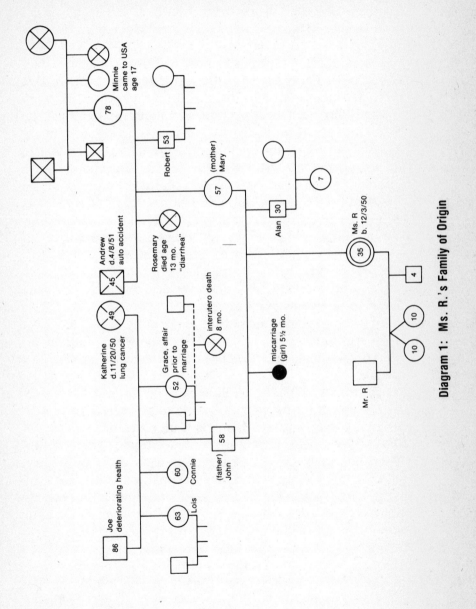

Diagram 1: Ms. R.'s Family of Origin

and protective of, her new daughter. As the genogram illustrates, the firstborn daughter in Mary's own sibling group (Rosemary) had died an untimely death, which undoubtedly further increased Mary's anxious preoccupation with her firstborn child.

Evidence of her mother's intense focus on Ms. R. was more than apparent. For example, until the birth of her brother Alan, she was frequently brought to sleep in her parents' bed when she fussed during the night. Mary's explanation for this practice was that Ms. R. was a fearful baby and child who "refused" to sleep alone when she was upset. John also participated in this arrangement, perhaps because the intensity of the mother–daughter dyad helped him maintain emotional distance from both females. John's withdrawal and Mary's focus on Ms. R. became fixed positions in this family. Ms. R. had once asked her mother whether she had ever considered working or having a career when she was younger; Mary had replied, "I would first be dead before I would leave my children with some stranger. And your father could never deal with you and Alan, so I had to be two parents in one."

This key triangle, consisting of distant father, a distant marital relationship, and overintensity between mother and daughter (see Diagram 2), became increasingly entrenched over time.

The arrows in Diagram 2 illustrate the circularity of family relationships. In other words, it is no more correct to suggest that her mother "caused" Ms. R.'s difficulties or father's outside position in the family than it is to say that her father "caused" her mother's overinvolvement with Ms. R. by creating an emotional vacuum in his relationships with both his daughter and his wife. Each side of the triangle is both the cause and the effect of the other two sides, and no family member, the mother included, has unidirectional power over the whole. The ability to fully appreciate the circular connectedness of family relationships helps the therapist avoid questions and interpretations that hold one family member implicitly responsible for another's symptoms and behaviors (Lerner and Lerner 1983).

After her marriage, Ms. R. participated in a similar triangle,

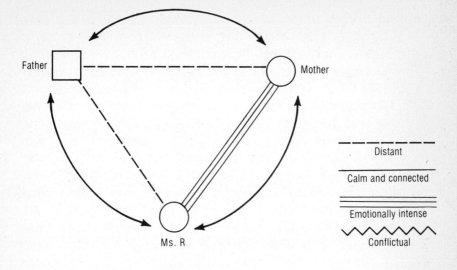

Diagram 2: Family Relationships

with her husband in the outside position. She frequently complained to her mother about her husband's domineering and unfair behavior in a manner that invited her mother to be her ally at the expense of both her marriage and her mother's relationship with her son-in-law. When marital tensions mounted between Ms. R. and her husband, she sometimes "disappeared" with her children to her parents' home. Mother went along with these disappearing acts (although there was no threat of violence), blaming Mr. R. for her daughter's difficulties and feigning ignorance when he telephoned looking for his wife and children. At these times, Ms. R.'s father managed his own anxiety through extreme emotional distancing. He did not ask his daughter why she and her children were temporarily camping out in their home, not did he clarify with either his wife or daughter his position regarding Ms. R.'s behavior and whether he was comfortable keeping such an important secret from his son-in-law. During these times, Ms. R. and her mother would have intense conversations about Ms. R.'s unhappy marriage; father would read in the next room, acting as if nothing was happening, solidifying his odd-man-out position in the family.

Although Ms. R. was not consciously sacrificing her own self to protect relationship ties in her family of origin, she nonetheless participated in patterns and triangles that thwarted her own growth and left her depressed. Her position in her family, as in her marriage, was an accommodating one in which she unconsciously went along with family roles and rules at the expense of differentiating a self. Much emotional energy went into being "for" her mother and protecting her father from dealing with emotional issues in his relationships with his wife and daughter. Like many daughters, Ms. R. had a radarlike sensitivity to underground issues in the family and unconsciously felt that significant changes on her part would threaten family stability and shatter the security of predictable family ties, including her parents' marriage and her fused relationship with her mother. She was also unconsciously aware of both of her parents' vulnerability to depression and of the important losses they each had suffered around the time of her entrance into the family.

In my clinical experience, therapeutic work derived from family systems theory (Bowen 1978) is especially useful in helping women to identify and move out of dysfunctional family patterns that contribute to de-selfing and depression in adulthood. One aspect of the work is gathering family facts, which allows the woman to put her current struggles and relationship patterns into a broader multigenerational perspective.[3] What follows is a brief picture of patterns in the previous generations that bear on the key triangle shown in Diagram 2, and on Ms. R.'s related difficulty assuming a more separate and differentiated position in both her first and second families.

Ms. R.'s mother, Mary, had an overly intense and enmeshed relationship with her own mother, Minnie (Diagram 3). Mary criticized Minnie constantly to other family members, yet accommodated to her demands and behaved as if she were

---

[3]Readers who are unfamiliar with systemic theory, which underlies the clinical use of the genogram, should see Kerr (1981), S. Lerner (1984), McGoldrick and Gerson (1985), and Ault-Riche (1986).

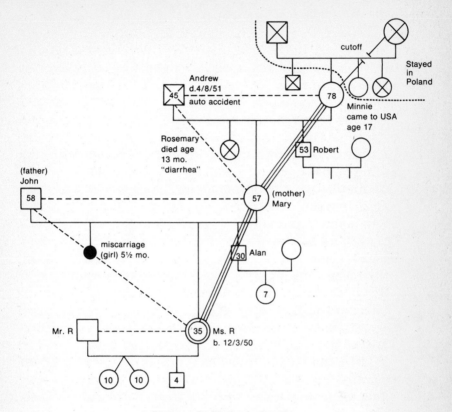

cutoff

Stayed
in
Poland

Andrew
d.4/8/51
45 auto accident

78

Minnie
came to USA
age 17

Rosemary
died age
13 mo.
"diarrhea"

53 Robert

(father)
John

58

(mother)
Mary

57

miscarriage
(girl) 5½ mo.

30 Alan

7

Mr. R

35 Ms. R
b. 12/3/50

10   10   4

Diagram 3: Mother's Family

single-handedly responsible for her mother's well-being.
Mary's longstanding sense of responsibility for her mother was
intensified following her father, Andrew's, death, at which
point Mary alternated between distancing from her mother on
the one hand, and trying to "fix" her loneliness and depression
on the other. When Ms. R. was born, Minnie had just become a
widow and Mary hoped that her new daughter, the first grand-
child, would cheer Minnie up and giver her a purpose for
living, thus contributing further to Ms. R.'s role as an over-
focused-upon child.

Grandmother Minnie had experienced a traumatic migra-
tion from Poland at age 17. After being sent to America with

her older brother, her parents and two younger siblings were unable to leave the country as had been planned. Minnie had been in love with a Polish farmer whom her parents had forbidden her to see and who died in a motorcycle accident the day following Minnie's one-year anniversary in America. Minnie told her children that she had married Andrew "for convenience, not love," and she confided in Mary that she had never gotten over the Polish farmer, whom she had known for all of a month. Undoubtedly, Minnie's emotional inability to let go of this young Polish man was connected to the devastating loss of her parents, two siblings, and her homeland. At the time of Minnie's marriage to Andrew, she burned a box containing all of her family photographs from Poland, stating that they were too painful to look at and "there was no point in dwelling on the past." However, she kept in her possession a gift from the Polish farmer. Not surprisingly, Minnie's marriage to Andrew was both distant and mutually dissatisfying.

The severe degree of geographical and emotional cutoff that Minnie experienced from important members of her family of origin emotionally overloaded her relationships with her children. The fact that Minnie had lost her firstborn daughter at 13 months of age further heightened both the anxiety and the fusion in Minnie's relationship with Mary. Minnie overprotected Mary as if she might disappear at any moment; Mary had slept with Minnie for much of her young life, each worrying about the well-being of the other. As an adult woman, Mary remained her mother's child, maintaining the fusion between them by failing to openly define differences or address significant relationship issues. For example, Mary did not attend church regularly but lied to her mother about this and other facts, claiming that Minnie would be "too upset" by the truth.

Over time, Ms. R. explored the ways in which her relationship with her mother was similar to her mother's relationship to Minnie, and she obtained a clearer, more factual picture of the broader context that had shaped family relationships over several generations. In so doing, she became increasingly observant of her own part in repeating a multigenerational triangle in which mothers and daughters were especially intense

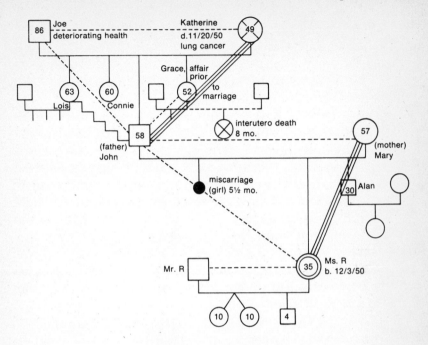

Diagram 4: Father's Family

and mutually protective at the expense of father–daughter relatedness, marital satisfaction, the pursuit of personal goals, and the clarification of self.

Ms. R.'s father, John, was the third child and only boy in a sibling group of four. He was his mother's "special son," whom she both overprotected and turned to as her "best friend" in the family (Diagram 4). John's pattern was also one of overintensity with his mother and a complementary distance from his father.

John's special position with his mother, Katherine, emotionally charged his relationships with his three sisters. Lois, the firstborn, was particularly vocal about John's being "spoiled" and privileged, while she had excessive family and domestic responsibilities. Because John was also looked to by Katherine as her "advisor," Lois received the burdens but not the benefits of her firstborn status. When Ms. R. began therapy, her father and Lois were involved in a heated struggle about managing their aging father's care. In the children's growing-up years, Lois was the closest to her father and often assumed the role of justifying or trying to explain his behavior to other family members.

John's parents, Katherine and Joe, managed intensity in their relationship through marital distancing and child-focused triangles, in which John played a key role. Katherine's role in her marriage was an accommodating one; she failed to voice her own needs or complaints, and she did not articulate her own life goals or plans. Marital dissatisfaction and anger was bound by her intensifying her relationship with her son John and turning to him as a special ally and confidant.

This pattern, beginning early in John's life, continued into his adulthood. For example, Grace, John's youngest sister, became pregnant out of wedlock the first year she moved from the family home to a distant city. She made plans to give the child up for adoption, but aborted a month short of full term. Katherine warned Grace against sharing this information with other family members, including Joe, who did not even know of the pregnancy. Mother then confided the whole story to John but forbade him to talk about it. John, on his part, failed to take a stand with his mother that he would not be able to keep such a big secret, and more than three decades later he had never discussed it. This example was one of many illustrating the entrenched and toxic triangle in which John had an overly intense tie with one family member (in this case, Katherine) at the expense of other crucial family relationships. Now, in his second family, married to Mary, he had flipped positions from "insider" to "outsider," replicating the position of his own father; the basic triangle, however, remained intact.

FAMILY OF ORIGIN WORK

Over the course of therapy, Ms. R. began to view her unsatisfactory marriage in the context of the broader family picture. The legacy of the previous generations included unsatisfying marriages managed by fathers/husbands through distancing and by wives/mothers through child-focus. Ms. R. entered the family at a time of loss for both her parents, which further intensified this triangle; when Ms. R. entered therapy she was solidly entrenched in the role of her mother's emotional ally while collaborating with her father's distant odd-man-out position; the triangle stabilized her parent's marriage but thwarted the growth of all involved.

Rather than working to challenge the status quo in her own marriage, Ms. R. complained to her mother and therapist in a manner that replicated the old triangle and only served to hold the clock still. The invisible threads that bound mother and daughter together were tightened as the two women consolidated their closeness around their disappointment in, and exclusion of men. The men in turn participated actively in creating and maintaining their part in this drama, which had deep roots in their own families of origin as well as in the prescriptions of culture. Ms. R.'s symptomatic depression similarly kept her bound to her mother, who focused her "worry energy" more on her daughter's depression than on her own problems. Because Ms. R.'s depression kept her stuck in all arenas, it also served as an oath of fidelity to her mother that Ms. R. would never really grow up and leave home.

Ms. R. was able to think clearly about her own situation and perceive new options for her own behavior after she obtained a picture of the multigenerational system and understood the current interactional context in which her symptomatic depression occurred. At the same time, the seemingly simple task of obtaining family facts inevitably forced a shift in entrenched patterns. For example, Ms. R. learned about her Aunt Grace's pregnancy and loss, as well as other family "secrets," by questioning her father and his siblings about their family history. In so doing, she herself moved against the long legacy of father–daughter distance and began, for the first time, to address emotionally important issues with John. This experience allowed her to observe firsthand the extremely high level of anxiety and resistance that was evoked in all family members, herself included, by this change; it also challenged her fused position with her mother since the overintensity in this relationship was inextricably interwoven with a complementary disengagement from her father.

Over the course of therapy, Ms. R. slowly continued to change her own part in the entrenched family triangle; for example, she stopped engaging her mother in intense marathons about her depression and miserable marriage, in which both women implicitly or explicitly agreed that Ms. R.'s husband was to blame and that Ms. R.'s father should not be told. Instead, Ms. R. connected with each of her parents separately, and, in a calm, factual way, shared something of her perspective on her marital difficulties and her own contribution to them. She stopped telling her mother "secrets" that were not for father's ears, and she slowly challenged the legacy of secret-keeping in the extended family. When her marriage heated up, she still sought temporary distance from her husband, but she no longer took her three children to her parents home or otherwise invited them to join with her in an alliance against their father.

As Ms. R. made these and other changes, previously unconscious material became accessible. For example, as she worked toward establishing more of an emotional connnection with both her father and husband, an underground sense of guilt and disloyalty toward her mother emerged. Ms. R.'s fears that her moves toward greater separateness and differentiation would injure her mother were reinforced by strong "change back!" reactions from both parents, as well as by Ms. R.'s own separation anxiety and resistance to change that she projected onto mother, which further increased Mary's fragility in Ms. R.'s eyes. In addition, Ms. R.'s changed behavior destabilized the family and, predictably, had profound reverberations throughout the system. First, marital issues between her parents surfaced full force as Ms. R. moved out of the old triangle. Ms. R.'s father confessed to his wife that he had been having a homosexual affair for several years, and the couple began a marital therapy process that continued on after Ms. R.'s terminated. Ms. R.'s mother was confronted with emotional issues in the relationship with her own mother, Minnie, as Ms. R. began to interact with both her mother and grandmother in a more differentiated fashion. Her father had a similar challenge of renegotiating relationships with persons on his family tree as his daughter began to challenge a long legacy of cutoffs and secret-keeping. For example, shifts in John's hostile, blaming relationship with Lois and in his distant relationship with his younger sister, Grace (with whom he had never discussed her traumatic pregnancy and loss), occurred over time as Ms. R. worked to establish a person-to-person relationship with each of her aunts that was relatively free from the intense emotional field of her father's reactivity to both. Certainly Ms. R. could not have successfully initiated or sustained the significant changes she made in her family of origin until after she had spent considerable time in therapy gathering family facts, understanding multigenerational patterns and triangles, and gaining a calm and more objective perspective on the part she played in them.

As a result of the work Ms. R. did in her own family of origin, she was able to consolidate a clearer, more separate sense of self, and her depression lifted. She adopted a more thoughtful, responsible, and less reactive stance to her marital problems, and she was able to better observe marital interactions, free from the screen of old family scripts (e.g., her need to be "for" mother at the expense of other relationships). Yet as Ms. R.'s clarity and objectivity about marital issues sharpened, her resistance to moving out of the role of the accommodating and de-selfed spouse also mounted. I wish to briefly focus on one underpinning of resistance that is frequently overlooked or minimized in therapeutic work derived from a psychodynamic or family systems model. I refer here to the far-reaching implications of women's economic dependence on men.

IMPACT OF ECONOMIC DEPENDENCE

Ms. R.'s lack of economic independence was a crucial factor underlying her unconscious dread of clarifying a bottom-line position with her husband. ("These are the things that must change in order for me to continue in this relationship. These are the things that I will no longer do.") As noted earlier, Ms. R.

dared not make waves in her marriage until she was confident that she could survive without it, if need be. Even after she had worked through internal barriers to change, an unacknowledged factor in Ms. R.'s stuck position in her marriage was her fear of joining the new underclass of poor divorced women with dependent children.[4] I believe that this fear is universally operative for unemployed homemakers or those locked into low-paying jobs. While women tend not to articulate this dilemma to themselves or others ("Doing what I need to do for myself might eventually lead to the dissolution of my marriage, which would plunge me into a condition of poverty and insurmountable stress"), they may be blocked from moving forward until it is identified and addressed in the therapeutic process.

In Ms. R.'s case, I kept the issue out on the table by continually questioning the implications of either changing or maintaining her current economic situation. These questions were raised in the context of Ms. R.'s own complaints that she seemed unable to do the very things in her marriage that she eventually recognized as necessary for her to move beyond her depression and accompanying feelings of anger and bitterness. For example, one obvious source of Ms. R.'s depression stemmed from her overfunctioning and overresponsible position on the domestic scene. Over the course of therapy she became aware that this situation would change, not as a result of her symptomatic position and tearful arguments with her husband, but rather as a result of her own resolve to stop overfunctioning in this arena. However, when she planned even a small specific change in this direction (e.g., telling her husband that she would no longer make his lunches or do his laundry because she was tired and needed to take better care of herself), she would not stay on course. In response to Mr. R.'s predictable anxiety and countermoves, Ms. R. would reinstate the status quo and lapse back into depression and bitterness. At such times I would engage in careful systemic questioning

---

[4]The current divorce rate is almost 50 percent, and the rate of divorce in remarried families is projected to reach 60 percent in this decade. It is women and children who tend to become impoverished by postdivorce arrangements. Divorced women and their children suffer a decline of 73 percent in living standard, while divorced men experience an increase of 42 percent (Carter 1986, Hare-Mustin 1987).

designed to clarify exactly how Ms. R. saw the consequences of such changes on this relationship system. Through such questioning, Ms. R. came to recognize that her worst fear was that continued changes on her part might cost her her marriage.

I did not shy away from asking specific questions about how Ms. R. would take care of herself if she ended up without a husband and exactly what short- and long-term plans she would make for herself. I was clear that I was not predicting divorce but rather taking her own anxieties seriously, particularly in light of current divorce statistics and the facts available about the poverty conditions of divorced mothers with dependent children. The more I specifically questioned her in this area, the more clearly it emerged that Ms. R. simply did not think in terms of planning life and career goals for herself. The product of generations of sex-role socialization, Ms. R. had been raised to believe that she would marry and be taken care of, and that all her needs would be met through her husband and children. Instead, she found that she was taking care of everybody else and no one was taking care of her—except for the minimal secondary gains that her symptomatic depression evoked. Yet she could not begin to take care of herself when she feared that changes on her part might destabilize a marital arrangement that was for her not only a crucial emotional relationship but also a matter of survival.

I believe that a woman cannot save an unhappy marriage until she can save her own self. I also believe that nothing is more important for women than having a life plan that neither requires nor excludes marriage. This statement reflects more than my conviction that both men and women without long-term personal and work goals are especially vulnerable to depression and other symptoms and dysfunctional behaviors. More to the point, the issue is that of economic survival. Statistics suggest that if current trends continue, single women with dependent children, as well as older women, will constitute almost all of our nation's poor by the turn of the century. While it is not a psychotherapist's job to encourage women to seek employment, it is my experience that careful systemic questioning (which includes questioning about the legacy of work and career in the previous generations of women) will lead patients to eventually think through their own position on this issue, based on a need neither to conform to nor to rebel against cultural pressures and the wishes and expectations of others (Lerner 1987).

In Ms. R.'s case, she chose not to formulate career plans during the course of her work with me. She did, however, more clearly articulate her fear that she was one husband away from a welfare check, and she explored the impact on her marriage of her economic dependence and her choice of having all her eggs in the basket of one role. As her self-esteem and belief in her own resources mounted, she became more confident that she could find a way to survive on her own if need be, and she no longer needed to maintain her marriage at whatever cost to herself. She was thus able to relinquish her role of blaming her husband while accommodating to him, and to assert herself on a number of hot issues in their relationship, including her overresponsible position on the domestic scene. Although her changed behaviors did precipitate a marital crisis, which included the threat of divorce from her husband who started a brief affair, their marriage eventually weathered the stress of change and was ultimately strengthened. A year following Ms. R.'s termination from treatment, she wrote me that her family had relocated because of her husband's job promotion. She was entering a master's program in counseling psychology and, although she was struggling, she was far from clinically depressed.

DEPRESSION AND ANGER

In both the popular (Rubin 1970) and classical psychoanalytic literature (Abraham 1927, Freud 1956), depression has been linked to the avoidance of the awareness and expression of anger. Depression has been conceptualized as "anger turned inward" or "anger turned against the self," as if repressed aggression is the actual source of depression and depression, in turn, can be lifted by the mere venting of one's anger or rage at the appropriate object. More recently, the old anger-in/

anger-out theory, which states that "letting it all hang out" offers protection for the psychological hazards of keeping it all pent up, has been challenged by both empirical data and clinical experience (Tavris 1982, Weissman and Klerman 1984, Lerner 1985).

Obviously, the ability to voice anger and protest on one's own behalf is essential for maintaining one's dignity and self-regard and is a crucial vehicle for both personal and social change. Before the second wave of feminism, depressed women, like Ms. R., felt personally to blame for their own unhappiness and presented in our consulting rooms with a single-minded focus on their personal neurosis or, alternately, they blamed their mothers. In contrast, contemporary women, recognizing that "the personal is political," have begun to challenge and change the roles and rules that have falsely defined, constricted, and misnamed women's lives. Short of this process of consciousness raising and social-political change (in which the awareness of anger plays a crucial role), depression is nothing less than a universal aspect of the female condition. Bernardez-Bonesatti (1978) was the first to explore the powerful internal and cultural prohibitions against female anger and the psychological consequences of such injunctions, of which depression is one.

While depression may serve as an indirect form of protest, it may also bind anger and obscure its sources. In Ms. R.'s case, her symptomatic depression forced change in the marital relationship (e.g., Mr. R. began to do housework and to care for the children in order to fill in for his underfunctioning wife), but it also protected Ms. R. from clearly articulating her grievances and openly challenging the status quo. Ms. R.'s position as the sick one or the depressed patient in the family further lowered her self-esteem and sense of competence, making it even less likely that she would have a sense of legitimacy about voicing her complaints and taking a new and different action on her own behalf.

At the same time, venting anger does not offer women protection against depression. Ms. R., for example, was not helped by the fact that she blamed her husband for her unhappiness and solidified her bond with her mother by complaining about him. Depressed women frequently participate in endless cycles of fighting, complaining, and blaming that go nowhere and only reinforce their feelings of helplessness, powerlessness, and low self-regard.

Feelings of depression, low self-esteem, self-betrayal, and even self-hatred are inevitable when women fight but continue to submit to unfair circumstances, when they complain but participate in relationships that betray their own beliefs, values, and personal goals, or when they find themselves fulfilling society's stereotype of the bitchy, nagging, bitter, or destructive woman (Bernardez-Bonesatti 1978, Lerner 1985).

In Ms. R.'s case, as in most, her depression was not mitigated by voicing her anger at significant others, such as her husband for his sense of entitlement and patronizing attitude, her mother for her possessiveness and overinvolvement, and her father for his distance and emotional unavailability. Rather, her anger was a piece of a larger process in which Ms. R. became a better observer of larger relationship patterns and became more aware of the necessity for her to change her part in them. For example, Ms. R.'s repetitive angry complaints in therapy regarding her father's emotional absence did little to help her depression. What was significant was her ultimate ability to slowly connect with him over time despite the high level of resistance evoked from within and without. Such a change on Ms. R.'s part was possible only after she had spent considerable time in therapy, gathering information about family facts, patterns, and triangles, which allowed her to put father's distancing in a broader systemic framework in which no one individual was viewed as the cause of family problems.

In sum, depression is not anger turned inwards, although the denial of anger and lack of awareness of its sources can reinforce depression and mitigate against effective action. *Clinical depression and chronic anger and bitterness occur together, often signaling the necessity for change in a relationship system that is unconsciously viewed as lacking the flexibility to tolerate that change.* Although anger is other-directed ("If it weren't for him, . . .") and depression is self-directed ("What's wrong with me?"), both forms of emotional reactivity become less intense when the woman is able to identify and change her part in the relationship patterns and triangles that keep her stuck and when she is able to become an expert on the needs, wants, and priorities of the self.

If feelings of depression or anger ultimately move the woman in the direction of positive change, they have served a crucial purpose. Repetitive expressions of emotional intensity, however, have little inherent therapeutic value and often block the patient's ability to think about her dilemma rather than simply react to it. Therapists who work to uncover angry feelings in depressed patients as a therapeutic end in itself or operate primarily as sympathetic listeners to their patient's grievances about other family members may replicate a dysfunctional triangle in which therapist–patient closeness operates at the expense of the patient's relationship with that other family member who is viewed as bad, sick, or the one to blame (Lerner and Lerner 1983).

Depression and Women's Relationship Orientation

Feminist writers suggest that women differ from men in their stronger need to affiliate with and care for others (Miller 1976, Gilligan 1983). The notion that emotional ties are more central to a woman's sense of self than they are to her male counterpart has been evoked to explain research findings indicating women's greater vunerability to depression—a vulnerability that cuts through both economic class and all phases of the life cycle (Scarf 1980). Although feminist theorists view women's affiliative stance as a strength rather than a weakness, their work has nonetheless been interpreted to suggest that a primary commitment to relationships is an emotional health hazard and a key factor in female depression. Some experts (Scarf 1980) suggest that women have a biologically based "people orientation" that predisposes them to depression when relationships fail, while other authors have invoked nurture rather than nature in concluding the same (Braverman 1986).

Although there is indeed a link between female depression

and women's position in relationships, the connection between affiliation and vulnerability to depression has not been
clearly articulated. The valuing of marriage and family, intimacy and attachment is a mental health asset, not a liability; a
strong relationship orientation will hardly predispose an individual to depression, even when that relationship ends. In fact,
research unequivocally demonstrates that women do far better
without men than men do without women, despite women's
financial disadvantages (Bernard 1973). As every insurance
company knows, men without wives are the single most
vulnerable group to an alarming range of emotional and physical disorders. Men need women as much as or more than
women need men, although male dependency needs are more
likely to be hidden (Lerner 1983, Eichenbaum and Orbach
1983). Contrary to popular mythology, the male sex is far more
vulnerable to dysfunction when alone.

   In sum, it is not women's affiliative needs or relationship
orientation that predisposes females to depression, for emotional connectedness is a basic human need as well as a
strength. Rather, it is what *happens* to women in relationships that deserves our attention. Here the structuring of gender roles and the profound impact of women's subordinate
and devalued status have far-reaching implications for a woman's vulnerable position in her family of origin and in marriage
(Carmen 1981, Lerner 1985). The ways in which women have
suffered from the traditional structure of family life—or its
dissolution through divorce—have been well documented by
scholars from numerous disciplines (Bernard 1973, Carmen
1981, Wheeler 1985) and need not be elaborated here. While
women's higher incidence of depression has many sources, the
primary valuing of relationships (when relatedness does not
occur at the expense of the self) is part of the solution, not the
problem.

POSTSCRIPT: "THE PERSONAL IS POLITICAL"

As a psychologist and psychotherapist, my primary focus in
working with depressed women is on intrapsychic factors that

are inextricably interwoven with dysfunctional family patterns. It is important to recognize, however, that individual
and family dysfunction are inseparable from the dysfunction
of patriarchal culture (Carmen 1981, Goldner 1985b, Hare-
Mustin 1987). Ms. R.'s position in her family of origin is a case
in point. The all-too-familiar dance—repetitively reenacted by
the distant husband/father, the child-focused wife/mother,
and the symptomatic daughter who is too loyal to grow up
herself—is prescribed and perpetuated by the patriarchal societal system just as this particular type of family organization
reinforces and perpetuates that same societal dysfunction. As
long as men are the makers and shapers of culture in the world
outside the home, as long as women are not free to define the
terms of their own lives, as long as society continues to convey
the message that mother *is* the child's environment, then the
basic dysfunctional triad of distant father, emotionally intense, overinvolved mother, and child with little room to grow
up is a natural outgrowth and microcosm of the culture
(Lerner 1978, Goldner 1985a).

Familial structure and societal structure form a circular,
self-perpetuating, downward-spiraling cycle (Lerner 1978).
The more women are blocked from proceeding with their own
growth and excluded from positions of power and authority
outside the home, the more they become excessively child-
focused. As emotional intensity and intimacy increasingly reside within the mother–child dyad, the distance and emotional
isolation of the husband/father become more entrenched. In
turn, children growing up within this context may develop a
dread of the "destructive" powers of women and, in a defensive
attempt to further confine and constrict women's spheres of
activity and control in their own adult lives, move toward
patriarchal solutions of their own. The "solution," of course,
only perpetuates the problem and contributes, among other
things, to the high incidence of female depression.

How does one disrupt such cycles, and where does one
intervene to effect change? With Ms. R., much of my work was
focused on the rigid patterns and structures that inhibited her
growth in her family of origin and in her marriage. In my
experience, individual work derived from a family systems

model is particularly effective in fostering the differentiation of self and in altering psychic structures and distorted internalized object representations that have origins in early family experience. Yet individual and family dysfunction cannot be understood without thoroughly examining the meanings and implications of patriarchal systems that give shape and form to the family and to the very process of differentiation of self. Surely the failure to attend to the consequences of patriarchal structure on individual and family functioning can only result in partial and inaccurate theories of female depression and limit our ability to be agents of change.

References

Abraham, K. (1927). *Notes on the Psychoanalytic Investigation and Treatment of Manic-Depressive Insanity and Allied Conditions.* Selected papers. London: Hogarth Press.

Ault-Riché, M. (1986). *Love and Work: One Woman's Study of Her Family of Origin.* Topeka, Kans.: Menninger Video Productions, The Menninger Foundation.

Bernard, J. (1973). *The Future of Marriage.* New York: Bantam.

Bernardez-Bonesatti, T. (1978). Women and anger: conflicts with aggression in contemporary women. *Journal of the American Medical Women's Association* 33(5):215–219.

Bowen, M. (1978). *Family Therapy in Clinical Practice.* New York: Jason Aronson.

Braverman, L. (1986). The depressed woman in context: a feminist family therapist's analysis. In *Women and Family Therapy,* ed. M. Ault-Riché, pp. 90–99. Rockville, Md.: Aspen.

Carmen, E., Russo, N. F., and Miller, J. B. (1981). Inequality and women's mental health. *American Journal of Psychiatry* 138(10):1319–1330. Also in *The Gender Gap in Psychotherapy: Social Realities and Psychological Processes,* ed. P. P. Rieker and E. Carmen, pp. 125–138. New York: Plenum, 1984.

Carter, B. (1986). Success in family therapy. *The Family Therapy Networker* 10(4):16–22.

Eichenbaum, L., and Orbach, S. (1983). *What Do Women Want?* New York: Coward McCann.

Freud, S. (1956). Mourning and melancholia. In *Collected Papers*, vol. 4, ed. E. Jones. London: Hogarth Press.

Gilligan, C. (1983). *In a Different Voice.* Boston: Harvard University Press.

Goldner, V. (1985a). Feminism and family therapy. *Family Process* 24(1):31–47.

—— (1985b). Warning: Family therapy may be hazardous to your health. *The Family Therapy Networker* 9(6):29–23.

Hare-Mustin, R. T. (1987). The problem of gender in family theory. *Family Process* 26(1):15–27.

Kerr, M. (1981). Family systems theory and therapy. In *Handbook of Family Therapy*, ed. A. Gurman and D. Knistern, pp. 226–364. New York: Brunner/Mazel.

Lerner, H. G. (1978). On the comfort of patriarchal solutions: Some reflections on Brown's paper. *Journal of Personality and Social Systems* 1(3):47–50.

—— (1979). Effects of the nursing mother–infant dyad on the family. *American Journal of Orthopsychiatry* 49(2):339–348.

—— (1980). Internal prohibitions against female anger. *The American Journal of Psychoanalysis* 40(2):137–148.

—— (1983). Female dependency in context: Some theoretical and technical considerations. *American Journal of Orthopsychiatry* 53(4):697–705. Also in *The Gender Gap in Psychotherapy: Social Realities and Psychological Processes*, ed. P. P. Rieker and E. Carmen, pp. 125–138. New York: Plenum, 1984.

—— (1985). *The Dance of Anger: A Woman's Guide to Changing the Patterns of Intimate Relationships.* New York: Harper & Row.

—— (1987). Work and success inhibitions in women. *Bulletin of the Menninger Clinic* 51(4):338–360.

Lerner, S. (1984). *Constructing the Multigenerational Family Genogram: Exploring a Problem in Context.* Topeka, Kans.: Menninger Video Productions, The Menninger Foundation.

Lerner, S., and Lerner H. G. (1983). A systemic approach to resistance: theoretical and technical considerations. *American Journal of Psychotherapy* 37(3):387–399.

McGoldrick, M., and Gerson, R. (1985). *Genograms in Family Assessment.* New York: W. W. Norton.

Miller, J. B. (1976). *Toward a New Psychology of Women.* Boston: Beacon.

Rich, A. (1976). *Of Woman Born.* New York: W. W. Norton.

Rubin, T. (1970). *The Angry Book.* New York: Collier.

Scarf, M. (1980). *Unfinished Business.* New York: Doubleday.

Tavris, C. (1982). *Anger: The Misunderstood Emotion.* New York: Simon & Schuster.

Weissman, M., and Klerman, G. (1984). Sex differences and the epidemiology of depression. In *The Gender Gap in Psychotherapy: Social Realities and Psychological Processes,* ed. P. P. Rieker and E. Carmen, pp. 160–195. New York: Plenum.

Wheeler, D. (1985). The fear of feminism in family therapy. *The Family Therapy Networker* 9(6):53–55.

Chapter 14

A Critique of the Feminist Psychoanalytic Contribution

In this final chapter I will critique key aspects of feminist developmental theory. My primary task is to illustrate that much of feminist psychoanalytic theory remains narrowly mother-focused at the expense of recognizing both circular causality within families and interlocking family process. In addition, I will share my concern that feminists may unwittingly contribute to polarized generalizations about gender that exaggerate differences between groups while minimizing differences within them. Much of my own work, presented in this volume, is not above the criticisms I present here; indeed, many chapters in this volume provide an apt illustration of the very problems I will discuss.

It has been relatively easy for feminists to revise traditional psychoanalytic theory and, understandably, more difficult for us to view ourselves and our feminist sisters with a critical eye. I have undertaken the task, however, because I believe that feminist theory will fail to advance if we cannot articulate our differences and disagreements in a public forum where others can join in and respond. I believe that the enormous strength and integrity of feminism lies in its diversity and that we pay our greatest respect to feminist theory by carefully attending to it. It is in this spirit that I offer this critique.

Mother-Focus in Feminist
Psychoanalytic Theory

Historians of motherhood remind us that since the industrial revolution, mothers have been glorified and blamed—either surrounded by an aura of romantic idealization or held up as a target of unmitigated denigration (Bernard 1974, Rich 1976). Psychoanalytic theory has both reflected and shaped popular culture, in that explanations of individual pathology still remain a linear, backward "whodunit" game, which ends by pointing the finger in the mother's direction. Whether the focus of psychodynamic attention is on the special qualities and sensitivities of the "good mother" (or "good enough" mother) or the pathogenic qualities of the "bad mother," the implicit or explicit assumption is that mother *is* the infant's and child's environment, especially during earlier and more critical stages of development.

To say that mother-blaming remains a problem in our work is not to imply that psychoanalytic thinkers harbor unconscious hostility toward women as mothers that shapes theory and practice, although this, of course, may occur. The point is rather that psychodynamic theory has remained entrenched in an epistemological framework that assumes that what happens to a child is largely the product of who the mother is and what she does and does not do. This assumption has led to an intense preoccupation with maternal power and with the mother–child dyad, at the expense of a broader, more objective understanding of family processes and of how male and female children navigate the process of differentiation within the family.

For over a decade, feminist scholars have challenged mother-blaming by drawing attention to the larger patriarchal context in which mothering occurs. In shifting the locus of causality from mothers to culture, it is argued that pathological mother–child interactions stem naturally from women's subordinate status and from the socially constructed fabric of family and work life. The feminist perspective has been invaluable in demonstrating that the mother–child dyad cannot be understood in isolation from culture and from the institution of motherhood as it has been defined by the dominant group culture. Rich (1976), in her classic book *Of Woman Born*, carefully articulates this crucial distinction between potential mother–child transaction and the distortions of this bond through motherhood as institution.

Although the feminist contribution on mothering is incalculable, it is nonetheless problematic. As late as 1982, Chodorow and Contratto noted that both popular culture and feminist theory remain preoccupied with fantasies of maternal power and perfectibility and rooted in irrational notions of maternal responsibility. Since idealization and blame are two sides of the same belief in the all-powerful mother, the authors view feminist theory as constrained by the fact that we have not moved far enough beyond the limits of our own primary process. "Feminist theories of motherhood have not been able to move further because . . . they are trapped in the dominant cultural assumptions and fantasies about mothering, which in turn rest on fantasied and unexamined notions of child development" (1982, p. 69). While feminists may view maternal behavior as a product of the mother's entrapment within patriarchy rather than as a reflection of her own personal neurosis, the authors remind us that we still continue to see the mother and child as an isolated dyad existing within a magic or cursed circle.

INTRAPSYCHIC AND SYSTEMIC CAMPS

While Chodorow and Contratto (1982) challenge us to place the two-way relationship between mother and child in the context of "manifold relationships with the rest of the world," Chodorow's own work (1978) does not reflect this broader, interactive view, nor (as I will illustrate later) do other theorists operating from feminist psychoanalytic perspective. The encapsulated unit of mother and child, or the oedipal triad of mother, father, and child, remains the primary, if not exclusive, framework of feminist observation and theory-building, so that the complexity of interlocking family relationships is obscured from our view. While the recent shift has been toward a positive reframing of female development (Herman and Lewis 1986, Jordan and Surrey 1986), there has been little movement toward understanding mother–child interactions and the process of self-differentiation within the larger nuclear and multigenerational family context.

In noting that our models of development do not locate mother and child within an interactive web of other relationships, Chodorow and Contratto (1982) fail to mention the existence of well-developed systemic theories that avoid the reification of intrapsychic self apart from interpersonal context, and that elegantly demonstrate that the mother–child dyad cannot be understood in isolation from the whole. It is important to point out that a family systems framework has nothing to do with whether a therapist sees one person individually or meets with a couple or family together, nor does it relate to whether treatment is short or long, symptom-oriented or in-depth. Systems thinking is, rather, an epistemological framework that rejects a linear model of causality (whereby one family member is viewed as the "cause" of another's problems or as having unidirected power over the whole) and, instead, views family members as elements in a circuit of interaction in which each member influences others and is in turn influenced by them. Understanding problems in female development and self-differentiation from a systemic framework necessitates careful questioning to elicit specific constellations of transactional sequences that deviate from normal family processes in ways that result in symptoms of dysfunction. One's field of observation or inquiry is the reciprocal, repetitive, circular patterns maintained by all family members (including past generations), rather than the quality of mothering or the mother–child dyad.

The issue at hand is not whether systemic thinking is more "correct" than other perspectives. Rather, my point is that feminist psychoanalytic scholars treat family systems theory with a conspicuous "not-thereness." The current feminist psychoanalytic literature still pays enormous attention to summarizing and criticizing the misguided notions of Freud and his followers, but glaringly omits the work of the Women's Project in Family Therapy (1982), or for that matter the contribution of *any* systemic thinker or feminist family therapist.[1] Since feminist theory is by nature contextual, it is remarkable that we have located the mother–child dyad in the cultural system but have leaped over systemic analyses of nuclear and multigenerational family processes. To accomplish this feat of illogic, we have relegated the intrapsychic and the systemic to discrete camps as if they were separable one from the other, which has left us locked in a narrow, linear perspective even as we strive to recognize the importance of interaction, flow, process, and context.[2]

LINEAR THINKING AND THE ATTRIBUTION OF CAUSALITY

A tendency toward linear and polarized thinking is our natural bent, feminist or not, and it is overcome only with difficulty, if at all. I was recently reminded of this fact while serving as a consultant to an experienced psychiatric team at a large eastern mental health center. The identified patient, Deborah, was in the second grade and presented behavioral problems at home. Diagram 1 illustrates the triad of mother, father, and daughter that is evoked and reinforced by culture and seen frequently in clinical situations. As typically occurs in family structure, there was a distant marital relationship, a distant father–daughter relationship, and an intense, conflictual mother–daughter relationship. Of relevance to this chapter is a brief summary of how each team member assigned responsibility for Deborah's symptomatic behavior and for the shape and form of family relationships.

The evaluating psychiatrist, who was ultimately responsible for the diagnostic formulation, viewed Deborah's symptoms as a product of faulty mothering. His report documented the mother's fluctuations from neglectful unavailability to

---

[1] B. Carter, P. Papp, O.Silverstein, and M. Walter constitute the Women's Project in Family Therapy.

[2] This is as much of a problem for those psychoanalytic theorists (e.g., the Lacanians) who *do* focus on the father or cannot emphasize his influence enough.

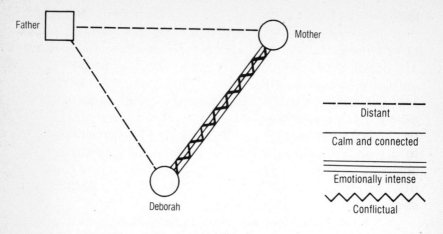

Diagram 1: Family Relationships

overstimulation and intrusion concluding that "mother's lack of attunement to her child's affective needs has impeded the development of self-images, self and other representations, and ego ideal. Deborah's symptoms worsened at a period of excessive maternal overinvolvement, which left daughter unable to negotiate separation-individuation without threat." Implicit in his formulation was the notion that Deborah's mother had set all three sides of the triangle in motion; her overinvolvement with her daughter "pushed father out" (hence the distant father–daughter dyad) and evoked a growing marital distance. His report noted that mother's problems could be traced back to her pathological relationship with her own mother.

The team social worker challenged the evaluating psychiatrist's attribution of causality and presented an equally compelling argument that Deborah's father was the responsible party. With carefully documented dates and family history, she illustrated that Deborah's symptoms immediately followed the father's depression and his concomitant emotional withdrawal from the family at the time of his own father's death when Deborah was entering second grade. According to the social worker, Deborah's symptoms served successfully "to rope father back into the family" and reconnect him with his wife around parenting concerns when the marital distance (and father's depression) reached threatening proportions. The social worker viewed the father not only as initiating and maintaining the marital distance but also as evoking mother's overinvolvement with her daughter ("Father's increasing marital withdrawal and absentee parenting caused mother to intensify her relationship with Deborah and to increasingly turn to her daughter to provide her with the emotional elements absent from the marriage"). Although not intending to attribute blame, the social worker's formulation labeled father as the starting point of the three sides of the triangle.

To further complicate or enrich matters, a psychologist of biological bent offered a third perspective. Although Deborah had not become openly symptomatic until she started the second grade, she was, from his perspective, a difficult child from birth onward in terms of both affective and physical predispositions. The psychologist pointed out that infants and children bring their own stimulus value into a family and shape interactions as much as they are shaped by them. Because a difficult child places severe stress on a marriage, the marital distance was hardly surprising. Also, Deborah's difficult behavior evoked maternal anxiety and overconcern just as it pushed father away. In sum, the psychologist's reading of early maternal–infant interactions led him to conclude that, "The daughter and not the mother is faulty in this case." He noted that Deborah consistently had "elicited poor maternal responsiveness." From this perspective, Deborah herself might be viewed as the primary cause of all three sides of the triangle.

It was not the intention of this team to judge "the one to blame" or to decide "who started it" in regard to this symptomatic child. As theorists and treaters, our focus is always on diagnosing and understanding rather than on pointing the finger at a particular family member. It should also be noted that this team functioned well, not only in light of their careful formulations but also in regard to their ability to openly articulate differences and to recognize that each team member presented a valuable point of view that contributed to a larger picture. My point in sharing this condensed and partial summary of an evaluation process is simply to illustrate *how naturally we observe the territory that fits our map, and how easily we slip into linear, causal language that obscures the complex, circular, patterned ways in which relationship systems interlock.*[3]

Feminist psychoanalytic theory of female development currently operates from the same epistemological framework held by the evaluating psychiatrist in the case just discussed. On the one hand, specific formulations of Deborah's symptomatology and development might look quite different coming from a feminist thinker, who might view the mother–daughter interaction through a more positive lens (Herman and Lewis 1986, Jordan and Surrey 1986). Nonetheless, one is reminded of the famous saying translated from the French: "The more things change, the more they stay the same." The territory that fits the feminist map is still the mother–child dyad, and causality regarding normal or pathological functioning still resides in this highly encapsulated unit viewed as possessing a life of its own.

To further illustrate this point, I will briefly examine two samples from the current feminist psychoanalytic literature. The first is a nationally acclaimed book by Chernin titled *The Hungry Self: Women, Eating and Identity* (1986). The second is an article by Jordan and Surrey titled "The Self-in-Relation: Empathy and the Mother–Daughter Relationship" (1986). The latter recasts and reformulates current psychoanalytic thinking (including feminist theory) and presents a new "self-in-relation" model of female development. Although these two works by no means capture the diversity of feminist psychoanalytic thinking, they are important and influential contributions reflecting both the strengths and the problems of the current state of theory-building and clinical practice.

-----

[3]For an example of a systemic (circular) formulation of a child's symptomatic behavior and a description of therapeutic work derived from this framework, see the case of the "Kessler" family in Lerner (1985, pp. 162–180) and Lerner and Lerner (1983). Also, see Papp (1983, Chapter 2) for an excellent definition of systems thinking.

CHERNIN'S "THE HUNGRY SELF"
THE MOTHER–DAUGHTER DYAD
IN HISTORICAL CONTEXT

For Chernin, eating disorders and food obsessions reflect problems of identity that are rooted in a mother–daughter separation struggle. Like most feminist psychoanalytic thinkers, Chernin warns against mother-blaming by emphasizing the historical factors that have constrained mothers' lives. She writes eloquently of the dilemmas of daughters who are caught between their own lives of possibility and their mothers' lives of imposed limitations, and she provides an especially poignant picture of a new generation of women trying to enter a world denied to the women who came before them.

At the same time, Chernin's understanding of eating disorders and, more important, her analysis of failed female identity and development never extend beyond the mother–daughter dyad, which she depicts as singularly pathogenic in nature. Who the daughter is and what she becomes—from the establishment of "basic trust" to the exertion of her will and the belief in her own initiative—rests on how the mother responds and how she does or does not meet her daughter's earliest needs. In this regard, Chernin does not depart from the traditional Kleinian emphasis on the preoedipal mother, and she concludes that "our most fruitful understanding of female psychology will come from the exploration of the dual-unity, mother and child, mouth-to-breast dyad of earliest childhood." The mother–child bond is primary, circumscribed, and magical (e.g., "Infants feel what their mothers are feeling" [p. 122]); there is no mention of fathers or family process in her entire text.

Of significance is the widespread popularity of this best-selling book among feminist scholars. Whereas Friday's *My Mother/Myself* (1977) has been criticized by feminists for being a litany of mother-blaming recriminations, disappointments, and complaints, Chernin's work has been hailed in feminist psychoanalytic circles as an inspired metaphor for

our age. On the one hand, her contribution is not to be minimized; Chernin writes like a dream and pays careful, ongoing
attention to the historical context of women's lives. However,
the widespread appeal of her book, as I see it, also reflects the
degree to which popular culture (including feminist culture)
remains stuck in a linear, mother-focused mode of observing
and organizing the complexity of information that confronts
us as we try to understand human behavior in general and
female development in specific.

Chernin's work also illustrates how difficult it is to maintain a balanced, objective view of the strengths and weak-
nesses of women in the previous generations, especially when
these women are our own mothers and grandmothers. For
Chernin, these women have left little more than a legacy of
deprivation and impoverishment, although not of their own
making; she rarely mentions the special strengths, courage,
and valor of these same women, and says nothing of their
satisfactions and competence or their joy in their traditional
values and life-style. She writes: "A handful of cherished rec-
ipes, perhaps, a lifetime of broken dreams and disillusion—
that is what most women alive today can receive from their
mothers" (p. 42).[4] Again, polarized and partial views of women
as mothers (be they devaluing or idealizing in nature) run
through both psychoanalytic literature and popular culture.
My own work, like Chernin's, also reflects this polarity and
focuses far too unilaterally (as I now see it) on the drama of
maternal envy and unfulfillment and the daughter's related
sense of anxiety and guilt.

So, where have all the fathers gone? In the preface of
Chernin's book, she notes that her exclusive focus on mothers
is not meant to deny the importance of the father–daughter
bond, which she plans to address in a subsequent book. This
caveat aside, her theory of development and symptomatology
clearly locates causality in maternal behavior. More important,
from an epistemological perspective, *the notion that one can*

---

[4]This picture surely does not do justice to Chernin's own thinking. In an
earlier book (1984), she tells of rediscovering her mother's strength and her own
powerful legacy.

understand the mother–daughter dyad apart from the fa-
ther–daughter dyad, the marital relationship, and other in-
terlocking family relationships and triangles (which may
include grandparents and siblings) is a linear, noncontex-
tual view of human functioning that ignores the entire body
of family therapy literature. To illustrate this point, I ask the
reader to consider a brief example from my own clinical work
with a symptomatic daughter who was viewed by her pediatri-
cian as having a "potential eating disorder." My point is not to
do justice to the complexity of the case at hand, but rather to
describe a key family triangle, central to the daughter's symptoms and thwarted development, yet obscured from observation or intervention by any theorist or therapist operating
from a linear or dyadic framework.

Clinical Example

At age six, Sarah B. was brought by both parents to see
me at the Menninger Foundation. While her symptoms
included school problems (inattentiveness, excessive
shyness, and isolation from peers), they were less the
focus of parental concern than what Mr. B. described
as Sarah's "fussy eating, which endangers her health."
Sarah's problems actually emerged at approximately
age 2 and worsened when she entered kindergarten.
Evidently Sarah was not proceeding smoothly with a
number of developmental tasks appropriate to her age.
  My evaluation of historical events and current relational patterns revealed that Sarah's symptoms and
thwarted development emerged in the context of a repetitive, interactional sequence in which both parents
fought about her care. When Sarah was 2 years old,
marital issues between Mr. and Mrs. B. had emerged
full force, focusing increasingly on issues of parenting.
Sarah's father was on the side of "law and order," while
her mother's complementary stance was one of per-
missiveness and distancing, which she described as a
"live-and-let-live attitude." By the time Sarah was
brought to therapy, the parents' positions had become

rigidly polarized, with each spouse evoking and maintaining the behavior of the other (e.g., the more her father would move in quickly and intensely to discipline Sarah, the less her mother would take initiative or exercise competence in this arena; the more her mother would fail to voice concern about Sarah's difficulties, the more her father would overreact). This entrenched child-focused triangle was fueled, in part, by a chronically high level of anxiety in both parents as each of them failed to process marital issues and work on crucial events and issues in their own families of origin.

At the time Sarah was brought in for an evaluation, the sequence of interaction around her symptomatic eating behavior would go somewhat as follows: Sarah would fuss with her food at the dinner table or claim not to be hungry. Mr. B. would rush in to make rules ("No dessert if you don't finish your salad!") and to openly voice anxieties about his daughter's health, which ran the gamut from concern that Sarah lacked vigor to viewing her as having the precursors of a life-threatening eating disorder. Sarah's mother predictably stepped into the middle of her husband's attempts to regulate Sarah's eating, with a "leave-her-alone" stance that infuriated Mr. B. and led him to shift his intense focus from his daughter to his wife. Marital fighting then ensued, and Sarah would retreat from the dinner table with a stomachache. This triangle had been operative since Sarah was two, and was manifested in various forms and content areas. When Sarah entered kindergarten, the pattern just described was moving in increasingly repetitive and intense cycles, focusing largely, although not exclusively, on the subject of food.

Loyalty issues, especially intense for Sarah, blocked her ability to navigate developmental tasks appropriate to her age. At times she was in the role of her mother's ally, with her father in the outside position in this key family triangle. For example, Sarah's mother would offer Sarah "secret" desserts and "junk food," swearing her to secrecy about these treats. She would also allow Sarah to disregard the father's rules ("No jumping on the white couch") when he was not present, thus undermining his attempts at authority. Sarah's father would similarly invite Sarah to join with him at her mother's expense and repeatedly communicated to his daughter that her mother was not competent to manage her care. At the time of the psychiatric evaluation, things had intensified to the point that Sarah's choice of salad versus a cream puff had become an anxiety-ridden dilemma unconsciously associated with "whose side" Sarah was on in the ongoing child-focused marital struggle.

Although a multiplicity of factors doubtlessly contributed to Sarah's symptomatology and thwarted development, I wish to emphasize that the interactional sequences just described (as well as other more covert triangles and coalitions) cannot be observed, nor elicited through questioning, nor deemed significant if one's theory of symptoms (be they food-related or otherwise) and impaired female development rests on a fixed idea that the "real" drama of development and differentiation unfolds between mother and child. Not only is father's crucial role obscured from view during the preoedipal years, but dyadic thinking blocks one's ability to identify actual relational processes and triangles, past and present, that are the building blocks of family process and of male and female development.

The exclusion of fathers from central focus in our theories merits further comment. For example, in Sarah's case, the father (Mr. B.) was not the more peripheral or emotionally distant parent. From the time of Sarah's birth, Mr. B.'s involvement with her was emotionally intense and colored by projections derived from his experience in his own family of origin, in which significant women (including his mother and older sister) prematurely "dropped like flies" and could not be counted on to survive. These two traumatic losses were neither emotionally processed nor successfully mourned within the family, leading to Mr. B.'s subsequent involvement in a toxic family triangle with his father and stepmother, parallel to the one he now participated in with his wife and daughter. Further, these unprocessed losses fueled Mr. B.'s heightened reactivity to Sarah, his firstborn daughter, as well as his anxious and protective stance regarding her health and eating behavior. However, even if Mr. B. had managed anxiety and emotional intensity through defensive distancing (as do many men), this would not have made him a more peripheral player in the drama of early family life. *Distance and disengagement have no less impact on family relationships than do their flip sides of overinvolvement and fusion. It is imperative that we carefully examine our tendency to render men to the position of the peripheral "other" in the domestic sphere, just as women have been so rendered in the public domain.* Similarly, we must guard against static and circumscribed beliefs about the role of father (e.g., fathers provide "non-mother space" or facilitate the loosening of a symbiotic mother–child union), which only serve to block our ability to objectively observe a triadic and circular process as it unfolds in a particular family.

Chernin's "lens setting" for understanding female identity and development represents much of current feminist psychoanalytic thinking, which combines reflexively with dominant cultural assumptions to avoid a systemic or contextual view of developmental phenomena. The problem, as I see it, is a reflection of our persistent compartmentalization of data derived from the retrospective methods of psychoanalysis and the systemic observations of family systems thinkers. The implications for treatment are profound, since intervention and clinical technique flow naturally from theory. If mothers and daughters are viewed as the primary source of one another's unhappiness—if a daughter's symptomatology is the outcome of her mother's limitations and lack of emotional competence—questions and interventions will be so guided. And if mothers are entirely responsible, yet at the same time are blameless victims, then what is the therapeutic task for women? For Chernin, to move beyond mother-blaming is to become conscious of our anger, frustration, and sense of abandonment. "And then, having lived through the shock of acknowledging our rage at the mother, we must learn how to place it in a social context." Admittedly, placing mother-rage in a social context is far better than having no context at all. I question, however, whether women in therapy can obtain a positive and balanced experience of either self or other when mother–daughter interactions are not located within the context of the other family relationships in which they are embedded.

"The Self-in-Relation Theory"
A New Model of Female Development

Self-in-relation theory, postulated by Jordan and Surrey (1986), puts forth a new model of female development and identity based on a reinterpretation of current psychoanalytic theory and a search for principles of self-development not based on a male model. While the richness of their formulations cannot be summarized here, their central thesis is that "women organize their sense of identity, find existential meaning, achieve a sense of coherence and continuity, and are motivated in the context of a relationship" (p. 102), be it an actual, current relationship or an internalized one. They contrast their model with the usual theoretical emphasis on the attainment of autonomy and separation as hallmarks of emotional maturity—a perspective that the authors view as a male model which does not fit women's unique experience. Self-in-relation theory emphasizes the development of mutual empathy in the mother–daughter dyad, which they believe proceeds in a relatively more smooth and untroubled fashion than is the case with mother and son, thus facilitating women's special investment and comfort in relatedness.[5]

Self-in-relation theory typifies a different line of feminist thinking than is represented by Chernin's work. Chernin does

---

[5]Jordan and Surrey's concept of self-in-relation grows out of Miller's work and reflects a larger collaborative group effort on the part of women at the Stone Center (Wellesley, Mass.) to reformulate female psychology and development. A list of all *Stone Center Working Papers* on women may be obtained by writing the Stone Center, Wellesley College, Wellesley, Mass. 02181

not depart significantly from current psychoanalytic and Kleinian theory; rather, her contribution lies in her ability to carefully attend to the influence of social and historical factors on women's lives and to add this to the psychological picture. In contrast, Jordan and Surrey's work follows the tradition of Miller (1976) and Gilligan (1982), who argue for the development of new concepts and language to describe female experience. Here, the task is not simply one of moving beyond the "deficiency" model of female development and accounting for the social context. Instead, Jordan and Surrey put forth a new model of female development that positively rather than negatively describes the vicissitudes of mother–daughter interaction and reaffirms traditional female values of nurturance and connectedness. Their positive description of early mother–daughter relatedness is in striking contrast to Chernin's more familiar characterization of this dyad as colored primarily by aggression and conflict.

From my own perspective, the contribution of self-in-relation theory is multifaceted. First, the intellectual courage and integrity of the authors in formulating new theory, as well as their respect for women and their obvious ability to speak in their own voice, serve as a model for theorists and practitioners, as does the earlier pioneering work of Miller (1976). In addition, Jordan and Surrey challenge a deeply embedded psychoanalytic leaning toward pathologizing female development in general and the mother–daughter relationship in particular. A major contribution of self-in-relation theory is the authors' positive redefinition of the developing mother–daughter bond, which lends balance to existing theories (including much of the feminist contribution) focused primarily, if not exclusively, on the "darker side" of this dyad.

It is the authors' exclusive focus on the mother–daughter bond, however, (and the theoretical assumptions that follow from such a focus) that I see as problematic. Self-in-relation theory neither departs from nor broadens the notion that the establishment of identity and self as an organizing psychological structure (and the associated capacity for empathic relatedness) develops within the context of early mother–child interaction. While Jordan and Surrey explicitly value a systemic, interactive perspective, and even state at one point (p. 88) that they do not intend the model of self-in-relation to be viewed as specific to the nuclear mother–daughter relationship, this broader vision is not woven into the fabric of the theory itself. As with Chernin, the invisibility of fathers and of basic family process is striking. Again, this problem runs through all feminist psychoanalytic thinking, perhaps because our *ideal* of appreciating the web of interactive relationships that affect development is not achievable when reality is constructed solely through a psychoanalytic lens.

For example, Jordan and Surrey note that Newtonian physics, with its emphasis on static structure and discrete, bounded objects, has given way to the "new physics" and quantum theory that emphasizes flow, waves, and interconnections. It is this growing appreciation of process, relationship, and interaction that the authors explicitly strive for in their theory of female development. Thus, they reject the old unidirectional model of development, in which the mother shapes the infant in a linear fashion, for a model of emphasizing two-way interaction. Similarly, they do not formulate the concept of the self as a contained, separate unit, noting that "systems theorists have recently applied to development the idea of a set of interacting units with relationships among them" (p. 84). Yet the authors then proceed to isolate the mother–child dyad from family process (as well as from patriarchal social context) and to treat it as a discrete, separate entity wherein the development and maintenance of self-images, sense of identity, motivation, and structures of the self are assumed to unfold. I shall comment briefly on implications for theories of gender.

Mother-Focus and Gender Dichotomies

From a systemic perspective, the development of self or identity and the related capacity for empathic connectedness develop in the context of complex family processes, which are, in turn, given shape and form by the cultural context in which the family is embedded. While boys and girls look toward the same-sex parent as a model of what it means to be male or female—man or woman—basic psychological structures are not formed within an isolated dyad. Rather, relational capacities and the structure of self reflect many interacting factors, including key family triangles, the relationship between parents, the level of differentiation of each parent from his or her own family of origin, and each parent's capacity to form an emotionally close bond to the child, relatively free from marital issues and other relationship issues, past and present. The infant's and child's task of differentiating self and sorting out self from other (while maintaining emotional connectedness to key family members) includes a clarification of how he or she is similar to and different from *each* parent and the degree to which expressions of difference are acceptable within the family. From a systemic perspective, family members are both the cause and the effect of each other's behavior, and the functioning of one or two family members cannot be understood apart from the whole.

This partial and simplistic summary is meant only to provide a contrast or backdrop to psychoanalytic assumptions regarding the primacy and exclusivity of the preoedipal mother–child dyad. If one assumes that the core process of development and the structure of identity occurs between mother and child, certain generalizations and polarized assumptions about gender differences naturally follow. *The basic given, reified as truth, is that males are differentiating and developing self–other structures with a cross-sex parent, while girls are proceeding with this same task with a same-sex parent.* For certain feminist psychoanalytic theorists, this core assumption is founded on the socially constructed fabric of family and work life (and would thus change in the face of gender equality and shared parenting); for others, this given seems to transcend the particulars of patriarchy and prescribed sex roles. In either case, polarized and dichotomous notions of maleness and femaleness follow. Which sex is viewed as having the edge on something good or bad depends on the slant of the particular theorist. For example, Chodorow

(1978) assumes that the preoedipal girl is seen as an "exten-
sion or double of the mother herself" (p. 109) which leads to
"boundary confusion and a lack of a sense of separateness in
the world" (p. 110). My work (1980) also has focused narrowly
on the special difficulties mothers and daughters have in navigating the differentiation process due to gender sameness. In
contrast, Jordan and Surrey (1968) postulate that mother–
daughter sameness facilitates empathic relatedness and leads
to girls' heightened relational capacities. Because males are
assumed to develop psychological structures with a cross-sex
parent, they are characterized by "a basic relational stance of
disconnection and lack of identification" (p. 90).

While most of feminist theory (as well as antifeminist theory) pays special attention to women's capacity for affiliation,
caretaking, and orientation toward relationships, Jordan and
Surrey approach this subject with exceptional sensitivity and
depth. Unfortunately, they do not locate male–female differences in any social context. For example, after describing the
mutual attentiveness and capacity for empathy that Jordan
and Surrey believe flows naturally between mother and daughter, they state, "The contrast with the development of this
capacity in boys is shown by a male patient's description of his
childhood experience as 'learning not to listen,' learning to
'shut out my mother's voice, so that I would not be distracted
from pursuing my own interests' " (p. 89). Of significance here
is that the authors do not present this example to illustrate
individual, family, and/or cultural dysfunction, but rather to
illustrate the "different" line of development that males follow.
It is notable that whereas Miller (1976) carefully links sex
differences to gender inequality and the complex nature of
dominant and subordinate groups; whereas Kanter's (1977)
research demonstrates the overriding power of the work context in determining an individual's relative leanings toward
ambition and affiliation; and whereas Chodorow (1978) argues
that gendered personality differences arise within a particular
family form that is prevalent in capitalist industrialized society—Jordan and Surrey do not appear to take these into
account in their paper. Rather, their central thesis that women

find meaning and motivation in relationships and caring while men forge their identity in autonomy and separateness echoes Gilligan's (1982) work, which is rooted in the premise that these gender differences are something akin to universal givens. What is thus called for is not social reform or a reorganization of the structure of family and work life that would facilitate, for both sexes, a more adaptive and flexible balance of the "I" and the "we," of work and of love. Instead, social changes might rather reflect a "separate but equal" doctrine that recognizes, validates, and facilitates women's different developmental line and superior nurturing abilities.

The self-in-relation model represents a particularly valuable line of theory building in terms of both content (which brings us closer to the positive realities of womens lives) and feminist spirit of inquiry. The author's emphasis on the heretofore undervalued quality of empathic relatedness and their description of the relational self, unfolding within the ongoing context of mutual connectedness and empowering is, I believe, a model for all human development. For Jordan and Surrey, however, as for other psychoanalytic theorists, gender differences are polarized and seem to rest on implicit assumptions about the primacy of early mothering and the related belief that interactions with same-sex or cross-sex children will lead to different, if not opposite, developmental pathways. Because Jordan and Surrey pay careful and respectful attention to the process of mothering and to the positive, adaptive aspects of the mother–daughter relationship, it would require a great deal of imagination to label their work "mother-blaming." Indeed, their theoretical contribution is in quite the opposite direction. *Yet, I wish to underscore my belief that any mother-focused, nonsystemic framework for understanding behavior implicitly holds mothers responsible (even if intended otherwise), in that the locus of causality, or "where things happen" (whether one's focus is on normal or pathological development), is assumed to reside primarily within the early mother–child dyad.* This belief, on which object-relations theory is founded, does not do justice to the existence of fathers— nor to the complexity and diversity of actual interactional patterns in real families.

A POSTSCRIPT ON POLARITIES

What needs to be critically examined in recent feminist literature is a full-circle return to the reification of dichotomous notions of masculinity and femininity and polarized views of male and female development. On the one hand, the redefinition and validation of women's relational skills is an essential contribution of feminist scholars, since traditional feminine attributes have been devalued in our competitive, warring, male-dominant society, where measuring up and moving up too often take precedence over human relationships and even lives. Yet recent theories on the psychology of women reify and exaggerate gender differences without keeping the larger family and social context in view, which leads to a false polarization of the sexes in ways that violate both the precision of science and the richness and diversity of human experience. Statements such as "For women, the self develops within a context of relatedness; for men, by separating from it," or "Women define identity by their social and family networks; men through a process of individuation, autonomy, and achievement," or "Women's basic orientation is caretaking" speak to our deep-rooted human tendency (from which feminists are not exempt) to dichotomous and polarized modes of thought.

In regard to self-in-relation theory, I agree with Jordan and Surrey's belief that women organize identity and find meaning within actual or internalized relational contexts. However, the implication that men, in contrast, do *not* develop self and find meaning in the context of relationships is a puzzling one, as *all* people develop within the context of ongoing family relationships and fail to flourish in the absense of human connectedness. Similarly, any dichotomous characterization of affiliation and nurturance versus autonomy and achievement reflects an obvious conceptual muddle, since mature and successful intimacy requires a high level of differentiation and separateness (i.e., the ability to define the "I" within the "we") as well as the ability of each partner to formulate personal goals and ambitions apart from the relationship. We also know that given sufficient opportunity, status, and access to money and power, both men and women may have a hard time curbing personal ambitions in order to tend to important relationships. Getting one's life "in balance" is a lifelong struggle for both sexes, and the circular overfunctioning/underfunctioning reciprocity of the sexes in the domestic and public spheres leads to a mutually reinforcing circular process that is difficult to disrupt.

This is not to render issues of gender invisible or unimportant, nor to deny that gender is a crucial variable in the organization of human experience. Nor is it to discourage us from putting forth generalizations about how the sexes differ. In a particular couple, for example, it is more likely than not that the man will manage anxiety and intensity through distancing and disengaging and that the woman will react by pursuing or seeking greater togetherness. Similarly, it is more likely that the man will develop personal and vocational goals at the expense of family ties and responsibilities and more likely that the woman will do the reverse. It is also the case that historical factors have combined with traditional family structure to create parenting roles that tend to affect each sex differently. For example, many men have been raised by physically and emotionally unavailable fathers and by omnipresent mothers (blocked from the pursuit of personal goals) whose very qualities male children are then encouraged to repudiate within themselves. Such a family structure is hardly conducive to the establishment of a firm male identity and the associated capacity for intimacy. Finally, biological differences between the sexes add further to the picture.

Those of us interested in gender differences and the psychology of women are thus faced with a difficult challenge. The study of group differences of any kind requires us to make generalizations for which there are many exceptions. We do this not to obscure the diversity within groups, but rather to appreciate the different filters through which people see the world. Unfortunately, these same generalizations tend to stereotype or simplify people, to emphasize or exaggerate intergroup differences while minimizing similarities and commonality of experience, and to create static notions of what is natural, healthy, God-given, "right," or best for a particular group.

Thus, generalizations about gender are both necessary and inherently problematic. Take, for example, Jordan and Surrey's basic premise that mothers feel more comfortably and affectively connected to daughters and that it is within this bond that accurate empathy is more likely to unfold. These authors write, "Since being a man is not something with which the mother has had immediate experience, she must act as she has seen others act with males or must imagine what should be done" (p. 88). This generalization, like others of its kind, is valuable and worth considering, but only if one recognizes that it may have nothing to do with what actually occurs in a particular dyad or family. For example, a mother who is the older sister of brothers in her family of origin may tend to be especially comfortable with sons, perhaps more so than with daughters. Further, the specifics of family history often override gender considerations.

For example, I am currently seeing a woman in therapy who has a chronically symptomatic older sister who was an intense and unrelenting focus of parental concern. A younger brother was relatively free from the family projection process and sailed through childhood and young adulthood without major disruption. When my patient married and had two children, she predictably became focused upon and negatively reactive to her firstborn daughter, whom she fused in her mind with her own underfunctioning older sister. Early interactions with her son were much calmer, less fueled by anxiety and projection, and more characterized by accurate empathy and an ability to accept and recognize him for what he was, rather than what she wished or feared him to be. Obviously, predicting accurate differences about mother–son or mother–daughter relationships in a particular case would require studying a complete family genogram and having access to important facts about family history. Information would also be needed about the marital relationship and the father–child relationship since these shape the mother–child relationship just as they are shaped by it.

I am not sharing the above fragment of clinical information to criticize Jordan and Surrey's important assumptions about mother–daughter relatedness. Their careful attention to the positive unfolding of interactions within this dyad is an essential and long overdue contribution. I am rather attempting to underscore the problematic nature of making generalizations about gender, while recognizing at the same time that generalizations are unavoidable when discussing group differences. When generalizations are formulated about subordinate group members (e.g. blacks, women, ethnic minorities), there is an additional risk that these generalizations will be offered out of the context of the group's subordinate status in ways that will be used to justify or reinforce the status quo and obscure the necessity for social change.

Gilligan's (1982) work, as it has been widely interpreted, illustrates the problem at hand. In my role as consultant for organizations and executive seminars, I frequently hear Gilligan's research interpreted as demonstrating that women on the job care primarily about people's feelings and personal ties, whereas men think in rational, logical, and abstract terms and are primarily oriented toward the task at hand. If such an absurd generalization were grounded in facts, no sensible employer would hire women, since the primary function of an organization is to ensure its own economic viability and to get the job done; organizations do not exist to create affiliative ties and attachments among employees, although ideally this will be facilitated. While Gilligan herself expresses dismay at the way her work is used to reinforce old stereotypes, the language of her generalizations and her failure to connect gender differences with the fundamental inequality of power and authority between the sexes may lend itself to the problem and contribute to a further polarization of the sexes that exaggerates differences and obscures similarities.

What then can we do to minimize the problems associated with the study of gender? First, we can watch our language. To state, "Women's identity is rooted in nurturance and caretaking, while men's identity is rooted in achievement and self-development" presents endless problems. If we want to compare the sexes, we would be far more accurate in saying, for example, "More women than men root their identity in nurturance and caretaking," or "More men than women pursue ambitious strivings at the expense of intimate relatedness and caretaking."

Second, we can recognize the circular reciprocity between the sexes. That is, there is a mutually reinforcing dance between women's overfunctioning position in relationships and caretaking, and men's underfunctioning in this realm (Lerner 1985). Similarly, there is a circular interconnectedness between women's outside position in the public sphere and men's outside position in the domestic sphere. *From a systems perspective, we can predict that the more we continue to reify and glorify women's nurturant and caretaking abilities as a "separate but equal" line of development, the less likely it is that men will identify and utilize their own competence in this arena.*

Third, we must recognize that gender differences involve relationships between dominant and subordinate group members and thus must always be grounded in this broader sociocultural context. For example, the very traits, qualities, and behaviors that Gilligan, Jordan, and Surrey label as being specific to women are those that research has shown to be characteristic of any subordinate group. Surely Gilligan's conclusions look quite different if interpreted through the broader framework of Kanter's (1977) research on contextual variables in the workplace or Hare-Mustin's (1987) emphasis on power and hierarchy. In psychoanalytic circles, Miller's (1976) classic text, *Towards a New Psychology of Women*, remains an excellent example of a view that identifies and affirms women's affiliative strengths in a balanced way that neither devalues nor glorifies female psychology, and that carefully places women's special strengths and problems within the context of dominant and subordinate groups.

Finally, we must recognize that gender differences need to be understood not only in the broader sociopolitical context but also in the broader family context. The psychoanalytic assumption that gender differences can be studied from the narrow perspective of the mother–child dyad, or that any dyad can be understood apart from the whole, is deeply problematic, reflecting the polarity between psychodynamic and systemic thinking and the dramatic degree to which we have chosen to remain ignorant about systemic family process. If we continue to formulate research and generate theory from this narrow focus, we will become much like the proverbial man who lost his keys in the alley but searched for them under the lamppost because the light was better.

Although a good antidote to the problems at hand is for psychoanalytic feminists to become serious students of family process, being credentialed as a "family therapist" or "systems thinker" hardly ensures a position of greater clarity, complexity, or virtue (Luepnitz 1984). As Bograd (1986) and other family therapists point out, systemic language often cloaks linear explanation, and circular causality or recursiveness frequently gives way to mother-blaming. Further, family therapists have until quite recently virtually ignored the subject of gender (Goldner 1985, Taggart 1985, Hare-Mustin and Marecek 1986), which is simply the flip side of the psychoanalyst's obsessive and reductionistic focus on it. Hare-Mustin (1987) notes that few of us find a middle ground between what she calls the alpha prejudice (exaggerating gender differences) of psychodynamic theories and the beta prejudice (minimizing or ignoring them) of systemic approaches.

Finally, I want to emphasize that the questions I have raised here are ones that we all need to keep out on the table and struggle with. The works I have critiqued constitute valuable contributions to female psychology, despite the presence of still unsolved dilemmas that have no simple solutions. As Carter (1985) says so succinctly, "How shall we deal with the central role that mothers play in family emotional life? If we ignore or depose her, we are failing to acknowledge her efforts and importance; if we overfocus on her, we are blaming her for the problem and/or holding her responsible for change" (p. 78). Like Chernin, Jordan, and Surrey, Carter reminds us that mothers and daughters *do* form a central axis in family emotional life and that this relationship has not received the attention it deserves. Yet how do we proceed to attend to it while at the same time maintaining a family process perspective that does not minimize or obscure the role of fathers, the complexity of interlocking relationships, and the impact of culture and women's subordinate status? And how do we create a language that allows us to discuss sex difference or evolve a "psychology of women" in a manner that does not reify stereotypes or construct gender as a dichotomy, at best reductive, and at worst prescriptive? Certainly I do not pretend to have the answers, which I trust will evolve from the continued collaborative efforts of us all. I hope I have asked some of the right questions.

REFERENCES

Bernard, J. (1974). *The Future of Motherhood.* New York: Dial.
Bograd, M. (1986). A feminist examination of family therapy: what is woman's place? *Women in Therapy* 5(2/3):95–106.

Carter, B. (1985). Ms. intervention's guide to "correct" feminist family therapy. *Family Therapy Networker* 9(6):78–79.
Chernin, K. (1984). *In My Mother's House: A Daughter's Story.* New York: Harper & Row.
—— (1986). *The Hungry Self: Women, Eating and Identity.* New York: Perennial Library.
Chodorow, N. (1978). *The Reproduction of Mothering.* Berkeley: University of California Press.
Chodorow, N., and Contratto, S. (1982). The fantasy of the perfect mother. In *Rethinking the Family: Some Feminist Questions,* ed. B. Thorne and M. Yalom, pp. 54–75. New York: Longman.

Friday, N. (1977). *My Mother/Myself.* New York: Dell.

Gilligan, C. (1982). *In a Different Voice.* Cambridge: Harvard University Press.
Goldner, V. (1985). Feminisim and family therapy. *Family Process* 24(1):31–47.

Hare-Mustin, R. T. (1987). The problem of gender in family therapy theory. *Family Process* 26(1):15–27.

Hare-Mustin, R. T., and Marecek, J. (1986). Autonomy and gender: some questions for therapists. *Psychotherapy* 23(2):205–212.

Herman, J. L., and Lewis, H. B. (1986). Anger in the mother-daughter relationship. In *The Psychology of Today's Woman: New Psychoanalytic Visions*, ed. T. Bernay and D. W. Cantor, pp. 139–168. Hillsdale, N.J.: The Analytic Press.

Jordan, J. V., and Surrey, J. L. (1986). The self-in-relation: empathy and the mother–daughter relationship. In *The Psychology of Today's Woman: New Psychoanalytic Visions*, ed. T. Bernay and D. W. Cantor, pp. 81–104. Hillsdale, N.J.: The Analytic Press.

Kanter, R. M. (1977). *Men and Women of the Corporation*. New York: Basic Books.

Lerner, H. G. (1980). Internal prohibitions against female anger. *The American Journal of Psychoanalysis* 40(2):137–148.
—— (1985). *The Dance of Anger: A Woman's Guide to Changing the Patterns of Intimate Relationships*. New York: Harper & Row.

Lerner, S., and Lerner, H. G. (1983). A systemic approach to resistance: theoretical and technical considerations. *American Journal of Psychotherapy* 27(3):387–399.

Luepnitz, D. (1984). Cybernetic baroque: the hi-tech talk of family therapy. *Family Therapy Networker* 8:37–41.

Miller, J. B. (1976). *Toward a New Psychology of Women*. Boston: Beacon Press.

Papp, P. (1983). *The Process of Change*. New York: The Guilford Press.

Rich, A. (1976). *Of Woman Born*. New York: W. W. Norton.

Taggart, M. (1985). The feminist critique in epistemological perspective: questions of context in family therapy. *Journal of Marital and Family Therapy* 11:113–126.

Women's Project in Family Therapy. (1982). *Mothers and Daughters*. Monograph Series 1(1). See also (by same authors) *Mothers and Sons, Fathers and Daughters* (1983). Monograph Series 2(1). Washington D.C.: The Women's Project.

Index